"Martyn Lloyd-Jones said, 'I spend half my time telling Christians to study doctrine and the other half telling them doctrine is not enough.' J.D. Greear's book on the Holy Spirit explains why doctrine is not enough, yet grounds all its clarion calls—to experiential communion with God, to relying on the Spirit for doing greater works, to seeking transformative revival for the church—in biblical doctrine at every point. This is a readable, practical guide to the Spirit's relationship to the individual believer and the church."

—**Tim Keller**, Senior Pastor of Redeemer Presbyterian Church, New York City

"If you are wanting a clear understanding of the Holy Spirit, J.D. Greear's important book, *Jesus, Continued...*, will open your eyes to the personal and powerful Spirit that dwells within followers of Jesus. Experiencing the presence of God through his Spirit will empower you to live in freedom, worship with intimacy, and tap into God's supernatural strength."

—**Craig Groeschel**, Senior Pastor of LifeChurch.tv and author of *From This Day Forward*

"I have witnessed many great movements of God over the course of my life. Yet I believe God's greatest works lie ahead. He waits for his people to surrender their lives fully to him before he works mightily through them. J.D. Greear has pinpointed the issue. The need is not for Christians to try harder. Rather, God's people must comprehend the enormous power that is available to them through the indwelling Holy Spirit. There is no limit to what Christ can do through one ordinary life, wholly surrendered to him. As you read this book, be sensitive to Christ within you, urging you to surrender your life fully to him so you are in a position for him to impact the world, through you."

—**Dr. Henry Blackaby**, Author of *Experiencing God*

"I can't tell you how thankful I am for this book, especially at this time when fear and confusion about the Spirit's work abound. With deep wisdom, clarity, and a strong reliance on the Word, J.D. Greear brings a theology of the work of the Holy Spirit in light of the good news and located in the church. As he writes, it's time for us to stop lamenting that Jesus has left us alone and start rejoicing that his Spirit dwells within us."

—**Elyse Fitzpatrick**, Author of *Good News for Weary Women*

"The Spirit inside you is better than Jesus beside you." What a challenging and life-transforming statement! I love how J.D. Greear inspires us in *Jesus, Continued...* to recognize how real and relevant the power and presence of God is for us today."

—**Mark Batterson**, Author of *The New York Times* bestseller *All In*

"A much needed reminder of how Christianity suffers when we ignore God the Holy Spirit."

— **Jim Cymbala**, Senior Pastor of The Brooklyn Tabernacle and author of *Spirit Rising*

"Most of us believe God is at work somewhere, but have a hard time seeing how he is working in our lives. In *Jesus, Continued...*, my friend J.D. Greear uses his story to explain how God is vitally present with his people today, and how understanding our relationship with the Holy Spirit will help us experience God's presence in a powerful and personal way."

— **Steven Furtick,** Lead Pastor of Elevation Church in North Carolina and *The New York Times* bestselling author of *Crash the Chatterbox; Greater;* and *Sun Stand Still*

"Wow! I am so proud of J.D. Greear and the transparency that he writes in *Jesus, Continued....* We know that Jesus is alive and working in the world and in our lives, but having someone expound on the power of the Holy Spirit and how he interacts and changes us is so encouraging. J.D. gently reminds us that Jesus doesn't need us, but that he *chooses* us to help build his church for our benefit. If you've ever struggled with feeling crushed under the pressure to always 'do more' or wondered how to better understand the Holy Spirit, this book is for you."

— **Perry Noble,** Senior Pastor of NewSpring Church in South Carolina

"*Jesus, Continued...* is a brilliant, biblically grounded, convicting book that points us to the greatest source of inspiration—God's Spirit. J.D. Greear shows what a resource the Holy Spirit is to our daily lives and gives clear insight on how to live in the Spirit. *Jesus, Continued...* is a message we desperately need for a more powerful and active faith."

— **Jud Wilhite**, Senior Pastor of Central Christian Church in Nevada and author of *Pursued*

"J.D. Greear wants us to want the Spirit—to be filled with his presence and power as we proclaim the glory of the crucified and risen King Jesus. This is a book that challenged and convicted me—and ultimately led me to repentance for the many times I have overestimated my own ability and vision and underestimated the magnitude of what God can do through us when we yield to the Spirit. Read this, and be refreshed."

— **Trevin Wax**, Managing Editor of The Gospel Project and author of *Gospel-Centered Teaching; Clear Winter Nights; Counterfeit Gospels;* and *Holy Subversion*

"J.D. Greear writes masterfully as a pastor-theologian. I'm very grateful for his book and pray that people will take it to heart. *Nothing* happens without the Holy Spirit."

— **Bob Roberts Jr.**, Senior Pastor of NorthWood Church in Texas and author of *Bold as Love*

"In *Jesus, Continued...*, my friend J.D. Greear has produced an engaging, accessible, and *practical* theology of the Holy Spirit that rightly emphasizes the Spirit's work to glorify Jesus and empower believers to participate in God's mission to the nations. Once again, J.D. demonstrates why he is one of the leading pastor-theologians of this era."

— **Thom S. Rainer**, President and CEO, LifeWay Christian Resources

"In *Jesus, Continued...*, J.D. Greear brings to light with great clarity and passion why it's far better to have the Holy Spirit in us than Jesus beside us. The power of the Spirit is not a religious cliché; it's a life-changing reality available to all who follow Jesus. If you want to better understand and experience the Spirit's guidance and power in your life, this book is for you."

— **Larry Osborne**, Author and Pastor of North Coast Church in California

"For twenty years I have known J.D. Greear to be a thoughtful and passionate pastor, writer, and friend. But he seems to have tapped into a deep well of insight and application in *Jesus, Continued....* This book is as rich and deep as you'll ever find regarding the person and work of the Holy Spirit, but it's unparalleled in its helpfulness to Christians of every stripe. It's practically applicable to missionaries, pastors, college students, stay-at-home moms, new believers, and seasoned saints. It's a fresh approach to an ancient truth; the Holy Spirit is real, powerful, tangible, and you don't need to be afraid of Him. Run, don't walk, and get this book as soon as you can."

— **Clayton King**, President of Crossroads Camps and Crossroads Missions, Campus Pastor of Liberty University, and Teaching Pastor of NewSpring Church in North Carolina

"Finally, a biblically based, Jesus-centered book is written on the power of the Holy Spirit. This book will ignite your faith, enlarge your vision, and empower you to believe God for the impossible."

— **Dr. Ronnie Floyd**, President of the Southern Baptist Convention and Senior Pastor of Cross Church in Arkansas

"J.D. Greear has given us a much-needed book on the Holy Spirit that drives us into the Word, ignites our hearts for the mission of God, and stirs our affections for Jesus. In *Jesus, Continued...* you will find the precision and balance this subject deserves, while helping create a longing for more of the Spirit of God in your life."

—**Matt Carter**, Pastor of Preaching at Austin Stone Community Church in Texas and coauthor of *The Real Win*

"Jesus, Continued... by Pastor J.D. Greear is important for several reasons. First, Greear, a well-trained theologian, as is clear in the careful documentation, nevertheless writes like a college minister, and therefore identifies with a younger audience in a most effective fashion. Second, the book addresses a subject that, as Greear notes, is too often addressed in terms of side questions and too infrequently approached in the way that God's Word actually emphasizes. But this young pastor has understood the biblical emphasis and has brought it skillfully to light in these pages. Looking for a book that makes the work of the Holy Spirit come to life in the day-by-day world of the true believer? Here you will find it in *Jesus, Continued....*"

—**Paige Patterson**, Southwestern Baptist Theological Seminary, Fort Worth, TX

"A hugely helpful book that I highly recommend. If only every Christian realized what (or better put, who) we have in the Holy Spirit!"

—**David Platt**, *The New York Times* bestselling author of *Radical*

JESUS,
CONTINUED...

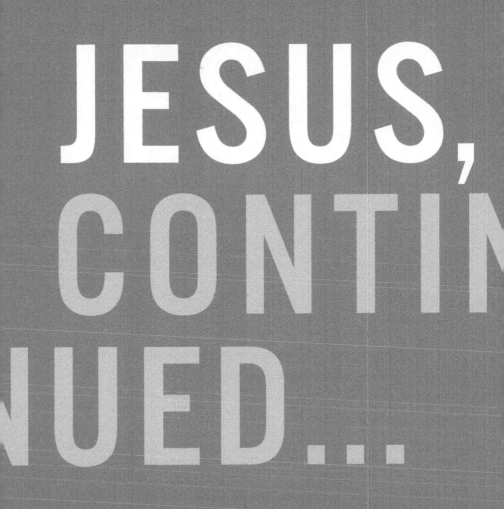

JESUS, CONTINUED...

WHY THE SPIRIT INSIDE YOU IS *BETTER* THAN JESUS BESIDE YOU

J. D. GREEAR

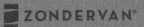

ZONDERVAN®

ZONDERVAN

Jesus, Continued
Copyright © 2014 by J. D. Greear

This title is also available as a Zondervan ebook. Visit www.zondervan.com/ebooks.

Requests for information should be addressed to:

Zondervan, 3900 Sparks Drive SE, Grand Rapids, Michigan 49546

ISBN 978-0-310-33776-8

Published in association with Yates & Yates, www.yates2.com

Cover design: Dual Identity
Interior design: Matthew Van Zomeren

First printing September 2014 / Printed in the United States of America

Contents

PART THREE: SEEKING THE HOLY SPIRIT

Introduction

A few years ago a young man sat in my office feeling deeply frustrated with his faith. Although he knew a lot of truths about God, he sensed very little relationship with God—at least, not the dynamic relationship he wanted. God seemed distant.

It seemed that everything God had done, he had done in the past: he created the world, died on a cross, and then inspired a Bible to tell us about it. Then he gave us a mission and left through the clouds. God seemed like a busy teacher who had given an assignment and then stepped out of the room, leaving his students to get it done on their own.

So this guy was busy at work, trying faithfully to learn the lessons, follow the instructions, and complete the assignments. He had a "relationship with God" in the sense that he prayed about his problems and tried hard to trust that God was working somewhere, somehow, to help him. Yet he lacked any vibrant *interaction* with that God.

But as he read the Bible, he saw a God who interacted with his people, spoke to them, corrected them, and comforted them. In the days of Moses, God had taken up residence among his people, first in the pillar of cloud and fire that guided them through the wilderness and then in the glory that settled down permanently on the Tabernacle. Throughout the rest of the Old Testament, God spoke to his people

11

through prophets, warning them, encouraging them, and instructing them. He was present.

Then there was Jesus—Jesus had not merely given his disciples a body of doctrine to learn, but also escorted them on a guided tour of its application. How awesome would that have been? And then came the book of Acts. You get the sense reading Acts that the church is being blown about by this mighty, rushing wind called the Holy Spirit. He shows up fifty-nine times in Acts, more than twice per chapter, and in nearly forty of those times he is speaking.

"Where was *that* God?" the man asked.

Must be for a different time and place, he assumed. *Maybe one day in heaven, I'll relate to God like that.* But for now, he thought, "I better just get after the assignments. After all, the teacher is coming back."

But a problem was developing. He told me he was feeling increasingly burned out by the weight of "the assignment." There was always one more person who hadn't heard, one more language group without a copy of the Bible, one more orphan in need of adoption. The weight of the assignment, which once had inspired him, now felt paralyzing. In a world of seemingly infinite need, how could he ever feel like he had done *enough*?

So his life oscillated between summers of feverish, radical activity and winters of paralyzed despair. He gradually began to tune out the heart-wrenching stories of global need. He knew that was wrong—but he simply didn't know what else to do.

And then another problem began to develop. His sense of disconnect from God left a boredom and yearning in his heart that made the dark appetites of the flesh all too appealing. He knew these sinful indulgences were wrong ... but at least they felt *real*.

He sat in my office a weary, burned-out man, wondering if there really was a God who could be *experienced*.

What would you say to such a guy? I confess that I didn't know what to say to him. I mean, what unexpected, spine-tingling insight can you share ... with *yourself*?

Yes, *I* am the guy in this story. For many years, even as a pastor with a PhD in theology, I sensed a relational disconnect with God. It wasn't that I didn't understand that God had reconciled me to himself in Christ, and I was "in him" and he "in me." I understood all that and had embraced it.

But how to interact with that Infinite now living within? I was clueless.

Do you ever feel that way? Do you ever feel like God is someone you know *about* more than someone you *know*—like he's *more of a doctrine than a person?* Does God feel truly present in your life? Do you interact with him *personally?* Do you read the book of Acts and say, "Yeah, that's similar to my experience," or does that world seem like a completely different one than the one you live in?

In this book I want to tell you what I was missing, how God restored it to me, and how you can have it too. I want to show you how you can have a deep, satisfying relationship with God through the Holy Spirit, on the basis of the finished work of Christ.

Better than Jesus beside You

The Holy Spirit tends to be the forgotten member of the Trinity. Most Christians know he's there, but they are unclear about exactly what he does or how to interact with him—or if that's even possible. Yet *something* was so important about the Holy Spirit that Jesus told his disciples it was to their advantage that he go away—if his departure meant the Spirit came. The Spirit's presence inside them, he said, would be better than himself beside them. In fact, they needed the Spirit's presence so much that Jesus told them not to so much as a raise a finger toward the Great Commission until that Spirit had arrived.

Do you consider *your* connection to the Holy Spirit so strong and real that you regard his presence *in* you to be a better advantage than even Jesus himself *beside* you?

Be honest. Seriously.

I've written this book to help you experience that kind of relationship with God through the Holy Spirit. Personal relationship, you see, has always been God's plan.

From the very beginning, he has passionately expressed a profound desire for a close, growing relationship with his people. In the garden of Eden, God walked with Adam and Eve in the cool of each evening. Many centuries later, he directed his people to construct a temple in the heart of their nation so he could *dwell* among them. Through the prophet Micah he told us that what he requires of us is not simply that we "*do* justly," but also that we "*walk* humbly" with him (Mic. 6:8, emphasis mine). In the same way, Jesus told us, "*Follow me,*" not just,

"Obey my teaching." In other words, he didn't want us merely to follow a plan or learn a doctrine, but to *follow* him. That requires real, personal *interaction*. Like any other relationship.

He has always been a God who is close and present — but only since Jesus returned to heaven has he taken up residence *inside of us*.

And that makes him closer than ever.

This is not to say that the Christian life is a series of spine-tingling experiences, inner voices, or burning bushes, and that there are not times when we must walk through dark, silent valleys by faith alone. As I'll show you, walking by faith often means staying the course when you can't see or feel anything, and to suffer through times of dryness when you have nothing to cling to but the promises of God. But that is not the same thing as saying that God is *absent* during those times. In the Holy Spirit, God is literally with us until the end of the age, and he has promised never to go away, forsake us, or leave us stranded (Matt. 28:20; Heb. 13:5; John 14:18) In our darkest moment, he is as real as the breath in our lungs.

Do you interact, personally, with God? Think about this question very carefully:

> Is Christianity more of a set of beliefs to which you adhere and a lifestyle to which you conform, or is it a dynamic relationship in which you walk with the Spirit and move in his power?

Jesus birthed the Christian movement by sending his Spirit like a mighty, rushing wind into his disciples. The place where they met shook with God's power, and as a result they turned the world upside down. The first church was not primarily a study group, a self-discovery seminar, or a building program. It was a mighty movement of the Spirit that propelled Jesus' followers into the whole world, preaching the gospel. Acts is the story of disciples following that Spirit, being filled by that Spirit — trying to keep up, but feeling like a kite in a hurricane.

Does that metaphor characterize your church? Does it characterize *you?*

Through the pages that follow, I want to help you experience that very real presence of God. *How* you experience him may surprise you; much of what I learned differed greatly from what I expected. But his presence in those things is real — I can assure you.

And just to manage your expectations, you should know that I'm still not the guy who gets up every morning and sees God spell out his daily assignment in my Alpha-Bits. The Virgin Mary has never appeared to me in a grilled cheese sandwich. God doesn't put a strange restlessness in my spirit when I need to change the oil in my car—I have to check the little sticker on my windshield for that. But the presence of God is every bit as real to me, and as powerful, as the presence of God I see with his people in the past.

This is a book about the Holy Spirit, though perhaps not a typical one. Many books about the Holy Spirit seem to me to get stuck in secondary questions that, while important, never focus on the truly essential issue—how is God present with his people today? How do we perceive his movements? You see, we can disagree on some of the secondary questions (like whether the gift of tongues is in operation today, or even the distinction between baptism and fillings with the Spirit) and still agree on this one, central truth: *God wants to be vitally present in and through his people.*

So that's what this book is about. I have not written this book to tell you everything anybody ever learned about the Holy Spirit. I've written it to help you experience his presence and power in a personal way.

Our generation of Christians—mission-driven, but burned out, weary, and longing for joy—desperately needs to recover the dynamic presence of God. The good news is that God wants us to know it. He created us for that very purpose.

You see, maybe you've never realized it, but you yearn for it.

Maybe you picked up this book knowing very little about God but sensing a disconnect in your life that you suspected had something to do with needing to know God better. Maybe you picked this book up as a last, desperate attempt to find something worth living for in this world—something that goes beyond the drab and dulling pursuit of pleasure, something that takes you far beyond yourself. I hope that in this book you will discover the God who has reconciled himself to us in Christ and offered himself to us in the Holy Spirit. *He* is that purpose you have always been looking for.

So let's get started. An infinite amount of power and possibilities await us.

We all see problems in the church. We don't need another book to point those out. We need the faith to believe that the solution is really quite simple: The Holy Spirit. — *Francis Chan*

PART 1

THE
MISSING
SPIRIT

"Did you receive the Holy Spirit when you believed?"
They answered, "No, we have not even heard that there
is a Holy Spirit." — *Acts 19:2*

CHAPTER 1

A False Dilemma

"Nevertheless, I tell you the truth: it is to your advantage that I go away, for if I do not go away, the Helper will not come to you. But if I go, I will send him to you." —*John 16:7 ESV*

… Religion is what happens when the Spirit has left the building.
—*Bono*

I have a friend—I'll call him Brennan—who served for several years as a leader in our church. A bright young college senior, Brennan was well-spoken, well-regarded, and a leader both on his college campus and in our church. But Brennan had a dark secret he had shared with no one. He had a same-sex attraction that led him into pornography and eventually to a string of hook-ups with random guys he met in Internet chat rooms.

By the time Brennan finally confessed his sin to his campus leader and me, he was a broken young man. He had already desperately tried everything he could think of to fix himself. He had memorized Scripture, made vows, and even gotten rid of his Internet connection. Yet his "problem" was getting worse. So together, we plotted out a course of recovery that involved professional counseling, more Scripture, and high accountability. Brennan progressed a little, and for brief seasons it looked as if he was gaining victory ... only to fall back down into the same dark valleys. Eventually he checked himself into an intensive ministry that helps believers get control of the lusts of their flesh.

Brennan showed up at my house eight months later, noticeably different in his demeanor. I asked him what he had learned. "I didn't *learn* anything new," he said. "I learned to *lean* on the Holy Spirit. I always knew he was in there, but I didn't know how to relate to him." Brennan told me he had been surprised at how frequently the counselors at this ministry, all of whom had come through their own struggles and sexual addictions, referred to the Holy Spirit. They talked about him like he was *real*, like someone they met with daily. For them, the Spirit was not a theological concept, but a Person with whom they interacted and on whom they depended.

Brennan, who had grown up in Baptist and Reformed circles, knew all *about* the Holy Spirit. He knew the Holy Spirit came into his heart when he trusted Christ and that he was in there, helping out somehow in the sanctification process. But never, he said, had he been taught to seek the Holy Spirit like these believers did. They sought his presence as if their lives depended on him. Brennan began to understand that he needed more than "right beliefs" to subdue these lusts of his flesh. He needed power. Resurrection power. And a constant Companion who would always be there to help.

"And this discovery," he said, "marked a turning point in the struggle with my sin." He added, "These temptations are still with me, and I suppose always will be. But I have found in the Spirit of God a power more potent than the lusts of my flesh. Being filled with God the Holy Spirit has done more for me than all the seminars I sat through or coping techniques I mastered."

Do you know the Holy Spirit in this way?

Just before Jesus ascended to heaven, he told his disciples, "I will not leave you as orphans; *I* will come to you" (John 14:18, emphasis mine). At the ascension Jesus did not become an absentee God. He, as God, simply came to his disciples as a different Person. The mystery of the Trinity is that only one God exists in three Persons. Each person is distinct from the other two, but in experiencing one, you experience the one God who *is* them all. (If your mind feels as if it just exploded, that's okay. Christian theologians have been wrestling with that for centuries!)

In the same way that he could tell his followers, "If you have seen me, you have seen the Father," so it would be true for him to say, "When you hear from the Spirit, you hear from me." And, remarkably, he told his disciples that his presence *in* them would be even better than his presence *beside* them. Wow. Think about that.

This Spirit, he said, would bring to their minds all that he had said and taught. In other words, he would make the Word of God come alive in their hearts, *applying* that Word to their questions and doubts. The Spirit would lead them through the Word, and they would gain the ability to obey that Word by his power.

An Eternal Partnership

In Scripture, the word of the gospel and the power of the Spirit always go together. The Word is God's revelation to us, profitable for rebuke, for correction, for training and instruction in righteousness, capable of making us complete, sufficient for any and all good works (2 Tim. 3:16–17). But only through the ministry of the Spirit, Jesus said, could we ever understand or obey that Word:

> "When the Advocate comes ... he will testify about me." (John 15:26)

> "He will glorify me because it is from me that he will receive what he will make known to you." (John 16:14)

> "But the Advocate, the Holy Spirit, whom the Father will send in my name, will teach you all things and will remind you of everything I have said to you." (John 14:26)

> "When he comes, he will prove the world to be in the wrong about sin and righteousness and judgment." (John 16:8)

> "Apart from me you can do nothing." (John 15:5)

The Spirit makes the living Word come alive *in us*. He brings it to our remembrance at the times we need it. He explains it to us. He gives us spiritual eyes to see God's beauty in it. He empowers us to obey it. He shows us specific ways we are to apply it.

Paul believed the study of the Word without this illumination was useless. That's why after expounding the gospel in great detail in the first three chapters of Ephesians, he stops explaining and starts praying that the Spirit would enable the Ephesian believers "to grasp how wide and long and high and deep is the love of Christ…that surpasses knowledge" (Eph. 3:18–19). Do you catch his play on words? He prays they would understand something that is *beyond all knowledge.* Isn't that a contradiction?

Not at all. We arrive at certain kinds of "knowledge" not through the accumulation of more cognitive facts, but personal experience. There are two words for "knowledge" in Greek. *Oida* refers to facts, data, and cognitive pieces. *Ginosko* refers to an internalized knowledge gained through experience. In asking God to help believers *know* the love of Christ, he used *ginosko.* Paul wants us to have a knowledge of the love of God that we *experience* deep within our soul.

It's like the "knowledge" of color that comes into blind eyes opened for the first time, or the "knowledge" of sweetness that comes with a tongue's first taste of honey. It is the knowledge of a lover who cannot only tell you *about* her beloved, but knows the joy of his presence and the warmth of his embrace.

When we know God's love this way, Paul says, we will be "filled with all the fullness of God" (see Eph. 3:18–21 ESV; see also Rom. 5:6–8). The Spirit of God takes the revelation of God in his Word and consumes our hearts with it, so that "the love of God is shed abroad in our hearts" and we overflow with it (Rom. 5:5 KJV), our hearts burning with its warmth.

Two Extremes

Christians, you say, tend to gravitate toward one of two extremes regarding the third person of the Trinity. Some pursue experience in the Spirit apart from the Word. They listen for voices in their hearts or seek "signs" from God in the heavens. They always seem to be talking about what God "said to them" through a stirring in their spirit or in a strange confluence of circumstances.

Others, however, seek to know and obey the Word without any interaction with, or real dependence on, the Spirit. These Christians might know who the Holy Spirit is and that he floats around in their hearts somewhere. They might even know that he produces "spiritual fruit" in their lives, but they relate to him in ways similar to how I relate to my pituitary gland: I know it's in there somewhere, and that it's necessary somehow for bodily growth and life, but I have no real "interaction" with it. I've never spoken to or heard from my pituitary gland. Its work remains invisible and undetected, even though I know it's essential.

Once, as Paul taught on the Christian life to a group of new disciples at Ephesus, he mentioned the importance of the Holy Spirit. They immediately interrupted him: "Wait ... *who*? We have not even heard that there is a Holy Spirit!" (Acts 19:2, my paraphrase).

Many Christians might well still be in the same place, functionally speaking. Though they have *heard* of the Holy Spirit in a doctrinal sense, they have no real interaction with or dependence on him. Functionally, they live in ways "unaware" that there is a living, moving Holy Spirit. These Christians have all but excised the Holy Spirit from the Trinity; instead, they believe (functionally speaking) in "Father, Son, and Holy Bible."

But the Spirit and the Word work inseparably. One without the other leads to a dysfunctional Christianity. Just as a toaster without a plug is useless, biblical knowledge apart from the Spirit is impotent.

The Floodlight Ministry of the Spirit

Let's talk first about how walking with the Spirit depends on knowing the Word.

We cannot know the Spirit apart from the revealed Word. That Word, Jesus said, was all about him (John 5:39). The Spirit points to *Jesus'* words and works, not his own (John 16:14). In fact, there is a certain irony in how the Spirit operates; whenever he is really present, you are not thinking about him, you're thinking about Jesus. The Spirit's work is to direct you to notice something else.

If you've ever driven into Washington, DC, on Interstate 395 late at night, you've seen the magnificent splendor of the Washington Monument like a shining ivory needle illuminated against the night sky. Hundreds of thousands of dollars' worth of lights shine directly on the stone pillar, memorializing the father of our country. Yet I doubt you have ever noticed, or maybe even thought about, those expensive, brilliant lights. That's because they are there to illuminate something else. If they are doing their job, you're not thinking about them; you're thinking about the Washington Monument.

The same is true of the Spirit of God. His purpose is to illuminate the gospel and bring glory to Jesus. J. I. Packer calls the work of the Spirit a "floodlight" ministry, quietly turning everyone's attention away from himself and to the Savior.[1] Theologian Dale Bruner calls him, in fact, the "shy member of the Trinity," because he doesn't like attention on himself![2]

This means that when someone claims to be filled with the Spirit and yet spends most of his time talking about his own experiences with the Spirit, you have reason to doubt whether he really is filled with the Spirit. When the Holy Spirit speaks through someone, you tend to forget about the person speaking. You don't even really think about the Holy Spirit. You find yourself thinking about Jesus.

As we saw at the beginning of this chapter, the fullness of the Spirit comes as we plumb the depths, heights, widths, and lengths of God's love as revealed in the gospel. The more he comes into us, the more we know his love; and the more of his love we know, the more of his fullness grows within us (Eph. 3:17–19). The Spirit moves us in the Word. The Spirit moves us to go deeper into that Word.

So do you want more of the Spirit? If so, then seek greater knowledge of God's love through the Word of his gospel. As you do, Paul promises, you'll experience the "fullness of God."

Where the gospel is not cherished, the Spirit will not be experienced. And, on the flip side, where the Spirit is not sought, there will be no deep, experiential knowledge of the gospel. The two always go hand in hand. Jesus said, "The words I have spoken to you—they are *full of the Spirit* and life" (John 6:63, emphasis mine). Spirit and Word, inseparably united.

Seeking experiences with the Spirit apart from the Word leads not only to confusion, but to disaster. Leviticus 10 records a chilling event involving Nadab and Abihu, the sons of Aaron the High Priest. These two men offered "strange fire" before the Lord. God had prescribed a certain way to offer sacrifices, but Nadab and Abihu thought they had discovered an alternative way. Their new fire burned just like the old fire, and it seemed to accomplish the same purpose ... but God killed them for their presumption. God's not looking for a "new thing." God has laid out very clearly how his presence is to be sought and experienced. If we want to experience the fire of God's presence, then we must seek it in exactly the way he has appointed.

We Cannot Fulfill the Word Apart from the Spirit

Just as there is no real experience with the Spirit apart from the Word, so there can be no true obedience to the Word apart from the Spirit. "Apart from me," Jesus said, "you can do nothing" (John 15:5). *Nothing* is a big word, and I'm sure Jesus chose it intentionally. Without his divine presence living inside of us, we cannot truly accomplish even the first word of his commands. This means we cannot overcome sin without his presence. We cannot love others. We cannot win others to Christ. We cannot raise our children. We are like an appliance unplugged from the socket. We can do *nothing*.

Jesus told his disciples that if they truly understand that the Holy Spirit was so essential to their lives and would be such a help to them, they would be glad Jesus was returning to heaven, because only then would the Holy Spirit come:

> "Nevertheless, I tell you the truth: it is to your advantage that I go away, for if I do not go away, the Helper will not come to you. But if I go, I will send him to you." (John 16:7 ESV)

Think for a moment about how absurd this idea must have sounded to those first disciples. It would be *to their advantage* for Jesus to go away? What would it have been like to walk around with the all-knowing, miracle-working, God of the universe—and then to have him tell you that you shouldn't feel sad over his departure because it was to your *advantage?*

Really?

Apparently so.

> "For if I do not go away, the Helper will not come to you. But if I go, I will send him to you." (John 16:7)

Jesus claimed that having the Holy Spirit *in* them would be better than having him *beside* them. Wow. Let that sink in for a moment. I mean it. Go back and read that sentence again.

Now, be honest with yourself: Is *your* experience with the Holy Spirit like that? Do you feel as though your relationship with the Holy Spirit is *better than* if you had Jesus for a personal companion? Is the Spirit's presence inside you really preferable than having Jesus beside you?

I said, "Be honest."

Or, to raise the stakes a bit: Does your experience with the Holy Spirit validate Jesus' promise—that it is to our *advantage* that he go away, if it means we get the Holy Spirit? And if not, doesn't that mean you are missing something ... and likely, something *important*?

Jesus believed that the Holy Spirit would be a better teacher than even he was. That may sound hard to believe, but the Spirit, Jesus explained, could apply the Word more powerfully than he did, because he could speak it into the deep recesses of our heart at just the right moments (John 14:25–26; 16:5–14; 1 John 2:27–28).

Only through the Holy Spirit can we live victoriously over sin. In Romans 8, Paul's great chapter on how to live the victorious life, he refers to the Spirit twenty-two times. (To put that in perspective, he mentions the Holy Spirit only ten other times throughout the other fifteen chapters of Romans!) The implication is clear: If we want victory over our sinful flesh, we must be filled with the Holy Spirit! Paul cannot conceive of victory over sin without him. Apart from him, we have no hope against our "wretched body of death." But with him, we are more than conquerors (Rom. 7:24; 8:37; cf. John 15:5).

And the Holy Spirit, Jesus promised, would be a better director of mission. He could supply the right words at just the right moment, whatever our circumstances (Luke 12:12). He would not be merely God beside us, coaching and inspiring us, but God inside of us, working in us and through us. And that was *better* even than sitting around a campfire each night with Jesus discussing your day.

In fact, the Spirit was so important that Jesus told the disciples not to lift a finger in pursuit of his mission until the Spirit came.

Your First Assignment: Do Nothing

I've always thought that Jesus gave a very odd first step to completing the Great Commission, basically telling them, "Do nothing until the

Holy Spirit comes upon you" (Luke 24:49, my paraphrase). With millions of people waiting to hear the gospel, he instructed the only ones who knew anything about it to sit and wait until he had sent them something mysterious from above. That meant they were not to write books. They were not to go out to try to make converts. They were not to plan. They were to do *nothing*.

Why? Until he came, they couldn't really do anything of value to the mission. Jesus had promised that *he* would build his church, and he could accomplish more in one moment through his Spirit than they could accomplish in 10,000 lifetimes on their own.

As you pursue God's mission in your life, do you live with that sense of dependence on the Holy Spirit? Do you really believe that you can do *nothing* without him? As a parent, as a spouse, as a friend, as a witness?

The book of Acts tells the mind-blowing story of how a group of underqualified, mostly blue-collar workers filled with the Holy Spirit can turn the world upside down. We're still reeling today from that first Christian century. New Testament scholars have pointed out that when later Christians gave a name to the book of Acts, they probably chose the wrong title. Rather than "The Acts of the Apostles," many say it should instead be "The Acts of the Holy Spirit." They say this because even a quick read of Acts reveals that the Spirit of God is the primary actor. *He* guides; *he* speaks, and *he* moves; the disciples are simply trying to keep up. *At their best*, they are conduits of this mighty, rushing wind. At their worst, they are obstructions. In fact, they seem to spend a lot of time in Acts arguing with the Spirit (see, for example, Acts 9:13–14; 10:14–16). He slowly drags them to victory. It becomes readily clear that the Spirit, not them, is the one accomplishing the mission Jesus gave in Acts 1:8.

Keep in mind that Acts is the only example God gave us of how Christians walk with Jesus in this present age. Of course, it is true that some unique, once-in-history things happen in Acts, and that means we need to approach certain stories with some caution (more on that later). Not all examples apply to us in exactly the same ways. I don't walk down the beach trying to heal people by letting my shadow fall on them, and I've never struck anyone dead for lying (Acts 5:4–5, 15). Though I've been tempted to try a couple of times. But since Acts really is the only example God gave us of how to walk with him in this age, doesn't it make sense that we can look to the stories for instruction in how to interact with the Holy Spirit? Are you telling me we are to have nothing in common with the only biblical account of people experiencing the Holy Spirit?

As the apostle John told the first Christians:

> We proclaim to you what we have seen and heard, *so that you also may have fellowship with us*. And our fellowship is with the Father and with his Son, Jesus Christ. (1 John 1:3, emphasis mine)

Fellowship means we have something in common. We should have the *same kind* of relationship to God that he and the other apostles had, a relationship of fellowship. We are to *commune with God*, not just obey him, just like John did with Jesus. That communing happens, he says, through the gospel, in the person of the Holy Spirit (1 John 1:6–9; 2:26–27; 4:13).

John Newton, the Puritan writer of the song *Amazing Grace*, wrote to a friend:

> Many ... who would not flatly contradict the apostle's testimony in 1 John 1:3 [i.e., that we should have fellowship with God in the Holy Spirit] attempt to evade its force by restraining it to the primitive times ... but who can believe that the very nature and design of Christianity should alter in the course of time? And that communion with God, which was essential to it in the apostle's days, should now be unnecessary?[3]

We depend as much on the Holy Spirit as they did, and the Holy Spirit wants to fellowship with us as much as he did with those first believers. Their experience is in many ways a model for ours.

You see, when I read the book of Acts, I don't have any problem seeing how the apostles would have considered the Spirit's presence *in* them to be better than Jesus *beside* them! They turn out, after all, to be much more effective witnesses *after* Jesus leaves! Think about it: The same Peter who denied Christ three times in one night before the Spirit came boldly tells a crowd in Acts 2, "You crucified Christ by wicked hands!" Then three thousand get saved and baptized on the spot. And while the Holy Spirit worked through Peter in Jerusalem in Acts 15, he was simultaneously speaking through Paul in Philippi in Acts 16. He was two places at once! Jesus in his incarnation couldn't have done that! Now that the Holy Spirit had come, God's power was not localized in one person in one place. He was in every believer, scattered all over the world with his power.

Now, maybe you still feel skeptical. You cannot understand how it possibly could be better to have an invisible presence inside of you rather than a bodily Jesus beside you. Fair enough. We'll get to that. But at least concede this: What Jesus said has to mean *something*, right?

Be encouraged. That "something" is what God has waiting for you.

The Word and Spirit Dynamic

Throughout the remainder of this book, I want to show you how God's Word and God's Spirit operate together in one powerful dynamic. While pursuing one without the other leads to spiritual ruin, pursuing one *in* the other leads to power and life. We see this interdependent relationship of Word and Spirit over and over throughout Scripture. Let me show you.

In the beginning, God established the world by his Word, but the Spirit hovered over the expanse and brought order and beauty to the firmament God had spoken into being. That's a good example of how the two relate: the Word issues the command and establishes the foundations; the Spirit quickens and makes alive.

The Spirit takes God's timeless truths and makes them come alive in us. He helps us understand them, shows us how to implement them, and empowers us to accomplish them. He transforms task lists into a relationship.

> *The Word is eternal and unchanging. The Spirit's direction is temporary and varied.*
> *The Word gives us promises. The Spirit compels us to risk in certain situations.*
> *The Word outlines the mission. The Spirit inspires a vision.*
> *The Word sets the standards. The Spirit guides the operations.*
> *The Word shows us the end game. The Spirit points to a starting place.*
> *The Word sets our expectations. The Spirit inspires our dream.*
> *The Word describes the character of God. The Spirit pulls us into his emotions.*

The Word recounts God's acts of salvation. The Spirit sheds abroad his love in our hearts.

The Word gives us the revelation. The Spirit illumines the explanation.

The Word provides the content. The Spirit brings the conviction.

The Word helps us to know. The Spirit enables us to learn.

The Word commands us to hear. The Spirit empowers us to listen.

The Word commands us to obey. The Spirit beckons us to follow.

The Spirit makes God's Word *personal* to us.

Has Christianity become *personal* to you? Have the doctrines and declarations turned into relationship? Has the Great Commission been translated into some specific vision for your life? Do you know you are walking with, and following, Jesus in the Holy Spirit?

Has the Spirit of God generated in you holy ambitions in ministry that function something like the arrow of a compass, pointing you to God's "true north" for you? Do you know your *specific* role in his kingdom? You see, that's a major component of his leadership: He shows us what part of the mission belongs to us specifically and assigns to us our unique role in his kingdom.

For example, while the responsibility to carry the gospel to the ends of the earth is the responsibility of the *whole* church, Paul felt called specifically to preach the gospel where Christ was not known (Rom. 15:20–21). That was his personal "ambition," and he considered that particular assignment to be his life's "race" (Acts 20:24).

Has part of the Great Commission become a personal assignment for you? Which part of the mission has become your passion? Have good ideas in your life been replaced by *God* ideas?

In my experience, it's better to discover those one or two "God ideas" for your life than to be marginally involved in a thousand good ideas. Because that's when Christianity explodes.

Christianity Ignited

I have seen this kind of "explosion" happen in the church I pastor. It came when we realized there were specific aspects of the mission the Spirit of God was calling us to give ourselves more fully to. We looked back through our history and realized the Spirit had given us a few "personal ambitions." Let me explain what I mean.

Back in 1962, over a decade before I was born, a man named Sam James planted our church. He worked with a core team for eight months, but on the Sunday the church officially launched, he left to become a missionary to Vietnam. That day he preached the only sermon he would ever deliver at that church. Using Isaiah 54:2–3, William Carey's famous missionary text, he explained that just as God had commanded Israel to "expand her borders" and "lengthen the cords of her stakes," so God had called this new church to expand her vision in order to bring the nations into God's tent of blessing. He sensed that this was part of what God had in mind when he moved that core team to plant the church.

Sam James then left for Vietnam and didn't return for forty years.

Sadly, the church wandered from the vision Dr. James had laid out. Like many churches, it turned its focus inward, tending the gardens of the faithful rather than storming the gates of hell.

I came to the church as pastor in 2002. During the interview process, I sensed God stirring in the hearts of the church leadership about international missions. I had never heard of Sam James and didn't know anything about the church's history. But it seemed clear by the questions the leaders asked me that God's Spirit had placed a call on this church for the nations. Yet they weren't really doing anything about it.

God had put a specific call on my life for international missions, so I began to preach about it. What surprised me was how quickly the vision took root in the church. After the first year, the International Mission Board of the Southern Baptist Convention recognized us as the highest missions giving church, per capita, of the 42,000 churches in our denomination. I'd love to say that was due to some unusual preaching or leading ability on my part, but that would be false. (I have tried to lead many things, even in our church, that never came close to this level of success!) It seemed as though, in this area, an unseen hand propelled us forward.

College students "discovered" our church in 2003. College students, if you don't know, travel in herds. So our attendance tripled in three weeks while our average weekly giving went up about $13.48. We learned that while we were not destined to be a rich church, we would have a lot of workers to mobilize for the nations.

Today, more than 190 of our members live overseas on one of our church-planting teams. In the last ten years, we have sent out close to 500 on domestic and international church-planting teams. Earlier this month, we commissioned another 100 college seniors who have given their first two years after graduation to serve on one of these teams, and 130 who will be leaving our church to plant churches in unreached cities around the United States.

I'm not being falsely humble when I tell you that I'm not quite sure exactly how all this has happened. I really can't figure it out; our success in this area has come too fast and too strong to explain it merely as the result of good leadership techniques.

Another reason, you see, explains it.

This is what God's Spirit had called this church to specifically. He put it in our DNA. He beckoned our church to follow him, and then waited. It took nearly forty years, but when we finally put up the sail, the mighty, rushing wind of the Spirit propelled us forward, like a dinghy in a hurricane.

A couple of years ago, I discovered Sam James was still alive (he is now in his eighties), and I brought him back to Durham for our church's fiftieth anniversary. For the first time, I heard his story. As he told it, a lot of our past ten years began to make sense. For the last decade that I've served as pastor, we've simply followed the Spirit's lead, according to a vision he put in Sam James's heart more than fifty years ago. It's not that we're doing this *for* God so much as we're doing it *with* him. He is working through us. And it sometimes feels like we're just along for the ride.

To be involved in international missions is, of course, the responsibility of *all* churches. The whole mission belongs to the whole church. And there is a sense in which we are each to be involved in every aspect of the mission. But the mission is bigger than any one person or any one church, so the Holy Spirit will highlight for each of us a few specific parts of the mission, calling us to engage with particular focus in those things. (A calling, you see, is usually just a specialization in an assignment given to all believers.) God gave difficult, unreached people groups, particularly Muslim people groups, as his "special assignment" to our church.

Recently, I've sensed the Spirit of God pressing this vision deeper into my heart. God's command in Psalm 2:8 feels like a personal invitation to me: "Ask me, and I will make the nations your inheritance." This verse belongs to *all* Christians, of course, but the Spirit of God has beckoned our church, in a special way, to believe it and take it for ourselves. As Paul had a personal ambition to take Christ where he had not been named, reaching Muslims is our ambition. So we have asked God to let us plant a thousand churches by 2050, to send out over five thousand members on church-planting teams, and to let us be a part of seeing a major gospel awakening in at least three countries.

I don't know what the future holds for our church, of course; I cannot even guarantee I'll wake up tomorrow! But I know that I have heard the Spirit's voice beckoning in this, *"Follow me."* And I feel more confident than ever. I am not merely obeying assignments laid out in the Scriptures; I am following the initiatives of the Spirit. His vision outreaches mine.

How about you? Has the mission of God translated into a specific vision for your life? Do you, like Paul, have a personal ministry ambition? Through his Spirit, God invites you to join the purposes for which he has created you specifically (Eph. 2:10). When you grasp this, the Great Commission becomes a focused burden for some person or group of people. Kingdom work becomes a personal calling. Good ideas get replaced with *God* ideas.

Led by the Spirit, Taught by the Word

I once heard a Christian leader say, "Better to spend one hour on your knees pursuing the Holy Spirit than ten hours studying the Bible." Tweetable, maybe, but very wrong. Better to spend one hour on your knees pursuing the Holy Spirit *through* the Bible. Scripture invites you into a relationship that involves both Word and Spirit, each being indispensable for the other.

Every word of Scripture is a revealed Word of God, but God desires more than for us to learn the doctrines and obey the precepts. He desires relationship.

Martyn Lloyd-Jones, a Reformed, British pastor of a previous generation, said, "I spend half my time telling Christians to study doctrine and the other half telling them doctrine is not enough."[4]

Many Christians, you see, function as deists. They act as if God rules from the heavens and has spoken in his Word, but does not act on earth or move in their souls—at least in any way that they can sense those movements. Yet, if the Holy Spirit is a *person*, shouldn't we expect him to move dynamically, and sometimes perceptibly, on earth? If he lives in us, should we not expect some kind of movement?

Lloyd-Jones described his relationship with the Holy Spirit this way:

> Those who have received the Holy Spirit are aware of a power dealing with them and working in them. A disturbance, something, someone interfering in our lives. We are going along, and suddenly we are arrested and pulled up, and we find ourselves different. That is the beginning; that is what always happens when the Holy Ghost begins to work in a human being. There is a disturbance, an interruption to the normal ordinary tenor of life. There is something different, an awareness of being dealt with—I cannot put it better; that is the essence of the Holy Spirit dealing with us.[5]

"But wait a minute," you say. "What does that kind of communion feel like? How do I know when the Spirit is moving in me? Should I hear a voice? Get goose bumps? If I don't feel those things, am I not walking with God?"

Excellent questions. Let's try to find some answers.

CHAPTER 2

Mystery and Clarity

"The wind blows wherever it pleases. You hear its sound, but you cannot tell where it comes from or where it is going. So it is with everyone born of the Spirit." —*John 3:8*

To profess to know a great deal about the Spirit of God is contrary to the nature of the Spirit of God. There is a hiddenness to the Spirit that cannot be uncovered. There is an immediacy of the Spirit that cannot be shoved into vision. There is an invisibility of the Spirit that cannot be forced into visibility. There is a reticence of the Spirit that cannot be converted into openness. For these reasons one feels helpless, inadequate, and unworthy to write ... about the Spirit.   —*Bernard Ramm*

Several years ago, a college friend and I dove into unpacking what the Bible taught about various spiritual gifts. We came from different church backgrounds and had conflicting views about some of those gifts. Neither of us had ever really studied it personally, so we agreed to meet together for several weeks with nothing but our Bibles, open hearts, and dependence on the Spirit.

We had just started to unpack some of the key passages when my friend called to say that he would no longer continue our study, because the Spirit had assured him that his church's views on the question were correct and that he needed to study the Bible no further. I asked how he knew the Spirit had really said that, and he replied, "I just know. I am as sure about this as I have been about anything."

And that was that.

Now, I have a hard time believing that the Spirit said any such thing. My reason is simple: We aren't told to seek the Spirit *apart* from the Word; we are to seek him *in* the Word.

I've met people with all kinds of theories about how to "know" when the Spirit is speaking to them. Perhaps you've known people who equate the voice of the Spirit with some strange set of phenomena: "You won't believe this! I was praying about whether to ask Sarah out, and driving on the interstate, I saw a billboard and the first letter on the billboard was the first letter of her last name and the last two digits of the phone number were the same as her age, and right at that moment, my favorite Christian song came on the radio ... and so I just KNEW God was telling me to ask her out! Jehovah Jireh!!!! God is good, all the time!" (Or, girls, maybe a guy has used some line like that to ask you out. If so, on behalf of all guys everywhere, I apologize.) *#manupanddonthidebehindGod*

Perhaps you've gone through a set of circumstances so strange you had to wonder, "God, are you trying to tell me something through this?" To be honest, I have. But how do we *know* when he is communicating with us? Does he use a voice to speak in our hearts, and if so, what does that voice sound like? Is it a strange sense of peace in your heart, a sense of calm that would make even a Buddhist jealous, or an inexplicable, burning urge—a holy hunch?

Later in this book we'll spend some time probing that question, but here I want to offer a biblical insight that will serve as something of a ground rule for our investigation: A certain mystery enshrouds the Spirit's leadership.

And I'll admit this much: as a type-A person who majored in mathematics and law in college—someone who likes to have everything in neat, tidy, spread sheets—this can feel more than a little frustrating to me. Generally, I don't like mystery. I like clarity.

But Jesus said there is a certain mystery to walking with the Spirit:

> "The wind blows whereever it pleases. You hear its sound, but you cannot tell where it comes from or where it is going. So it is with everyone born of the Spirit." (John 3:8)

Think about his imagery. When a gust of wind hits, you don't know exactly where it came from, where it's headed, or when it will come again. Experiencing the movement of the Spirit is, according to Jesus, something like that. While the Word that God gave to us in Scripture is clear, eternal, and unchanging, the Spirit guides us in ways mysterious and varied.

(And, to be clear, when I say that mystery enshrouds the Spirit's leadership, I'm not talking about some kind of New Age mysticism or a Christian version of reading tea leaves. I'm simply pointing out that the Scriptures never give us a clear, detailed description of the experience of being led by the Spirit. For whatever reason, we just aren't given a great deal of specificity on that.)

If we fail to acknowledge this mystery, we either reduce God's working to a formula that will cause us to miss the Spirit's genuine movement in our lives, or (and perhaps worse) we become over-confident in what we think he is saying to us, elevating our interpretation of his movements to a level of authority we should only give to Scripture. (The only thing worse than not being open to the Spirit's leadership is elevating your subjective sense of it to a level that obscures the objective revelation he has provided in his Word!)

Where God has given clarity is in his Word. So throughout Scripture, God leads his people through both the mystery of the Spirit *and* the clarity of the Word.

The Mystery in Acts

This mysterious leadership of the Spirit pervades the book of Acts. The Holy Spirit speaks at least thirty-six times at various places throughout the book, but we discover no "standard" way in which he does so. Typically, Luke does not tell us how he spoke, just that he did.

Here are some examples:

- In Acts 16, the Spirit of God guides Paul through a dream in which a man Paul had never met invites him to a country he's never visited. Paul "concludes" this is the voice of God (Acts 16:8–10).
- A few verses earlier, the Spirit of Jesus forbade Paul and Silas from preaching the gospel in a certain place. But Luke doesn't describe *how* the Spirit forbade them (Acts 16:6–7). Acts 19:21

says Paul "resolved in the Spirit" (ESV) to pass through Jerusalem and then proceed on to Rome. But what exactly does it mean for Paul to "resolve something" *in the Spirit*? That simply doesn't tell us.[1]

- In Acts 10, the Spirit tells Peter not to fear the Roman soldiers who have come to question him about the gospel, and to go wherever they take him (Acts 10:20). But *how* did the Spirit make this clear—was it a strange, peaceful confidence in his heart; did thoughts appear in his head; or did he hear syllables in his ears? The Bible doesn't tell us.

- In Acts 15, church leaders validate their instructions to new believers with the words, "It seemed good to the Holy Spirit and to us" (Acts 15:28–29). What does *this* mean, exactly? I'm not sure, but it doesn't sound like the Spirit wrote something out on the walls or spoke to them through a vision. It just "seemed good to them and the Holy Spirit." Did God give them such unusual insight or conviction that they just knew they had heard from God? Or did they conclude that this decision, which made sense to them after having prayed about it and searched the Scriptures, was also in line with the Spirit, since he had not guided them otherwise? Hmm. The text simply doesn't say! Paul made a similar statement in Romans 9:1: "my conscience confirms it through the Holy Spirit." What does your conscience confirming it "through the Holy Spirit" *feel* like? Paul doesn't exactly tell us.

- In Acts 8:29, Luke records that the Spirit "told" Philip he should go stand near a stranger in a chariot. How exactly did he *say* that? Is this what I sometimes feel when I sense God "telling me" to share Christ with the person sitting next to me on the plane? Why would we assume that God has ceased to guide us like that? "Ethiopian eunuchs" exist all around us.

- In Acts 16:13–15, Paul seems to assume that God's work in Lydia is an invitation for him to stay and continue to preach in Philippi, even though he started the chapter with clear, determined plans to go somewhere else.

- In Acts 21:10–14, a disciple named Agabus warns Paul through the Spirit that Jews would deliver him into the hands of the

Roman rulers if he went to Jerusalem, leading the other disciples to urge Paul to avoid the city.[2] Paul does not heed the warning, however, saying, "I am ready not only to be bound, but also to die in Jerusalem for the name of the Lord Jesus" (v. 13). He also seemed to be willing to go because he believed God had called him to go to Rome (19:21). Eventually, Paul ends up in police hands because of his Jerusalem visit just as Agabus had warned, but he also ends up in Rome, just as he had hoped. Both impulses turn out to be from the Spirit.

- In Acts 5, the Spirit gives Peter insight that Ananias and Sapphira have lied to God in their offering. How did he know his insight came from the Spirit? Did he hear a still, small voice whispering in his ear? Did he feel a strong "check" in his spirit? Again, the Bible simply doesn't say.

Paul's references to Spirit guidance in the epistles yield similar ambiguity. For example, when the apostle Paul lays out his future plans in 1 Corinthians 16, he says (my paraphrase):

> Yeah … when I arrive in Corinth, I'll see what everyone thinks about me going on to Jerusalem. I tried to get Apollos to come visit you, but he didn't think it was a good idea to do it now. So for now, my plan is to come to you after I go through Macedonia. I'll probably stay awhile, maybe even the winter. I want to take my time, if the Lord permits. I'm also going to spend some time in Ephesus because God seems to be doing some great things there.

Reflecting on this passage, Kevin DeYoung says,

> You're not getting the sense that Paul got angelic visits every other day and waited for his dreams, visions of his heart, and supernatural messages written out in the clouds to tell him what to do.… With few exceptions, Paul planned, strategized, and made his own decisions about the non-moral matters of his life.… Paul never sought out special words of knowledge concerning his future.… When he gets to a fork in the road, hesitating and pleading with God to know which way to go seems completely foreign to the apostle.[3]

Does that mean that the Spirit only *occasionally* led Paul and that the rest of the time he got on by himself? Certainly not! Paul thought of his whole ministry as led by the Spirit. Evidently, however, Paul's means for following the Spirit did not entail getting up each day and waiting on a message to spell itself out in the foam of his cappuccino. Paul based most of his decisions on wisdom he gleaned from the Scriptures, not on extra revelation supplied by the Spirit in "Magic 8-Ball" fashion. (You know where you peer into your heart and see what words float to the top, and you assume that's the Spirit.) Getting guidance by "revelation" was the unexpected exception, not the rule.

The disciples had clear, general commands given by Jesus in the Great Commission to obey. But as they did so, they had no choice but to look to the Spirit for power and guidance in pursuing those commands. Seriously—have you ever thought about the overwhelming nature of the Great Commission? At the beginning, they were only twelve strong, with no money, no power, and no people in strategic positions of influence. They were just a group of local, blue-collar workers with the entire world arrayed against them. Unless the Spirit guided them through this mission, they couldn't help but fail. They had no choice but to look to the Spirit for help.

Yet, even in this extreme dependence, they never reduced the Spirit's activity in their lives to some formula. They grounded themselves in the Word, obeyed Jesus' general commands, and looked to the Spirit to lead them—watching for him, but assuming he was leading even if they couldn't see or feel him.

The Mystery in the Old Testament

We see this mysterious interplay of Word and Spirit even in the Old Testament. The psalmist called God's Word a lamp to his feet and a light to his path (Psalm 119:105). The word, he said, established his foundation, made his paths straight and cleansed his way (Psalm 27:11; 119:9 KJV). Yet throughout the Old Testament, we see God guiding his people in various situations through special, extra-scriptural instructions. And here again, *how* he gave that guidance varied with the circumstances.

Sometimes, prophets delivered a special word of instruction. Sometimes, God spoke audibly.[4] Sometimes, he directed "regular" (non-prophet) people through dreams and visions.[5] At other times, he spoke through angels.[6] Frequently, he guided leaders through the casting of

"Urim and Thummim," a type of divinely ordained dice.[7] Once, he controlled the moisture content in a hand towel to bolster the wavering faith of a would-be general,[8] and another time he rebuked a wayward prophet through the mouth of a donkey.[9] Still another time, he chastised a whole nation by posting a message on a wall at a drunken king's party.[10]

Several times he simply put godly ambitions in the heart of his people — like Esther wanting to appear before the king to save the Jews,[11] Jonathan wanting to besiege a garrison of Philistines,[12] or David feeling provoked to fight Goliath.[13] Nehemiah deduced that God "put it on his heart" to rebuild the walls of Jerusalem (Neh. 2:12), even though we find no explicit command to that end. These were, John Piper says, invitations of the Spirit to "risk" an exploit for the kingdom.[14]

I'm not suggesting that God uses *all* these same methods to guide his people today. The book of Hebrews says that while God spoke in past times through "various means," he speaks to us in these last days primarily by his Son and through the Word (Heb. 1:1 – 4; 2:3 – 4; John 14:26). The testimony of the apostles has replaced a lot of what people depended on prophets to provide in the Old Testament. God's revelatory activities in the "Scripture" sense have ceased. Nothing in Paul's epistles directs us to consult the Urim and Thummim, leave hand towels outside overnight, or wait on our pets to speak God's will to us.

Nevertheless, in the book of Acts we see a church still actively being led in various ways by the Spirit of God. For example, the Holy Spirit said to the church in Acts 13, "Set apart for me Barnabas and Saul for the work to which I have called them" (v. 2). We aren't told exactly *how* he said it, but *that* he said it is beyond question. As the early church devoted itself to the apostles' teaching, its members were guided by the Holy Spirit in its application through dreams, visions, open and closed doors, prophetic words through others, yearnings, circumstances, and a number of other things. There is no doubt that the Holy Spirit *was* leading, but we cannot reduce how he led to a formula in which we simply plug in variables and pull out the answer.

A Model, Not a Formula

Regarding the guidance of the Spirit, Scripture gives us a basic *pattern*, but not a detailed *prescription*; a general *model*, but not a precise *formula.* We know that the Spirit leads and guides and acts in line with the Scriptures that God has already inspired. In his written Word, the Spirit of God is *always* speaking and *never* silent. Yet he also sometimes "breaks in" to our experience in unexpected ways to give us specific guidance, strength, or insight at particular times. The precise nature of this "breaking in" we can never script, demand, predict, or even anticipate. It is like the wind. The most that we can say is that it will never contradict, violate, or diminish the Word he already has given to us. This is the joyful, mysterious journey of the Christian life.

Wise is the theologian who recognizes and embraces the mystery, not the one who tries to remove it. One such theologian said it this way:

> To profess to know a great deal about the Spirit of God is contrary
> to the nature of the Spirit of God. There is a hiddenness to the
> Spirit that cannot be uncovered. There is an immediacy of the
> Spirit that cannot be shoved into vision. There is an invisibility of
> the Spirit that cannot be forced into visibility. There is a reticence
> of the Spirit that cannot be converted into openness.[15]

Reducing the Spirit's activity to a formula will likely cause you to miss when he actually does move. The prophet Elijah, for example, felt discouraged when God didn't move in the mighty ways he had for Moses and Job. Elijah expected God to speak in awesome ways, punctuating his thunderous voice on earth with earthquakes and bolts of fire. God took Elijah out to that same Mount Sinai where he had spoken in boisterous thunder to Moses, where he made a strong wind and an earthquake and a fire, all to pass before Elijah. "But the LORD *was not in* the wind ... the earthquake, [or] ... the fire." Instead the Lord spoke through a small, low whisper that Elijah heard *after* those things.[16]

The meaning? God's activity in our lives doesn't always come in the ways we expect or in the same ways it happened with others. God did his work in Elijah's time differently, but he was no less active than he was with Moses.

Scripture has given us parameters for how to expect the leadership of the Spirit, and we'll get into a few of those later. But I think it's really important as we begin to acknowledge the mystery of the whole enterprise before we even get started. Go outside, feel the wind blow against you, and say to yourself, "This in some way was to be like how I experience the Holy Spirit."

Honestly, as I admitted at the beginning of this chapter, this drives the Type-A in me a little crazy. I want a chart, or at least some Geiger-counter type of device—as they had in the movie *Ghostbusters*—that lets me know with absolute certainty when God is present and speaking. But God didn't give us that. Except in one thing.

The Clarity of the Scriptures

God did give us something in which he speaks to us with absolute clarity. We call it the Bible. The apostle Peter said these writings were the "completely reliable" word from God (2 Pet. 1:16-19). Peter even compares reading those Scriptures to his hearing the voice of God speak directly from heaven at Jesus' baptism. And Peter says that the *written word* of Scripture is even "more sure" than that voice (v. 19 NASB)!

Every detail of Scripture is accurate and every promise of Scripture is true. God breathed out each word, Paul says, and the Holy Spirit guided the authors infallibly in their recording of each word. When it comes to the voice of God, the Scriptures are in a class all by themselves.[17] God is always speaking clearly and reliably there. Want to hear the Spirit? Open your Bible.

A pastor friend of mine told me about hosting a rather well-known Christian leader whom he had invited to speak at a large, area-wide event. When my friend asked this guy what he planned to preach that evening, the man replied that he didn't know, the Spirit of God had not told him yet. That night, the man walked on stage and told the crowd that after spending several hours alone with God, he had received no "word" for the evening. "I guess God just does not have a specific word for us tonight," he said, and asked the music team to come back up to lead in worship.

My friend noticed the man had left his Bible, unopened, sitting on the seat beside him.

God *has* given us "a Word." Sixty-six books full of them, in fact. They are always relevant, always speaking. They are perfect, complete, fully sufficient for every good work, that we may be complete, not lacking in anything (2 Tim. 3:16–17).

The vibrant Christian life is a union of clarity in the Word and openness to the Spirit. If we seek the Spirit of God apart from the Word of God, our faith will end in shipwreck. More havoc has been wreaked in the church following the words, "The Spirit of God just said to me. ..." than any other phrase. God's Spirit *never* operates independently of his Word. Why would he? Think about it: Why would he call the Scriptures a "more sure word," "fully sufficient for every good work," and then proceed to ignore, abandon, or contradict it?

But, in the same way, if you seek to obey the Word apart from the power of the Spirit, not only will your spiritual life be lifeless and dull, you'll also miss out on the help God wants to give you and the most exciting things he has planned for you. You'll miss out on the dynamism of *relationship*.

So, seek the Spirit in the Word. His guidance functions something like steering a bicycle: It works only once you're moving. The Spirit steers as you obey God's commands. You start pedaling in obedience; he'll start directing.

Or here's another way to think about it: The Spirit of God draws upon our knowledge of the Word of God to counsel and encourage us like a gunner draws upon a stash of ammunition. If no ammunition waits in the chamber, the gunner simply has nothing to work with. The most powerful gun with no ammunition is impotent.

If you want to be led by the Spirit of God, then devote yourself to the Word of God.

The Word, the Spirit, and a Beautiful Girl

When I ponder how I met my wife, I can see the clear leading of the Spirit of God—but during that time I was simply obeying the Word of God. Veronica was both a counselor and a worship leader at a Christian camp at which I was the speaker, and I thought she was the most beautiful girl I had ever seen. I had this strange sense that I should go talk with her, even though forced, awkward conversations were not usually my style. I thought, "Is that strong impression from the Spirit of God? Or is it simply the forces of biology at work?"

I "obeyed" whatever it was. And ... our first conversations did not go well. In fact, in the middle of one of my sentences, she actually got up and walked off, seeing a friend she was more interested in talking to (I kid you not!). A less confident (or more sensible) guy would have assumed she had no interest; I, of course, just assumed she was nervous.

After striking out all week, I was walking my stuff out to the car when I had another strong sense that I ought to go back and try to talk with her. Again, was this from God, or just a type-A refusal to admit defeat? I didn't know. I did find it curious that I felt *so* strongly motivated by this urge to talk with her, despite being rebuffed all week. I stood at my car for a moment in indecision, and then thought, "Well, what have I got to lose?" And so I walked back to try one more time.

What happened, you ask? Well, over a decade of marriage and four kids later, you can probably figure it out. I went back, sat down with her on a deck overlooking the lake, and we got into a theological discussion about Calvinism. (Okay, you probably couldn't have figured out that part). We then recognized that I was going to be in her hometown for a two-week missionary training session, and so we exchanged phone numbers and agreed to get together. Then I left to go serve in Southeast Asia for two years, and during those years we filled cyberspace with enough emails to replace the *Encyclopedia Britannica*. We were married on July 28, 2000.

I have no doubts now that she is God's gift to me, and that God was leading in every detail of that fateful week in 1997. But during that week, I was *not* absolutely certain that my determination to talk with her came from the Holy Spirit. (And, by the way, even if I had suspected such a thing, I never would have admitted it, because that's just a really creepy thing to say to a girl! Seriously, guys. Restraining orders begin with such claims!)

What I did know for certain, however, was that God wanted me to pursue for a wife only someone who shared my love of Jesus and the ministry (Prov. 18:22; 1 Cor. 7:39; 2 Cor. 6:14). I knew I could depend on him to "supply all my needs" (Ps. 127:1 – 3; Phil. 4:19).

As I obeyed the clarity of those words, God led me in the mysterious specifics. On this side of the decision, it's obvious the Spirit of God was leading me, and that has been a great source of confidence for my wife and me, particularly in those difficult times that go along with any marriage. I knew the Spirit of God guided me to her and will supply all that we need to make the marriage he has given us work.

Most of the major decisions in my life had been made in much the same way as above—obedience to the Word and dependence on the Spirit of God, even as I assume that a lot of his work is in the background. Sometimes he leads very obviously (in biblical ways we'll discuss in chapters to come), but at other times, as in this situation, in ways that leave me unsure in the moment. (If Veronica had shot me down that last time, I would have had no choice but to assume that it was simply not God's will for me to pursue her and that the strong "urge" to talk with her was not his urging!)

So, again, let me be clear: Most of the decisions I have made in my life have not come out of strong, mysterious urgings, tingly feelings, or obscure revelations from the Spirit. I have simply obeyed the will of God as revealed in the Word of God and trusted that the Spirit of God was guiding me in the process, just as he promises.

Later we'll look more in depth on how to perceive the dynamic leadership of the Spirit, but for now, let me ask you to consider two related questions:

Are you obeying what God has revealed in the Bible?
Are you seeking to know his will more through diligent study of his Word?

You won't know the Spirit any more than you know the Word of God. So if you want to walk with the Spirit of God, get on your knees and open your Bible.

CHAPTER 3

The Mighty, Rushing Wind

His authority on earth allows us to dare to go to all the nations. His authority in heaven gives us our only hope of success. And his presence with us leaves us no other choice.   —*John Stott*

"You will receive power when the Holy Spirit comes on you; and you will be my witnesses in Jerusalem, and in all Judea and Samaria, and to the ends of the earth."   —*Acts 1:8*

Back when I was in high school, a tornado touched down close to a house where a friend of mine and I were staying. As it got closer, he ran outside to pull his bike into the house, but as he got out into the yard, the wind picked up dramatically. Trying to get back into the house, it looked like he was trying to walk through wet cement. The terrible sound of the approaching tornado terrified me. I never actually saw the funnel cloud, and I didn't want to. Eventually my friend made it, terrified and awed at the powers of nature. We survived that night, and I'll never forget it.

When the Spirit of God came upon the first believers, his descent sounded as if a "mighty, rushing wind" had filled the room. It's easy to skip right over that phrase, because Luke's wording doesn't translate well into English, but scholars say "mighty, rushing wind" implies something like a tornado.

In other words, this was no serene, peaceful breeze that filled the apostles with warm, happy God-thoughts and a sense of quiet calm. The Spirit filled them with the power of a tornado, taking up residence in their souls, filling them to be his witnesses. Jesus had started a worldwide revolution; they would continue it. Even the gates of hell would not be able to stop them.

This was the first "church."

I'm not sure what image comes to your mind when you hear the word *church*, but it's probably a good ways off from how those first apostles understood it on the day of Pentecost. The apostles understood the church to be a movement birthed by the mighty, rushing wind of the Spirit of God. Is that how you see your church? Most people today see the church as an institution, a place to go to, or something to sit through. How did that happen?

An Assembly, Not a Place

The word "church" in our English Bibles is the Greek term *ekklesia*. The term literally means "an assembly" or "a gathering" of people, called out for something (*ek-* means "out of;" *-klesia* comes from *kaleo* which means "to call out.") The first believers were an assembly called out to engage in mission.

Over the years, however, a terrible thing happened to Christians' concept of "church." In the Middle Ages, believers began to think of a "church" as a *place* that people went to for religious services, rather than a movement built around a mission.

Interestingly, our English word "church" comes from the German *kirche*, which means literally "a sacred *place*," rather than *ekklesia*.[1] By the time we English speakers conceptualized "church," we were already thinking of it as a place, not a movement.

People began to *go to* church rather than *be* the church.

But then God did something awesome. He raised up a group of people we now call the Reformers, who reasserted the centrality of the gospel mission in the church. The church exists, they said, to preach — to spread the gospel. One of those Reformers, a young theological student named William Tyndale, devoted much of his life to translating the Bible into English. Every time Tyndale came to the word *ekklesia* in the Greek New Testament he translated it "congregation" instead of "church" because he wanted to reclaim the idea that the church was *not* a place to go but a movement to join.

This infuriated the authorities, because in so doing Tyndale had undercut their power. Controlling the "places" of worship meant controlling the people, and so when Tyndale downplayed the "place," he diminished their control. Places you could control; movements you cannot. They tried Tyndale as a heretic.

During his trial, Tyndale said to one church leader, "If God spares my life, ere many years, I will cause the boy that drives the plow to know more of the Scriptures than you do." As he was burning at the stake, Tyndale's last words were, "Lord, open the king of England's eyes." (If you have a copy of the King James Bible, you can see that God answered that prayer![2])

In every age, the church faces the danger of degrading itself from a movement to a place, from a conduit of God's mighty, rushing wind to a sacred place where we seek serene, spiritual moments; from a rescue station to a spiritual country club. This is certainly true in our day. I've heard the average church in our day described like a football game: twenty-two people in desperate need of rest surrounded by 22,000 in desperate need of exercise.

The Spirit is a mighty, rushing wind, however, and those filled with the Spirit *move*. They move to those within their community in need of the gospel, to those outside of their communities who are broken and in need of hope, and to the ends of the earth in places that do not share their language or culture. Movements (by definition) *move*, and that means if you're *not* moving, then you're not really part of the movement. Where there is no movement, there is no Spirit.

Let's look at a few of the things the Spirit did when he came on those first believers. They show us what the Spirit moving in believers looks like.

Divided Tongues of Fire

And they saw what seemed to be tongues of fire that separated and came to rest on each of them. (Acts 2:3)

Throughout the Old Testament, whenever God's presence descended upon a place, he did so in the form of a flame:

- He appeared to Moses in a burning bush.
- He led Israel through the wilderness by a pillar of a flame:
- He consumed Mount Sinai in fire when he gave the law to Moses.
- The heavenly temple filled up with fire and smoke as Isaiah saw it filled with God's glory.
- Solomon saw the fire of God settle into the Holy of Holies when he commissioned the temple.

In Acts 2 the fire of God has come to sit atop the head of every believer. Every believer has become a burning bush.

In the Old Testament, if people wanted to be in the presence of God, they had to come to Jerusalem. But now, with the fire of God atop their heads, Jesus commands them to *go*. No longer must men and women come to Jerusalem to be in the presence of "the fire of God"; God is sending his believers to the nations with that presence inside them. "Come and see" has become "go and tell."

In the Old Testament, the fire of God's presence produced fear. Those who came into contact with it died. Yet, in Acts 2, when the believers encounter the fire of God's presence, they do not die; instead, they come alive! The fire of God's presence was no longer fatal because Jesus has absorbed the fullness of God's wrath by dying on a cross in our place. Consider the parallel: When the fire of God came down upon Mount Sinai in Exodus 19, three thousand Israelites died because they broke God's law. But when the fire of the Holy Spirit came in Acts 2, three thousand people came alive. Jesus already had died for our breaking of the law. He absorbed the fire of God's wrath so that we could receive the fire of his life and power. And now we are sent out, not with the terrifying fire of God's judgment, but with the cleansing, healing fire of his redemption.

Is it any wonder that Peter says angels "long to look into" the things of the gospel (1 Pet. 1:12)? The God of untouchable holiness now lives in the heart of sinful people! Angels cover their faces in the presence of the glorious holiness of God. Yet this presence now dwells inside of broken, fallen people, making them alive and bringing life to others through their witness. This is no gentle, sacred breeze. It is a mighty, rushing life-giving wind.

In All Languages

The mighty, rushing wind of the Spirit moved the believers out of the place where they were hiding into the open market square, where they began to proclaim the gospel in languages previously unknown to them:

> All of them were filled with the Holy Spirit and began to speak in other tongues as the Spirit enabled them. Now there were staying in Jerusalem God-fearing Jews from every nation under heaven. When they heard this sound, a crowd came together in bewilderment, because each one heard their own language being spoken. Utterly amazed, they asked: "Aren't all these who are speaking Galileans? Then how is it that each of us hears them in our native language? ... We hear them declaring the wonders of God in our own tongues!" (Acts 2:4–8, 11)

During this time of year (Pentecost), men and women from all over the world came to visit Jerusalem. They were astonished to hear ordinary Galileans, most of whom had never been fifty miles outside their hometown, speak their native languages perfectly. It would be something like hearing the cast of *Duck Dynasty* suddenly breaking out into flawless French and Mandarin. This phenomenon amazed that first audience, but its wonder should not escape us, either:

The first time the Spirit preaches the gospel, he does so in all languages simultaneously.

I can hardly overstate the importance of this. This was no mere random display of power! It was a sign. The gospel was not just a "Hebrew" thing; it was an "every people group in the world" thing. Other religious messages tend to bring their originating cultures along with them. Islam, for example, "Arab-izes" whatever people embrace it. That's partially because Muslims do not believe the Koran can be truly translated out of Arabic, and so if you want to hear the actual words of God, you must learn Arabic.

51

But not so with the gospel! The first time the Holy Spirit preached the gospel, he did so in all languages at once, because God intended the movement of the gospel to express itself in the richness of cultural diversity. (Have you noticed, by the way, that those churches that most focus on the ministry of the Holy Spirit seem also to be the most ethnically diverse? Sociologists have noted that Pentecostalism is the widest reaching, most culturally diverse movement in history. That's because the Spirit loves diversity, and Spirit-filled Christians possess an internal humility regarding their cultural preferences. They recognize that the Spirit of God is bringing people completely unlike them into the kingdom, and rather than feeling threatened by this phenomenon, it delights them!)

On the Day of Pentecost

That the Holy Spirit arrived on the day of Pentecost was no mere coincidence. "Pentecost" signified the culmination of the harvest. Scholars have long recognized the link between Passover and Christ's death: just as God's death angel passed over the homes protected by the blood, so God's judgment passes over us when we are under the blood of Christ. But quite often we fail to make the connection of the coming of the Holy Spirit to the Jewish festival of Pentecost. The Holy Spirit was given to harvest what Christ's death had purchased. Jesus had ransomed for himself a people from all nations, and the Holy Spirit had come to gather the harvest.

For the Purpose of Power

Jesus gave the Holy Spirit to empower the mission he outlined in Acts 1:8:

> "But you will receive power when the Holy Spirit has come on you, and you will be my witnesses in Jerusalem, and in all Judea and in Samaria, and to the ends of the earth."

Think about this: If you are a Christian, the Holy Spirit has come upon *you* to empower you for that mission. You are filled with the Spirit to be a witness. Jesus' words are a promise *to you*. In fact, read this verse again, inserting your name wherever it says "you":

But [YOUR name] will receive power when the Holy Spirit has come on [your name], and [your name] will be my witness in Jerusalem, and in all Judea and in Samaria, and to the ends of the earth.

How exactly does the Spirit empower you for that mission? Primarily in two ways.

1. Spiritual Gifts That Serve the Mission

We will discuss spiritual gifts more in depth in chapter 9, but every believer has been given spiritual gifts whereby others experience the actual touch of Jesus through us. These gifts, while diverse, have one, unified objective: to propel Jesus' gospel to the ends of the earth.

A pastor friend of mine once brought about ten people onto the stage at his church and assigned them roles to play on an imaginary fire truck. One person was assigned to drive; another controlled the siren; one manned the hose; and one turned that strange little steering wheel in the back. After getting them all in place and having them commence their roles, he asked each of them, "Now, what is your purpose, again?" Each answered by repeating the name of whatever job he had given them. After they were done, he said, "You're ALL wrong! Your purpose—every one of you—is to *put out fires!*"

Every spiritual gift serves the larger purpose of getting the gospel to the ends of the earth. We have different roles, but the overall mission is the same: preach Jesus more effectively.

You can apply this thinking to your "natural giftings" as well (business, teaching, organization, etc.). Not every believer gets called into full-time vocational ministry, but we each should think about our careers in terms of God's global mission. As I have studied church history over the years, one of my most surprising discoveries is that "regular" people have been the most effective carriers of Christianity around the world.

Luke (the author of Acts), for example, seems to go out of his way to demonstrate that the gospel traveled faster on the wings of business than it did through the journeys of the apostles. The first time the gospel left Jerusalem (Acts 8), he makes a point of telling us that the apostles were *not* the ones carrying it:

All *except the apostles* were scattered throughout Judea and Samaria.... Those who had been scattered preached the word wherever they went. (Acts 8:1, 4, emphasis mine)

The sermon that produced the scattering and was instrumental in early Christianity's most notorious convert, the apostle Paul, was preached by Stephen, who was a *layperson*, not an apostle (Acts 7:1–60).

Laypeople, not apostles, got the gospel first to Rome. I find it almost a little humorous: The last third of the book of Acts focuses on Paul's desire to get the gospel to Rome. Yet, when Paul finally arrives in Rome with the gospel, he is greeted by "brothers and sisters" in Christ who seem to have been there for quite some time (Acts 28:15). The Holy Spirit in the mouths of regular people moves faster than apostles on mission trips.

Luke seems to be trying to show us that the gospel goes forward the fastest when regular people, filled with the Spirit, carry the gospel with them "as they go" (a literal translation of Matt. 28:19). As historian Kenneth Latourette writes,

> The chief agents in the expansion of Christianity appear not to have been those who made it a profession or a major part of their occupation, but men and women who earned their livelihood in some purely secular manner and spoke of their faith to those whom they met in this natural fashion.[3]

A friend of mine likens Jesus to a spiritual cyclone: he never pulls you in without also, almost instantaneously, hurling you back out. The moment you are converted to Jesus, you are sent out into mission. You're either a missionary or a mission field. There is no third option.

2. Power to "Prophesy"

In the middle of Peter's Acts 2 sermon explaining the coming of the Holy Spirit, he quotes a prophecy from Joel:

> "In the last days ... I will pour out my Spirit on all people. Your sons and daughters will prophesy." (Acts 2:17)

Prophesying in the Old Testament was a big, big deal. Those whom God's Spirit filled to speak his Word were few and far between; they wore weird clothes and had books named after them like "Isaiah" and

"Ezekiel." Yet Peter says that with the coming of the Holy Spirit, *every* believer would prophesy. This does not mean that we compose Scripture, as Isaiah or Ezekiel or Paul did (this was a special class of prophecy, which we'll discuss later), but that the Spirit of God now fills the mouths of ordinary believers with his Word to proclaim it in power to others. Think about it: That which God reserved for heroes in the Old Testament becomes standard fare for believers in the New. In terms of preaching, you're in the same league with Isaiah and Jeremiah.

"But I'm not a great public speaker, or even an extrovert," you say. Are you not in the "all" Joel prophesied about? Even if you are the shyest person on the planet, you have been filled with the Spirit of God to speak the Word to others.

Every time the Holy Spirit fills people in Luke and Acts, they proclaim the Word of God to others, regardless of their personality type. Every time! For example:

- When the Spirit fills John the Baptist, he proclaims the coming of the Lord (Luke 1:15 – 17).
- When the Spirit fills Elizabeth, she proclaims a blessing over her relative, Mary (Luke 1:41).
- When the Spirit fills Zechariah, he prophesies about the coming glory of Jesus (Luke 1:67).
- When the Spirit fills the disciples at Pentecost, they declare the gospel in multiple languages (Acts 2:4).
- When the Spirit fills Peter, he preaches to the rulers that Jesus is their only hope of salvation (Acts 4:8).
- When the Spirit fills the disciples, they speak the word of God boldly in the face of persecution (Acts 4:31).
- When the Spirit fills Paul, he immediately begins to preach in the synagogues (Acts 9:17-20).

And on and on it goes. The Spirit of God in the heart produces the Word of God on the tongue. Every time.

So are *you* speaking the Word of God to others? If not, can you really claim to be filled with the Spirit?

"But I Just Don't Feel Comfortable Talking to Others about God"

There is not a better evangelist in the world than the Holy Spirit (D. L. Moody).

I can sense the objections beginning to form. Maybe you feel like "evangelism" is just not your thing—it's not your gift. You don't know much Scripture, you are not a natural salesman, you aren't good with confrontation, and you don't want to paint "Jesus Saves" down the side of your car.

Over the years, I've heard my fair share of excuses for why people don't proclaim the Word of God to others (and, to be honest, I've *made* my fair share of excuses as well). So let's consider some of the more common ones. I promise that none of these will end with you spray-painting anything on your car.

1. "I'm not sure I have what it takes."

Yes, you do. You have the Spirit of God. You may not have the speaking abilities of Billy Graham, but you've got something even better: the Spirit of the living God inside of you. Jesus said that his Spirit in you gives you greater position than even John the Baptist had, who was, in Jesus' estimation, the greatest prophet who ever lived. The Spirit has come upon you, Jesus said, to do "greater" things than even he did himself!

So, short answer: Yes, you have what it takes. The ability to prophesy lies not in your personality, nor your personal abilities. These come from the Spirit who now resides in your heart. He promises that the words you ought to say will be given to you in the moment you need them and that they will be filled with his power (Luke 12:12).

2. "Evangelism is just not my spiritual gift."

It's true that God has given some believers the gift to be "evangelists" (Eph. 4:11). But a spiritual gift is really just a specialization in an assignment given to *all* Christians. For example, those believers who have the gifts of "service," "generosity," and "faith" are not the only ones who should serve, share their stuff, or believe God. God gives some Christians an *extraordinary* effectiveness for those assignments, but they are the responsibility of all believers.

The same is true of evangelism. While the Spirit has made some people especially effective in bringing others to Jesus, he comes upon *all of us* to testify. A specialization for some does not negate a mandate for all.

And, by the way, there's nothing wrong with asking for a greater measure of that gift. If you've got to do it anyway, you might as well ask God to make you really effective at it! That's a prayer God loves to answer.

3. "I witness with my life."

In other words, "I think I bring other people to Jesus by being a really nice person." But the gospel is, in its essence, an *announcement* about what *Jesus did* to save people, not a presentation of what a good person you are. Sharing that announcement requires *words,* because you can't really explain what Jesus did through charades. Trying to share the gospel without using words is like watching a newscast with the sound turned off. I may realize that the newscaster looks excited, but I don't know why. And if he's telling me about danger headed my direction, I'd like to know specifically what he is saying.

Some Christians appeal to the quip attributed to Francis of Assisi: "Preach the gospel; when necessary, use words." With all due respect for St. Francis, how can you preach the gospel of Christ's finished work *without* words? That's like saying, "Tell me your phone number. If necessary, use digits." The announcement consists of words.

A generous, humble, gracious, sacrificial, holy life can wonderfully complement the proclaimed gospel, but it can never substitute for it.

4. "I don't have time."

We are a culture of busy people, that's for sure. Perhaps you say, "When would I possibly have time to go out and 'evangelize'? I get up, go to work, and after work, I come home, try to play a little with my kids, watch a little television, and then collapse into bed. Then I get up the next day and do the whole thing over again. I feel like I'm barely surviving in life with the time I have. I don't have time to *add* a program of evangelism."

One of our staff pastors frequently says this: "Oh, you're busy? Well, Jesus was busy, too. You know, saving the world and everything. The difference is that Jesus was busy *with* people." We live our lives *with* people; as we do, we testify to them. British pastor and author Tim Chester says that evangelism is "doing normal life with gospel intentionality."

I once heard a lady lament that she couldn't take her kids to soccer practice because she had too much ministry activity at her church. Why not look at soccer practice *as* the real place of ministry? Probably there are more "lost" people in the crowd of parents at soccer practice than there are at the church (At least, I hope so!)

In Acts the Spirit of God seems to spend more time taking believers *outside* the church than keeping them in it. Consider this: Of the forty miracles recorded in the book of Acts, thirty-nine of them occur outside of "church." So if you're walking with the Spirit, he just might be leading you to connect with people at soccer practice instead of attending another meeting *about* ministry at the church. Thirty-nine fortieths of what he wants to do is outside the church walls.

5. "Talking to other people about Jesus makes me feel weird."

Of course it does. It's a message about judgment and condemnation and an offer too good to be true. I've heard evangelism defined as "two nervous people talking to each other." But here's the thing: Isn't the message *important* enough for a little weirdness?

I heard a story several years ago about a man who was driving his car down an interstate outside of Los Angeles very late one evening. A significant earthquake rumbled through the region, and the man immediately pulled his car over to the side of the road to wait it out. The severe earthquake lasted just a few seconds, then ended. After the shaking stopped, the man pulled his car back onto the road and took a left to cross a bridge over a river. As he began driving across the bridge, he noticed the taillights of the car in front of him suddenly just disappear. He stopped his car, got out, and realized that a section of the bridge had fallen into the river below. The car in front of him had plunged nearly seventy-five feet into the water below.

The man turned around and saw several more cars headed toward the break. He began to wave his arms frantically, but people driving across a bridge outside of Los Angeles at 3 a.m. are not likely to stop for what looks like a crazy person on the side of the road. He watched helplessly as four drivers barreled right past him, off the bridge and to their deaths.

Then he saw a large bus coming toward the break. He decided that if that bus was going to go over the edge, it would have to take him with it. So he stood in the bus's path and waved his arms frantically. The bus honked its horn and flashed it lights, but the man would not move. The bus driver got out, saw the danger, and turned the bus so it blocked off the bridge.

Here's the question: What would you have done had you been the first one to see the break in the bridge? You probably would have done just what that man did — wave like a fool to get people to stop. Would you care that observers thought you had lost your mind? Probably not. Why? Because you see something that they don't — something that makes their ridicule insignificant.

To put it plainly, the gospel is worth the occasional awkwardness, or even the outright persecution, that goes along with sharing it.

Recently I have become friends with a very prominent imam (an Islamic religious leader) in our area. We both have young families, so one night we had their family over to our house for dinner. As we gathered around the table, I wondered about the appropriate thing to do regarding the meal blessing. So I said, "Should I just pray for my family, and you for yours?" He said, "Why don't we have our daughters do it?" His oldest daughter was eleven; mine was seven. I said, "Okay, you up to it, Kharis?" She stared at me for a moment and said, "Okay."

His daughter bowed her head and began to pray in Arabic. For over a minute. Which is brief, but when it's all in Arabic and you have four kids under the age of seven, it feels like a long time. She finally said something that sounded like "Amen," followed by silence. I peeked out of the corner of my eye, just in time to see my seven-year-old daughter lift her head and say, slowly, but in a distinct voice, "Dear God. Thank you for sending your Son Jesus to die on a cross for our sins so we could be saved. Thank you for leaving us your holy Word so we could all know about it. And thanks for this food. In Jesus' name, Amen."

I've never been prouder — or more mortified — as a parent than I was at that moment. But in a seven-year-old's mind, the message is important enough to take any opportunity to share it. And in that moment she became my instructor.

The message is worth the weirdness. It's worth *anything*.

Filled with the Spirit's Passion for the Spread of the Gospel

Do you really believe the gospel message is worth the social awkwardness, a change in lifestyle, the sacrificing of your comforts, and a rearranging of your priorities? Is sharing the message worth more than even your *life*? If so, that's an evidence of the Spirit of God at work inside you.

Paul, in Acts, would have said an unequivocal, "Yes."

> However, I consider my life worth nothing to me; my only aim is to finish the race and complete the task the Lord Jesus has given me — the task of testifying to the good news of God's grace. (Acts 20:24)

In fact, in one place Paul said he would be willing to go to hell himself if that would convince his friends and family to listen to the gospel (Rom. 9:1–3). That's tough, and I'm no quite sure I'm there yet. But this is what happens when the Spirit of God takes up residence in you and allows you to feel for the world what God feels for the world. God loved the world so much he gave up his Son for it. If his Spirit lives in you, that's how you'll begin to feel about it. What he went through for you, you will be willing to go through for others.

Devotion to the mission of Jesus and fullness with the Spirit of God, you see, always go hand in hand. If you are going to walk with the Spirit, you have to be going where he is going! And from the moment he came to earth he has been going to the unbelieving world. He is the mighty, rushing wind of mission. Churches and Christians not devoted to this mission are not filled with the Spirit, no matter how vibrant their worship, how sanctified their imaginations, or how sacred their demeanor.

A pastor-friend of mine said:

> [Some traditions believe the Holy Spirit is given] to make you healthy and wealthy; he's presented as the source of blessing to those who have faith. In more fundamental tribes, the Holy Spirit has two primary ministries: to write the Bible and convict us of sin.

Basically, you are a nail, the Bible is a hammer, and the Holy Spirit's job is to pound you.... In Reformed churches, you won't hear a lot about the Spirit, as they tend to attribute much of his work to the gospel and the sovereignty of God.[4]

The primary objective of God's Spirit is to complete the mission. To know him is to be devoted to that mission. Without him, we cannot hope to succeed. With him, we cannot fail.

The mighty wind continues to blow through the church. Have you discovered your place in his mission? Has he picked you up out of a comfortable life and hurled you into the vortex of his mission? Have you spoken the Word of God to someone today?

There is no such thing as a Spirit-filled Christian who does not become a mouthpiece for Christ.

Let me close this chapter with the words of Charles Spurgeon:

If Jesus is precious to you (as he is to the Spirit), you will not be able to keep your good news to yourself; you will be whispering it into your child's ear; you will be telling it to your husband; you will be earnestly imparting it to your friend; without the charms of eloquence you will be more than eloquent; your heart will speak, and your eyes will flash as you talk of his sweet love.... It cannot be that there is a high appreciation of Jesus and a totally silent tongue about him....

If you really know Christ, you are like one that has found honey; you will call others to taste of its sweetness; you are like the beggar who has discovered an endless supply of food: you must go tell the hungry crowd that you have found Jesus, and you are anxious that they should find him too.

Every Christian here is either a missionary or an impostor. You either try to spread abroad the kingdom of Christ, or else you do not love him at all.[5]

CHAPTER 4

Greater

"Very truly I tell you, whoever believes in me will do the works I have been doing, and they will do even greater things than these, because I am going to the Father." —*John 14:12*

Recently, driving through the countryside of North Carolina, I passed a tiny, storefront church building that could not have seated more than thirty (and that is provided that all thirty sat two to a chair). The church building, like many of the structures around it, was quite shabby. What did not look shabby, however, were the bright red, freshly painted letters above the door: "New Harvest World Outreach Headquarters."

I love it! "World Outreach *Headquarters*." Here is a small group of believers without enough resources to afford a paved parking lot, yet they still think of themselves as a "world outreach *headquarters*." Honestly, I'm not mocking it. Such ambition is entirely appropriate if you understand the promises Jesus gave about the Holy Spirit. When he left the earth, there was a fearful, partially trained band of fishermen, tax collectors, former prostitutes, and cowards. And yet he told them that through the power of the Holy Spirit they would see kings bow in worship.

How much impact do *you* plan on having for the kingdom of God? Don't mock those who overestimate their potential for the kingdom of God. mock those who *underestimate* it.

Think about how your life would change if you took Jesus' following two promises seriously!

Greater than John the Baptist

"Truly, I tell you," Jesus said, "among those born of women there has not risen anyone greater than John the Baptist; yet whoever is least in the kingdom of heaven is greater than he" (Matt. 11:11). Jesus saw John the Baptist as the greatest prophet who ever lived. And yet the *least* talented believer in his kingdom, he said, would be *greater* than John the Baptist.

Seriously?

Statistically speaking, someone alive right now is the least spiritually gifted Christian on the planet. Mathematically, that *has* to be true, right? Maybe it's even someone reading this book. You're reading this and thinking, "I wonder if it's me?" And God in heaven is nodding his head and saying, "Yep, it's you. You're at the bottom of the pile."

And yet, even if this were true, according to Jesus you are *greater* in position and potential than John the Baptist, the greatest of all the prophets! Why? Because you know the truth about Jesus' life, death, and resurrection (which John didn't fully know), and because you have the Spirit of God permanently fused to your soul (which John never experienced on earth).

Just as astounding is Jesus' promise to his disciples in the upper room before he died.

Greater Works Than I Have Done

"Very truly I tell you, whoever believes in me will do the works I have been doing, and they will do even greater things than these, because I am going to the Father." (John 14:12)

This is one of those promises that sounds so astonishing that I feel tempted to not really take it seriously. "Greater" works than *Jesus?* How is that even possible? Have you ever done a greater work than Jesus did? Ever raised someone from the dead? Walked on water? Multiplied a cheeseburger and small fries into a banquet to feed everyone in Madison Square Garden?

Assuming the answer is "no," what could Jesus have meant? New Testament scholar Leon Morris points to two things:

> What Jesus meant we see in the narratives of Acts. (1) There are a few miracles of healing, but the emphasis is on the mighty works of conversion. On the day of Pentecost alone *more believers were added* to the little band of believers than throughout Christ's entire earthly life. There we see a literal fulfillment of "greater works than these shall he do."
>
> (2) During his lifetime the Son of God was confined in his influence to a comparatively small sector of Palestine. After his departure his followers were able to work in widely scattered places and influence much larger numbers of men. But they did it all on the basis of Christ's return to the Father. They were in no sense acting independently of him. On the contrary, in doing their "greater works" they were but his agents.[1]

Leading someone to forgiveness of sins, you see, is a greater work than making a lame man walk, because the latter is temporary and the former is eternal. In fact, Jesus raised the lame man *to prove* he had the power to forgive sins (Mark 2:1 – 11). Forgiving sins was the point; healing lameness was just a sign. All of Jesus' miracles of healing were only signs of his greater and more significant work: reconciling us to God. So, when we persuade people to believe in Jesus, we are accomplishing the greater work.

Nik Ripken, who served for years as a missionary in Somalia, says that persecuted church leaders in Russia, who have experienced repeated, miraculous acts of deliverance (which Ripken describes as being of "biblical proportions"), only use the word "miraculous" to refer to someone's conversion and never to the amazing acts of deliverance.[2] All other "miracles," they say, merely assist in the greatest miracle of all: conversion from death to life.

Furthermore, unlike Jesus, our ministry is not restricted to only one geographical sector. When Jesus was on earth, his miraculous work was contained to wherever he was at the moment. Now that he is *in* us, his power is wherever we are. Thus, the extent of our works, which he does through us by the Spirit, is greater than anything he accomplished himself in his earthly incarnation.

Truly, truly, our works are greater than those of Jesus. The Spirit inside us is better than Jesus beside us.

Jesus, Continued

Gospel author Luke wanted us to see our ministry as an extension of Jesus' works, not as something we now do *for* him. In his introduction to his second book, Acts, Luke says:

> In my former book ... I wrote about all that Jesus began to do and to teach, until the day he was taken up.... (Acts 1:1)

The "first book" to which Luke refers is his Gospel, in which he recorded all that Jesus did during his earthly incarnation. Luke says that these things were only what Jesus *began* to do and teach, however. The book of Acts recounts what Jesus *continues* to do and teach—no longer through his incarnated body, but through his Spirit in the church.

In other words, it's not that *Jesus* worked while he was here and now *the church* works in his absence. *Jesus* worked then through his incarnation, and he works now through his church. He is as much at work through you in your city now as he was then in the streets of Jerusalem.[3]

Luke points out that even Jesus did his miracles by the power of the Holy Spirit. Didn't Jesus have his own power? Certainly. But Jesus seems to have the Spirit's power in his miracles. For example, in Luke 5:17, Luke sets up an encounter between Jesus and a paralytic and then says, "And the power of the Lord was with Jesus to heal the sick." I used to read that and think, *Well, duh. Of course, it was present to heal. Jesus was there, and he is the power to heal.* But Luke writes it in this way to show us that even *Jesus'* power to heal came from the Holy Spirit.

Why make that distinction? If Jesus had healed exclusively out of his own power, then he'd have a significant advantage over his disciples. But if the Holy Spirit empowered Jesus, then the disciples could do what he did, continuing the ministry he started. Believers, who now possess that same Holy Spirit, have access to that *same* power. Wow! That really blows my mind.

As Luke recounts the first activities of the early church, he draws a number of parallels between the ministry of Jesus and that of the church. (See chart on next page.)

Many more examples could be given, but do these at least help you see the comparison Luke is drawing between the ministry of Jesus and the ministry of his church? What the Holy Spirit did through Jesus in the Gospels, he continues to do in the world through the church.

But perhaps you say, "Luke is only talking about the apostles and the early Christians. They are a special class of people, living during a special time. Things are different now." Okay. I'll concede some of that. The twelve apostles *were* a specially selected group of men commissioned to give eyewitness testimony to the resurrected Christ and to faithfully record his works and teachings. And the book of Hebrews indicates that God gave them a special endowment of power to authenticate their testimony.[4] Furthermore, by the end of Acts, we even see the regularity of *their* more spectacular miracles fading. In Acts 3, for example, Peter could heal on demand, without even "asking" God to do it, and in Acts 5:15 his *shadow* heals people. But in 2 Timothy 4:20 (some of the last words Paul ever wrote), we see the mighty apostle leaving a traveling buddy behind because of sickness. In other words, things seem to have changed between the first chapters of Acts and the end of Paul's life.

But even as some of these spectacular miracles faded in frequency, the "greater" works of the apostles continued, and their *dependence* on the Spirit for power and direction in them remained constant.

Scholars have pointed out that the book of Acts never really ends, literarily speaking. The book concludes with a cliff-hanger, with Paul still awaiting release from prison in Rome so he can get the gospel to the corners of the earth. Meanwhile, people in Rome are getting saved by the dozens ... and *what happens*? Will Paul die, or go on another mission trip — to Spain, then maybe to China? But the book ends there.

When I was a kid, I liked to watch a TV show called *The Dukes of Hazzard*. It always seemed to end with the two main characters, Bo and Luke Duke, suspended in midair between two cars. Would they make it? You had to tune in the next week to find out. As Acts ends, Paul, and along with him the progress of the gospel around the world, are suspended in midair between death and success. What will happen?

LUKE

Jesus' birth comes through the Holy Spirit "overshadowing" Mary. His ministry begins when the Holy Spirit descends upon him at his baptism (3:22).[5]

Jesus' first sermon explains how the Spirit had come upon him to set the captives free (4:16–19).

Immediately after his baptism, Jesus is driven into the wilderness to be tempted by Satan. Luke notes that he did so "full of the Holy Spirit," which was part of the reason he so successfully resisted the temptations (4:1).

Jesus gets sent out by the Spirit to travel around Israel, preaching the gospel (4:16).

Numerous followers prophesy in the power of the Spirit about Jesus (e.g., 1:39–45; 2:25–35).

The Spirit of God fills Jesus to preach the gospel (4:14). He tells his disciples to depend on the Spirit for that same filling (12:11–12).

The Spirit of God comes upon Jesus to empower him to work justice and mercy on earth, to do things like "set the oppressed free" (4:18).

The Holy Spirit fills Jesus with joy so that he can rejoice in the midst of opposition and persecution (10:21–22).

ACTS

The church in Acts is born through the baptism of the Holy Spirit (2:1–4).

Peter's first sermon explains how the Spirit's power had come upon the church to testify to Jesus (2:14–36).

The apostles are baptized in the Spirit and almost immediately get dragged in front of the Sanhedrin, in whom the power of Satan is at work. The Holy Spirit fills them with boldness so that they can respond to their accusers (4:8).

Jesus tells the apostles that the Spirit will take them around the world, preaching the gospel (1:8).

Peter tells the first church gathered at Pentecost that the evidence that the Holy Spirit is on them is their prophesying about Jesus by the Holy Spirit (2:17–18). (This happens throughout Acts, e.g., 11:28; 21:11.)

The disciples experience this filling frequently (4:31; 7:55).

The apostle Paul frees a girl from material and spiritual bondage by the power of the Spirit (16:16–34).

The Spirit fills the disciples with joy in the face of grave danger (5:42).

How does the story end? We'll have to watch your life to see. *You and I* are the next episode. What Jesus began to do and teach on earth, and continued to do in the apostles, he *continues* to do in us.

Ordinary Obedience, Extraordinary Results

In the last year, two different guys I had known in college contacted me out of the blue. "Brad" was a senior psychology major I had met just before the end of my freshman semester. He had fallen on hard times, lost his apartment two weeks before graduation, and had to spend his last two weeks in a freshman dorm in the suite next to mine.

Brad was a rough character, and we had some long conversations. I told him all about Jesus — he'd never heard an explanation of the gospel. He vigorously disputed the Bible with me, sometimes even yelling at me. Yet he kept coming back to talk. Late one night, he burst into my room to tell me he had trusted Christ. Wiping sleep out of my eyes while he wiped tears out of his, I asked how and why, and he said it was because God had spoken to him. He had gone for a long walk, disgusted with the state of his life. He wandered through downtown, and as he walked, he yelled at God, "What do you want from me?"

"I had just finished yelling at God," he said, "when I turned a corner, and there was a sign on the side of a building with the words, 'Believe on the Lord Jesus Christ, and you will be saved.' In that moment," he said, "it all made sense. I literally crumbled to my knees. God had put me flat on my back so I'd finally be looking in the right direction. My whole life had been leading to this point. In the middle of the sidewalk, with people walking by me on either side, I gave my life to Jesus."

Brad graduated, moved out, and I never saw him again.

After more than ten years, he found me again and wrote a letter to tell me that my witness had pulled him out of the deepest despair, saving him from probable suicide. And (this blew my mind) God had called him to be a Christian counselor. He traced everything back to those two weeks when the Holy Spirit moved him into a room beside me. I was his "Philip," and that freshman dorm suite his dusty, desert road (Acts 8:26–40).

When you think about it, how is this not a "greater" work than merely walking on water?

I knew "Justin" for a brief period during my junior year. He also was very lost, but he had dozens of questions about God. So I bought him a Bible and invited him to begin reading it with me, which we did for nearly a month.

One day, however, Justin walked into my room to tell me he would no longer come to our Bible studies. He said he did not believe in God anymore and wanted nothing further to do with him. When I tried to ask why, he all but admitted it had to do with a new sexual fling with a girl. He walked out, and we never really talked again. For fifteen years.

Just last week, however, he contacted me. He told me that after college, God brought him back to that Bible I had given him. He started to read it, and, to make a long story short, he trusted Christ. Justin *also* has become a pastor, leading many others to Jesus. He wanted to thank me because I had given him his first Bible.

Greater.

Again, think about it: Are these kinds of encounters any "less" the Holy Spirit than the opening of blind eyes or the multiplying of loaves and fishes? Which is more significant, the opening of blind eyes by the pool of Siloam—physical eyes that would again one day cease seeing—or the opening of Brad's eyes to the beauty of the gospel for his *eternal* benefit? The feeding of five thousand hungry bellies which would grow hungry again the next day, or the satisfaction of my sexually promiscuous friend's soul on the Bread of Life?

Who knows what the Holy Spirit is doing through your "normal" obedience? Time and distance sometimes allow you to see that some of the most "random" events in your life were, in fact, orchestrated by a Spirit who had an agenda you often knew little to nothing about. And what he was doing through you is *greater* than anything else you've ever been involved with on earth.

He Still Does the Spectacular

I do feel pressed to point out, however, that even though some of the more spectacular incidents may have faded in regularity, we should *never* write them off entirely. Nothing in Acts nor in the rest of the New Testament gives us any reason to think that God has ceased working in spectacular, jaw-dropping ways.

Christians who believe that God has ceased miraculous activities are called "cessationists." Honestly, I started out as one, but after studying the New Testament carefully and reflecting on what I've seen personally, there is no way I could believe that God has "ceased" working miraculously on earth. At least three Muslims with whom I've shared Christ personally have experienced some kind of supernatural dream as a confirmation of the gospel. I'll tell you about just one.

"Can You Tell Me What My Dream Means?"

I spent two years living among an unreached people group in Southeast Asia. The day I left to come home, I got a visit from Ahmed, a man who had become one of my closest friends. I had tried a number of times to bring up Jesus to Ahmed, but he always seemed eager to leave the subject alone. He was as committed a Muslim as I had ever met. He volunteered his afternoons to serve underprivileged Islamic youth.

Whenever I would talk about Jesus, he would smile and say, "You, my friend, are a good man of faith. You were born in a Christian country, and you honor the faith of your parents. I was born in a Muslim country, and I honor the faith of mine. You were born a Christian and will die a Christian. I was born a Muslim, and I will die a Muslim. That is how it will always be."

The week before I left, I mentioned Jesus to Ahmed one last time. I told him that, according to the Bible, only those who have believed on Jesus Christ for the forgiveness of their sins can enter God's kingdom. For about fifteen minutes, he sat politely and listened as I poured out my heart to him. When I finished, he thanked me again for my friendship, and left.

I did not see him again until the day I got ready to return home. When he showed up at noon, I could tell something sat heavily on him, so I asked him what it was.

"Our conversation," he said. "After we talked the other day, I thought about how much I appreciated you for telling me so directly what you believed. But then I didn't think much of it ... 'He is a Christian, I am a Muslim,' I thought, 'that is how each of us was born, and that is how it always will be.'" He paused, then said, "But last night I had a dream."

He gathered himself and continued, "At first, I thought it was one

70

of those dreams that comes from eating strange fish. But I've had many of those kinds of dreams. This was something different.... This was a dream from Allah. I was standing on earth when suddenly, open before my feet, was the 'straight and narrow way' leading to heaven. As I looked up along this pathway to heaven, *you* were on it!" (He seemed so surprised by this that I felt a little offended.)

"You arrived at heaven's gates, but the way inside was blocked by huge, brass doors. I thought to myself, 'This is where his journey ends. Who has the power to open those doors?'

"But then, as I watched, someone from inside knew you and called your name. The doors then swung open wide for you, and you went in ... and then my heart broke because I really wanted to go with you. But then the doors opened again, and you came back out, walked back down the path a little ways, and stretched your hand out to me down here on earth. And you pulled me up to heaven with you."

He then looked at me and said, "What do you think my dream means?"

Now, understand that I was raised in a traditional, Baptist home. Dreams were not a part of our standard religious repertoire. But in that moment, I knew what to say: "Brother, you are so in luck. Dream interpretation is my spiritual gift!"

The Holy Spirit did not cease to work miraculously when John, the last living apostle, died. John may have gone to heaven, but the Spirit stayed here. He is every bit as alive and active today as he's ever been. The degree of sensationalism with which the Spirit operates may vary by situation and context, but his work is no less real. And it is *greater* today than it has ever been—if for no other reason than that there are more Christians with the Spirit alive today than there have ever been. And if you're one of them, he waits to do some of those "greater" works through you.

"Do Not Seek Me in Jerusalem"

Yet, when many of us think about great manifestations of the power of God on earth, we think *only* about what's happened in the past:

- "Wouldn't it have been cool to have heard Peter preach at Pentecost?"

- " ... to have stood before Caesar with Paul as he proved Jesus was the Messiah?"
- " ... to have been there when Martin Luther debated the cardinals at Wittenberg?"
- " ... to have sat in an audience as Jonathan Edwards preached with such power in the Great Awakening?"

But if Jesus' promises are true, why would we relegate God's greater works to a thing of the *past*? God's acts in the past should not only inform and inspire us, they should move us to seek more of his activity in the *present*. The Bible contains not only records of what God has done, but invitations for us to believe in what he *will* do. (There are, of course, some things that God *only* did in the past such as die for our sins and inspire the Bible. Those things will never be repeated, but his work of extending the knowledge of those things on earth is *not* done, and it continues in full force today!)

God rebuked the Israelites of Amos's day for thinking his great acts were only in the past:

> This is what the Lord says to Israel: "Do not seek Bethel, do not go to Gilgal, do not journey to Beersheba.... Seek the LORD and live." (Amos 5:5–6)

"Bethel," "Gilgal," and "Beersheba" are not just a random list of cities.

- At *Bethel*, Jacob had his life-changing encounter with God (Gen. 35:15).
- At *Gilgal*, the children of Israel finally emerged from their forty-year wandering in the wilderness, believed God, and took possession of the Promised Land. There, God "rolled away their reproach" (Josh. 5:9).
- At *Beersheba*, God delivered Abraham and first gave him possession of the land that would become Israel's home (Gen. 21:22-34).

These cities were three of the most spiritually significant places on earth to the Israelites. They were places heaven had touched earth. Yet God said to them, *"Do not* continue to seek me in those places. *Do not* stare with wonder at what I did in the past. Seek me *now* and live!" To look backward when they should have looked forward was not sacred; it was sinful and unbelieving.

Enshrining God's work in the past (and elevating it above anything he does today) may feel reverent and humble, but that kind of attitude displeases, even angers, God. In fact, the Lord destroyed a number of sacred places in Israel because Israel kept enshrining them. What God intended to *motivate* future faith they turned into monuments. Rather than inspiring them to action, these monuments lulled them into complacency. For example:

- He tore down the shrines the children of Israel had erected around the bronze serpent God had used to heal their suffering (2 Kings 18:4).
- He decimated Shiloh, the place in which his presence had first dwelt in the Promised Land (Ps. 78:60; Jer. 7:12).
- He hid the "Ark of the Covenant" and declared that it would never be found or re-constructed. I know many of us who grew up in the 1980s think that Indiana Jones found it and stored it in a warehouse in Washington, DC, but even if that were true (and I'm 94.3 percent sure it's not), God's power is no longer in it, and God has declared it has no role in our future (Jer. 3:16).
- The three cities in which Jesus did most of his "mighty works" no longer exist (Capernaum, Chorazin, and Bethsaida). We're not even sure of Bethsaida's location (Matt. 11:21 – 23).

Monuments to God's works are good when they serve as catalysts for continued faith. But when they become merely markers and memories, our admiration for them wearies God. He's not just a God of the past; he's a God mighty for his people in the present. His name is not "I was," but "I AM." "Seek me *now*," he says, "and live."

Charles Spurgeon said,

> We do our Lord an injustice when we suppose that he wrought all his mighty acts, and showed himself strong for those in the early time, but doth not perform wonders or lay bare his arm for the saints who are now upon the earth.[6]

So, when *you* think about great outpourings of the power of God, what's the first place you think about? Do you look backward, or forward?

I think God might say to a lot of us, "Do not look for my power on the Damascus Road, in the Philippian jail, in the halls of Wittenberg, in the pulpits of Puritans, or in the stadiums of Billy Graham. Seek me *now* and live!"

Jesus' salvation has not yet fully reached our world. Maybe it hasn't reached *your* family or friends. These are the "greater" works he's ready to use *you* to accomplish.

To accomplish these "greater" things, we must know how to follow his Spirit and how to attain his power. So that's where we're headed next.

But before we go *there*, we need to establish one more principle, one crucial to approaching our relationship to the Spirit correctly.

CHAPTER 5

God Doesn't Need You

Now the Lord is the Spirit, and where the Spirit of the Lord is, there is freedom.
—*2 Corinthians 3:17*

And we believe in the Holy Spirit, the Lord and Giver of Life, who proceedeth from the Father and the Son, who with the Father and the Son together is worshipped and glorified, who spoke by the prophets.
—*Nicene Creed*

I have spent a lot of my Christian life feeling guilty over what I am not doing in the kingdom of God. It's not that I am not committed to Jesus, living a sacrificial life, or intensely busy for the kingdom. I am—but there is just always so much more to be done, and sometimes I feel as if the needs of the world are crushing me.

I've found that many, if not most, committed Christians feel the same way. They've been told to be radical, full of "crazy love," followers of Jesus rather than fans—and these are all true, needed messages. And yet many of us, after a really zealous start, end up down a radical path, feeling paralyzed by the weight of it all. So we toggle between summers of feverish activity and winters of guilt and fatigue.

We read Jesus' words about the yoke being easy and the burden light, and we genuinely have *no idea* what he's talking about. Discipleship feels like drudgery. I've counseled many of these weary believers in college groups and pastors' circles, on the mission field, and in my office.

And as I said, I used to be one of them myself. No matter what I gave, there was always more that was needed. One more child to free from the sex trade ... one more unreached people group to target ... one more person to tell about Jesus!

How could I take my wife out to dinner with needs like that weighing on me? Or go on a *vacation*? In fact, how could I keep *any* money for my own enjoyment or pleasure when so many in the world die with nothing? If the price of a cup of coffee could really feed an Indian orphan for a week, was it right for me ever to have a cup of coffee? And why did I need a *hot* shower? Should I take only cold showers and free up another $20 a month in energy costs to house another refugee? John Wesley famously took down the pictures off of his wall, saying they were the "blood of the poor," unnecessary indulgences while people starve. Was my indulgence of hot showers depriving some poor person of their next meal?

My wife and I own a fairly modest house, but couldn't we have a smaller one? After all, my next door neighbors in Indonesia lived in a 400-square-foot, non-air-conditioned, aluminum-roofed hovel, and they were a family of *ten*. I don't know anyone in America who lives that way, but my Indonesian neighbors survived ... so wouldn't *truly* "radical" living require that I live that way, too, and give the excess money to missions? Was my insistence on living like a first-world American, with a nice home (even if modest), condemning many to starvation and hell?

Is *that* how God wants us to think about life? If so, where does this kind of thinking stop?

If every person I see is headed either to heaven or to hell, then shouldn't I spend every minute of every day interrupting them to make sure they know how to get to God? Don't they a*ll* need to know, *right now*? If it depends on me, shouldn't I interrupt them, *immediately*?

The burden of such a conviction nearly crushed me. Ironically, however, the more I dwelt on the need, the less I felt motivated to do. I know that's not the right reaction, but it seemed I had so little to offer in light of such great need—so why even start? Who wants to try to empty the ocean with a thimble?

My despair drove me to the Scriptures, and my despair eventually gave way to one of the most surprising insights I've ever had, one that has radically redefined how I see my service to Christ. This discovery turned drudgery and guilt into freedom and joy, and perhaps, ironically, has led to more generous living on my part than any resolve to "be radical" ever did.

Let me warn you, it's completely counter-intuitive. Here it is:

God doesn't need you!

Never has.

Never will.

For anything.

Ever.

It turns out that I had vastly *overestimated* what I had to contribute. I didn't have "more" I needed to give; I actually had nothing God needed to begin with. Nothing.

God is not now looking, nor has he ever looked, for "helpers" to assist him in saving the world. That doesn't mean he isn't calling us to give ourselves generously to that mission or be sacrificially generous with our neighbors; it's just that he's not looking for people to supply his needs. He's not short on money, talent, or time. He has never commanded us to go save the world *for* him; he has called us to *follow* him as he saves the world *through* us.

God's call to radical generosity begins with the good news that *he doesn't need us!*

If I Were Hungry, I Wouldn't Ask You

Thankfully, the weight of the mission sits upon the shoulders of a God who has no needs.

- He creates universes with words.
- He takes five loaves and two fish and feeds more people in five minutes than twelve men working full-time jobs could supply in eight months.

- He finds tax payments in a fish's mouth.
- He knocks down mighty giants with creek pebbles.
- He summons rich, pagan, enemy kings to pay for his building programs.

Through the prophet Asaph, God, in fact, mocked the idea that we'd ever think he needed something we have:

> "If I were hungry I would not tell you, for the world is mine, and all that is in it.... Call on me in the day of trouble; I will deliver you, and you will honor me." (Ps. 50:12, 15)

God doesn't call us from a place of need; we call to him. We get the grace; he gets the glory. *And we never switch roles.* If you do, you'll live a life of guilt-laden burnout instead of one of sustained, joy-filled, life-giving sacrifice.

He doesn't come to us with hat in hand, needing our help to save the world. If he did, we'd take some of the glory for saving it. And God insists he will share *none* of that glory. Besides him, he said, there is no Savior, and his glory he will not give to another (Isa. 42:8; 43:10 – 11).

Your First Assignment: Do Nothing

Let's go back to that moment when Jesus first laid the Great Commission on the disciples. He said: "First assignment, do nothing but *wait.*" (Luke 24:49, my paraphrase). Think about how hard (and humiliating) that instruction must have been! Every person on earth needed to hear the gospel, and these are the only guys who know anything about it. Some of the disciples had to be type-A.... Can't you just hear them murmuring under their breaths: "Uhh ... *wait?* But there's a world of great need out there, getting more lost by the moment! We need to raise money, *now!* Matthew, take up an offering! Peter, write some sermons! John, write a book! James, organize a pastors' conference! Thomas, get to work on an apologetics manual!"

Regardless of what they might have thought, however, they did just what Jesus told them to do. They waited. For ten days, they did absolutely nothing about thousands of unreached people groups languishing without the gospel, millions of people in slavery, and thousands of orphans in need of adoption.

They waited. For the Holy Spirit.

Why did Jesus make them *wait* for the Holy Spirit—why not give the Spirit immediately and have them get on with it?

Probably because he wanted them (and us) to learn that the Great Commission was not something they could accomplish *for him*. It was something he must do *through them*. "*I* will build my church," Jesus had said, "and the gates of hell will not prevail against it;" not, "*You* will build my church, and the gates of hell will admire it." He is the architect, we merely the unskilled laborers. We are conduits, not "co-Messiahs."

Let this sink in: The weight of responsibility for the mission does not rest on our shoulders, but on Jesus' shoulders. He leads; we follow. He commands; we obey. He supplies; we steward. He delivers; we worship. At our best, we are only unprofitable servants, *costing* God the blood of his Son. In other words, our contribution to the kingdom has been net-negative. And for that reason, he gets all the glory.

When Jesus fed the five thousand with a few fish and pieces of bread, he showed his disciples that he could do more to alleviate world hunger in fifteen minutes with one catfish po'boy than the richest man on earth could do in fifteen lifetimes. He meets the spiritual needs of the starving world not through the sufficiency of our supply but the strength of his saving power. It's not as if Jesus would have been able to do less with only four loaves and one fish! The staggering result had nothing to do with the size of the initial offering, but with the power of the one whose hands accepted that offering.

When God Multiplies Our Efforts

Just as Jesus multiplied the offering of the little boy who came with five loaves and two fish, so the book of Acts shows us how Jesus multiplied the meager offerings of the apostles in world evangelism. A group of under-educated, poor, powerless workers from the sticks in Judea "turned the world upside down" and started the largest religious movement in history (Acts 17:6). This happened as God took small offerings of faith and infused them with divine power. Consider just one stunning example.

In Acts 8, Philip finds himself in the middle of a citywide revival in

Samaria, with scores, hundreds, maybe thousands of people coming to faith in Christ. Then, without warning, the Spirit tells Philip to leave this hotbed of revival to go and stand along a dusty, desert road, all by himself. No crowds. No revival. Just tumbleweeds. If Philip were trying to build Jesus' church for him, this was *not* the move to make. The growth was happening in Samaria, not on this dusty road. Yet there he stands, obediently. Waiting.

Then, in the distance, Philip sees a lone chariot. The Spirit tells him to approach it, and when he does, he sees a man reading a scroll—which turns out to be the book of Isaiah. The section the man is reading prophesies of a coming "Servant" who would bear the sins of the world and make us right with God (Isa. 52–53). The man in the chariot is an important official from the distant land of Ethiopia, and Philip helps him see that this prophecy has just been fulfilled in Jesus. This official believes, is baptized, and returns home. Ancient church historian Eusebius tells us this eunuch and his band of servants became the first messengers of the gospel to Africa, establishing the first church there. Philip planted seeds of the gospel in sub-Saharan Africa that we are still harvesting today.

All this took place through one, simple act of obedience. Not one that looked strategic by our measure, but a Spirit-directed investment. Philip had placed the five loaves and two fish of his witness in the hands of Jesus, and Jesus multiplied it beyond his wildest imagination.

God can do more through one simple act of obedience than we can do through our most extravagant plans.

Working for God is not about what we can do for God in the world; it's about faithfully doing what God's Spirit leads us to do. We are to place all we have in God's hands. As we do, God works miracles.

So let me say it again: God did not place the weight of world evangelism on your shoulders. He only called you to follow and obey him. In fact, I find it interesting that after Paul builds an airtight case for why the only way people can be saved is if they hear about Jesus, he concludes:

> And how can they hear without someone preaching to them? And how can anyone preach unless they are *sent*? (Rom. 10:14–15)

Notice that he did not say, "And how can they hear ... unless we *go*," but "how can they hear ... unless we are *sent*." Paul's eyes are always on

God to send, not on us to go, because unless the Holy Spirit does the sending, our going does no good. Salvation, from start to finish, is *God's* work.

When we posture ourselves as co-Messiahs, we feel the strain of the world pressing down hard on our shoulders. And we can't bear it. *Of course* we feel burned out! We're trying to play God, a burden he did not design us to sustain.

God commissioned only one Messiah, and it's not us. He calls us to be servants, not fellow-saviors; stewards, not suppliers. He wants us not to be guilt-driven, but gift-driven; not only looking outward at the mission need, but inward at his empowering presence. The question is not just, "How much needs to be done?" but "What specifically has he empowered me to do?"

He Gives to His Beloved Sleep

Embracing our role as servants allows us the sweet peace of *rest*. As a dad, I sometimes feel the weight of responsibility to guide even my own family into godliness to be crushing. So I have clung to God's tender promise to dads in Psalm 127:

> Unless the LORD builds the house, those who build it labor in vain. Unless the LORD watches over the city, the watchman stays awake in vain. It is in vain that you rise up early and go late to rest, eating the bread of anxious toil; for he gives to his beloved sleep. (vv. 1–2 ESV)

According to these verses, what is the sign that I am beloved by God? Ha ha! I love it.

SLEEP.

But if I am sleeping, then who is protecting "the city"?

When we are resting, who is tending "the crops"?

The psalmist smiles and answers, "God is."

God expects no more of us than that we do what he has appointed us to do. He does the rest. And that enables us to rest. We obey his leadership, and then we sleep.

"But wait," you say, "doesn't God want radical generosity?" Yes, we'll get to that in a minute, but know this first: he doesn't call us to that because he has some needs that we must supply. He doesn't need us to spot him some cash.

Check the Address

Paul says that God distributes giftings for the ministry in his church according to *his* sovereign will (1 Cor. 12:11). *He* chooses what empowerment he gives to whom. This means not every assignment that comes from heaven has your name on it. (You may recognize that certain things need to be done in the world, yet God has not called you to be involved personally.) The burden of the whole mission belongs only to God; certain *parts* he assigns to each of us. So you support and pray for others as they serve in other ministries, and you focus (primarily) on what God has given *you* to do. (This doesn't mean we ignore needs God brings to us, even if they are outside our skill set. No matter who we are, Jesus expects us to help the stranger beaten up on the side of the road—Luke 10:25–31. More on that later.)

There's no reason to feel guilty over what you're not doing if you're doing what God has commanded you to do. We must faithfully steward what the Holy Spirit has put *our* names on. He's given us all an assignment in his kingdom, a way to share in the ministry of the cross. He has appointed us each to suffer in his way. His sovereign will determines what way that is.

In the same way, God will not ask us all to make the same level of sacrifice. Sometimes I look at the assignments given to other people and say, "Lord, am I inferior? In this season I'm not being asked to sacrifice like them." I've never had to watch my family be fed to the lions. If God asks that of me one day, I hope I will endure it faithfully. Until he does, however, I should neither seek it out for myself, nor should I feel guilty that God has not assigned it to me.

Jesus squashed this comparison mentality when Peter asked Jesus what would happen to John, since Jesus had just hinted that Peter would die by being strung out on a cross. Peter nodded over toward John and said, "Well, what about him?" Jesus replied, "What is that to you? *You* follow *me*."

"But Jesus, ummm, well, I have to die on a cross, while John gets to expire of old age on the Mediterranean island of Patmos, writing books and letters!"

Jesus' reply? "Yes."

(Though tradition says that John first got boiled in oil—so this was no beach vacation.)

The point is, Jesus doesn't want us comparing sacrifices. He wants us obeying assignments. "Now it is required," Paul says, "that those who have been given a trust must prove faithful" (1 Cor. 4:2).

Faithfulness, not degree of sacrifice, is our measure of "success."

Few people in Christian history have been used as powerfully as Martin Luther. Yet many in Luther's day criticized him for not suffering more, calling him "Dr. Easychair."[1] True radicals for Jesus, they said, live in poverty. Luther, who could have defended himself by pointing to the myriad places where he had suffered, instead responded by saying that just as it was wrong to avoid the cross when it came, so also it was wrong to seek out suffering for its own sake. The point, he said, is simply faithfulness in all things.

I've had to learn this the hard way. As I noted earlier, I have spent most of my life feeling guilty about what I was not doing, rather than feeling grateful and joyful in doing what God *had* told me to do. But as I have begun to discover what it means to walk with the Spirit, I have learned to focus on staying more attentive to him, more in tune with his heart. Sometimes faithfulness to God yields me a painful cross; at other times, it brings multiplied earthly blessings. Blessed be the name of the Lord.

Let us receive both with thanksgiving. Paul said that in Christ he knew both "how to be abased" and "how to abound" (Phil. 4:11–13 KJV). Obedience will at different times bring both. If God "Jobs" us (the Old Testament hero who suffered tremendously), then we must bear it patiently. If he "Abrahams" us (a significantly rich man by the standards of his day), we should prove faithful. We can do *all these things*, Paul says, through Christ who strengthens us in the Spirit.

Continually in a Posture of Waiting

We no longer "wait on the Holy Spirit" as the first apostles did, since he comes into each believer at conversion (1 Cor. 12:13), but we must never abandon their posture of humble dependence on God, looking for his guidance in the mission. Nor are we sitting around in idleness, waiting for a "holy hunch" to move us to action. Ours, you see, is a posture of *active* waiting, in which we gratefully offer ourselves in full surrender to God to be used in his mission. As we do that, he guides. We pedal with love for God and others; he steers.

In the next chapter we'll unpack more fully what that looks like. But for now, let me encourage you to take inventory of your life. Are you feeling burned out in your family, your job, or your ministry, because you have taken upon yourself burdens that belong only to God? Have you taken responsibility for "building the city," rather than leaving that weight to God?

Constant feelings of guilt, paralysis, and restlessness are dead give-aways of the co-Messiah complex. Of course, there's always more that you could do ... but you're just a creature. And an unprofitable one, at that (Luke 17:10)! Until you get off the saving throne and back into the position of creaturely servitude, you'll always be out of balance—because in your zeal to be a help to God you make the mistake of trying to be God. You'll never have the slightest idea how to balance rest and labor, enjoyment and sacrifice—in fact, the very ideas of balance and rest will seem ludicrous to you. And of course, you can't sleep, because gods can't nap. They have a universe to run.

But thank God, we serve a God who doesn't lack for resources. Because he never slumbers or sleeps, I can (Ps. 121:4). He blesses those whom he loves with the ability to sleep, even when work remains to be done in the city, because, ultimately, he's the one in charge of building it (Ps. 127:2). This means that many of his earthly blessings—such as food and vacation and friends—can and should be enjoyed without guilt (1 Tim. 6:17), because enjoying them does not mean that we are robbing the world of a needed provision. God is an infinite supply of provision.

Martin Luther pointed out that God "sets forth a feast for the *sparrows* and spends on them annually more than the total revenue of the king of France."[2] He does so because he is an endless supply of resources and loves to shower his creation with good gifts. Don't insult God by refusing to enjoy some of them.

What Makes Them Such Effective Mobilizers?

I recently learned that Pentecostal Christians more effectively mobilize people for mission than any other group on the planet. They produce more missionaries, by percentage, than anyone else! Yet, very few of the "famous" missions speakers are Pentecostals. The most sought-after missions speakers seem to be experts at hammering home the worldwide need, leaving listeners with a deep sense of the weightiness and urgency of the task. We need to hear that. But Pentecostal missions speakers tend to focus on what the Spirit of God has gifted and is calling *you* to do. In addition to directing our attention outward, to the enormity of the task, they direct it inward, to the empowerment of the Spirit. "I may not be able to do everything," the hearer realizes, "but God is sending me to *that* person, to *that* unreached people group."

Again, both emphases are crucial. We *need* to understand that more than 6,600 unreached people groups exist around the world, consisting of people just like us—created in the image of God—for whom going to hell will be every bit the tragedy that it would be for one of our own children. We *need* to understand that 100,000 children died just last week of preventable, hunger-related diseases. Our hearts need to break over those things and we need to look to heaven and say, "Please, Lord! Here am I! Send me!"

But we also need to remember that God has no need of our help. We need to offer our lives to him because the gospel demands it, not because he needs it. And then we need to look inward to discover *where* and *how* the Spirit of God has called us specifically to help. Instead of being *guilt-driven,* we need to become *grace-driven* and *gift-driven.*

The burden of the Christian mission is *heavy*—we are, after all, trying to bring life to a broken world underneath the condemnation of death—but even a Herculean burden is "easy" when it sits upon the shoulders of the infinitely strong Savior with whom we are co-yoked (Matt. 11:30). Engaging in the mission of God is not just about asking, "What would Jesus do?" but also, "What does Jesus want to do through me?"

Those Are *My* Four Children

I have a friend, Tony, who has adopted five kids, four from Ukraine and one from Kenya (and he says you have no trouble telling which ones are which!). The four from Ukraine he adopted at once. When I asked how he came to that, he replied that one summer he and his wife set out to study the book of Romans together. They felt struck by Paul's admonition that those who know the gospel should become like the gospel. The more he learned about his own salvation, he said, the more he longed for a way to respond to Jesus for his great grace.

But how should they do this? As Tony and his wife prayed through that question, he came to Paul's teaching in Ephesians 1:5 that God has adopted all believers into his family; then he read Paul's command in Ephesians 5:1 for believers to imitate their God. "What better way to put the gospel on display," Tony thought, "than to adopt an unwanted child?"

Tony asked God for the opportunity to do just that, and did God ever open *that* door! Tony went on a mission trip to Ukraine. While there, the orphanage director told Tony that someone had just brought in a set of four siblings. The kids, ages two through eight, were about to be split up and placed in orphanages around the country ... unless someone came forward to take all four. When a worker brought the kids out to Tony, he saw four scared little children, all holding hands. They thought they were being called in for discipline. In that moment, Tony knew the Spirit of God had answered his prayer. "Those are your kids," the Spirit said.

"I know I can't take care of all the orphans in the world," Tony said. "But God told me to take care of these four. I know adoption is not God's will for every family. But it was clear it was the Spirit's direction for us. We wanted to respond to the gospel, and this is the way the Holy Spirit directed us to do that. We didn't adopt because we couldn't have children; we did it because this is the way the Spirit of God directed us to respond to the gospel."

The Spirit's leadership in our lives begins with a desire to pour out your life for his kingdom and a willingness to do whatever he says.

Is your heart ready to be led?

Since that's such a significant question, let's probe it a step further.

CHAPTER 6

God Steers Moving Ships

He died for all, that those who live should no longer live for themselves but for him who died for them and was raised again.
—*2 Corinthians 5:15*

Let me remark that being "led by the Spirit of God" is a remarkable expression. The Bible does not say, "As many as are driven by the Spirit of God." No, the devil is a driver, and when he enters either into me or into hogs he drives them furiously. —*Charles Spurgeon*

God turned down David's offer to build him a house.

David lived in a really nice house himself. Second Samuel calls it a "house of cedar," an Old Testament way of saying "blingin'." Meanwhile, God dwelt in a drafty old tent, so David thought he would do a favor for God and upgrade his abode. But God said,

"In all places where I have moved with all the people of Israel, did I speak a word ... saying, 'Why have you not built me a house of cedar?' ... I took you from the pasture, from following the sheep, that you should be prince over my people Israel. And I have been with you wherever you went and have cut off all your enemies from before you. And I will make for you a great name.... And I will give you rest from all your enemies.... Will you build me a house? The LORD declares to you that he will make you a house." (2 Sam. 7:7–14 ESV, v. 14 paraphrased)

God did not need David to build a house for him. In fact, God was building one for David.

God said David's offer did please him, however (2 Chron. 6:8), because it revealed two things about David's heart—two things that should characterize any believer's heart: he was filled with a desire to sacrifice for God's kingdom, and he was completely yielded in surrender to God. These two characteristics embody the posture of "active waiting" I brought up in the previous chapter. Let's look at them one at a time.

Posture 1: A Desire to Sacrifice

David felt so overwhelmed at what God had done for him that his heart overflowed with a desire to give back to God. This pleased God, so while God told David he could not build the temple, he did allow him to collect the materials that his son Solomon would use to build the temple. The writer of Chronicles records that David provided "a large amount" of materials, more than could be counted, and "at great pains" to himself (1 Chron. 22:4, 14).

A heart that truly understands the gospel overflows with gratefulness to God. Extravagant grace produces extravagant givers.

David knew he had been nothing when God chose him to be king: a shepherd, the lowliest occupation in Israel, and the "least" of eight sons. God gave him *everything*. And even more than an earthly kingship, God gave him forgiveness of sins and an eternal inheritance in heaven.[1] David's heart burst with thanksgiving. "Who am I, Sovereign LORD, and what is my family, that you have brought me this far?" (2 Sam. 7:18). He had to do something. Something big.

Have you ever stopped to think about how much you "owe" to God? Where would you be had Jesus not come to earth to save you? He had no obligation to come. What were you when he came for you? You were condemned, having sold yourself to sin. Yet, "God demonstrates his own love for us in this: While we were still sinners, Christ died for us" (Rom. 5:8). He voluntarily absorbed the sting of your rejection and died in shame upon a cross in your place, going through hell itself for you, just so you could live with him in indescribable joy forever.

When you understand that in your heart, it changes your attitude toward what to do with your life. How could it not?

Realizing the love of God for us produces love for God in us. Imagine you arrived home one afternoon to find a friend waiting on the porch. As you unlocked the door to go inside, he says, "Oh, while you were out, a creditor came by, demanding that you pay your debt. So I paid it for you."

How would you react to that person?

If your friend had paid some undue postage on a letter, you might slap him on the back and say, "Thanks, buddy." But if the IRS had shown up, claiming you owed $900,000 in back taxes, and they were there to take you to jail, but your friend paid that debt off, you would probably fall on your feet and say, "Command me, my lord." Extravagant generosity compels extravagant response.

When we realize how great a debt we owe to God, we become willing servants, eager to be poured out for God and his kingdom. If we do not feel that way, we might never have truly understood the gospel.

Gifts that please God express a heart of deep gratefulness and passionate worship. Jesus praised the woman, for example, who poured out the expensive perfume on his feet, not because he needed that perfume — after all, it sweetened the air for only a few minutes, and was wasted in an economic sense — but because it expressed his priceless value to her. Jesus didn't need the perfume; it was she who *needed* to wash his feet with her tears and offer her most expensive possession. Jesus would wash her soul with his blood; she needed to declare his worthiness.

God calls us to be generous, not because he has needs, but because he wants us to become generous, as he is. Generosity is not something God wants *from* us, you see, as much as something he wants *for* us. He wants us to be consumed with his glory and filled with compassion, just like he is, moving instinctively to a world of need around us.

Toward the end of his life, David wanted again to give something to God — a field on which God would construct the temple. The owner told David he could just have it. But David responded,

> "No, I insist on paying you for it. I will not sacrifice to the LORD my
> God burnt offerings that cost me nothing." (2 Sam. 24:24)

David would not give to God an offering that cost him nothing, because by this point he understood well that his offerings were not about meeting God's needs, but about expressing God's worthiness. If the gift had been about meeting God's needs, then a free field would suffice. But to give God a gift that cost David nothing would not express to God how he felt about him.

So, is your heart ready to be led? The first question to ask is this: Have you offered your life to God in grateful sacrifice?

God steers moving ships — ships driven by the winds of worship, gratefulness, love to God for what he's done, and compassion for those he cares about.

Posture 2: Complete Surrender

Not only did David present his life back to God as a grateful sacrifice. He also yielded himself to God in complete surrender. Whatever God would command, David stood ready to obey. So later, when the prophet Nathan told David what God wanted from him, he obeyed with great zeal. His exuberance in obedience became so contagious that he brought all of Israel along with him into his offering (1 Chron. 22:2 – 19).

Following Jesus means a full surrender of our wills to God. David likely remembered how his predecessor, King Saul, had failed so badly in this. Rather than giving God what he asked, Saul had offered a substitute — although a generous one — in place of surrender. God rebuked Saul with these harsh words,

> "Does the LORD delight in burnt offerings and sacrifices as much as
> in obeying the LORD? To obey is better than sacrifice, and to heed
> is better than the fat of rams." (1 Sam. 15:22)

At the end of the day, obedience is what God desires most from us.

The first command Jesus gave for those who follow him is the complete surrender of our wills. He said, "Whoever wants to be my disciple must deny themselves and take up their cross and follow me" (Matt. 16:24).

"Deny yourself" means a total surrender of every desire in your heart to God. Every dream, every desire, every ambition. You say "no" to all that you want from life so that you are ready to say "yes" to all that he wants from it.

"Take up your cross" means you embrace his agenda in life rather than your own. The cross is the best-known Christian symbol, but for many Christians it has become little more than a sentimental piece of jewelry to hang around their neck. For the first disciples, it was no piece of jewelry. The cross was an instrument of oppression, torture, pain, and death. usually people they knew had died on them. Crosses struck fear into the hearts of all who beheld them.

Imagine that you went to someone's house and above the dining room table hung a picture of a man being electrocuted. In the family room you saw a life-size lethal injection table. Above the baby's crib you see a small hangman's noose dangling from a mobile. I'm guessing that you probably will not send your kids over for a play-date! Yet this is the image Jesus says should characterize the lives of his followers.[2]

To follow Jesus means that you die to any control you maintain over your life. Like a man on a cross, you place yourself under Jesus' complete domination, with no more dreams of your own. Dead men have no more ambition for their lives.

Have you ever presented your life to God that way—with no conditions, no restrictions?

This Is the Will of God for You

Grateful sacrifice and complete surrender. When Paul summed up in Romans 12:1 what God wants from us, he called for those exact two things:

> Therefore, I urge you, brothers and sisters, in view of God's mercy, to offer your bodies as a living sacrifice, holy and pleasing to God—this is your true and proper worship. (Rom. 12:1)

We are to offer our bodies as living sacrifices to God as an *act of worship*. Notice that we do this in response to something—*the mercies of God*. The mercies of God in the gospel, Paul believes, should cause us to be so overwhelmed with gratefulness that we joyfully die to everything we have wanted from life so that we can live to fulfill his desires.

This offering is both extreme and total. Don't let the beauty of Paul's prose keep you from the gruesome imagery he employed. Animal sacrifices are hard to watch. I saw one firsthand when I lived in a Muslim country. Seven men held down a large bull as the city's religious leader slit its throat. Blood sprayed everywhere—all over the imam, the men holding down the bull, and me. The poor animal, helpless and agonizing, squirmed and wheezed and moaned for the incredibly long minute it took him to die.

As I watched this hideous scene, two thoughts entered my head, one of which filled me with horror, the other with grateful joy. The first was that, according to Romans 12:1, this was the picture of what God wanted from my life: daily, living sacrifice. The second was that this is what God had voluntarily done for me, to save my soul from hell. Wonder at his sacrifice for me compels my sacrifice for him, making it a joy and delight.

So again, I ask you to consider: Where would you be without Jesus? Short answer: Lost. Forever. The only way others will hear about the gospel is through us. Others are at exactly the same place that we would be without Jesus. As Martin Luther said, "It wouldn't matter if Jesus died a thousand times if no one ever heard about it." It is *impossible* to understand that and not have your heart rise up to say, "Please, Lord, send me! Use me! I'm ready! Give your command."

Later we will discuss how we can know, specifically, what God wants us to do; but before we can know that, our hearts *must* be in a posture to hear from him—a posture of thankfulness and surrender. Until this happens, we will likely get the Holy Spirit's direction wrong. We will turn the Holy Spirit into a divine butler instead of a mission commander.

The Spirit is not a life coach helping you reach your potential, nor a concierge for a life of ease. The true Spirit of Jesus serves the mission of the cross. His goal is to make the cross larger in our hearts and to compel us to yield our lives in service to its purpose. *The Holy Spirit,* you could say, *is always leading to the cross or from it, to carry its message of healing to others.*

Waiting on the Holy Spirit

We are continually to be in that same posture of waiting in which Jesus left his first disciples. Our waiting is not passive, however; it is extremely active. Because we already have the Holy Spirit, we don't sit around in inactivity, waiting on Jesus to send something from heaven.

We've already got it. We aggressively offer our lives in living sacrifice to his mission, looking to him to *steer* us in the where and how.

Consider this: The question is no longer *whether* God wants us involved in his mission, only *where* and *how*. The gratefulness and surrender of Romans 12:1 is the gateway to hearing from the Holy Spirit! As Jim Elliot, missionary martyr in Ecuador, clarified, "Before we can ever hear his voice, we must heed that verse [Romans 12:1, to offer your bodies as living sacrifices]."

And this offering, by the way, will not be a onetime occurrence. "Living" sacrifices are hard to sustain because a "living" sacrifice always tries to crawl off the altar. As the heat and pain of sacrifice intensify, you want to quit. At least, that's how it is for me. I must *daily,* as Paul instructs, renew myself in the mercies of God for me, reminding myself of how far Jesus went to save me, and how much he gave up to do so. As I do, I gladly climb back on the altar, again and again, as an act of worship. I find myself pleading with Jesus to use my life for his purpose of saving others, just as he used his every breath for me. I want his glory to become my cause; the prosperity of his people, my passion; bringing home the lost sons and daughters he died to redeem, my agenda. Knowing he engraved my name upon his heart engraves his mission upon mine (Isa. 49:15 – 16).

My Story

My experience with being led by the Spirit began when I quit asking God what his will for my life was and started offering my life to him as a sacrifice for the pursuit of his will on earth.

It all started with a wrong prayer.

I surrendered my life to God right before going to college. I told God I would do whatever he wanted.

I chose a career path in law, because I had a natural proclivity toward it and knew I could make good money in it. I figured that if God wanted something different from me, he'd tell me. I'm not sure how I thought he would do that, but I assumed it would involve some kind of "Damascus Road" experience in which he knocked me out of my car and told me what to do, or at least spelled it out in my Cheerios. Something like, "J.D., take the gospel to Afghanistan." But nothing like that ever came. No bright lights. No voices. All my Cheerios ever spelled out was "oooooooooooo."

My junior year of college, I read through the book of Romans several times. On my third time through, Romans 2:12 seemed to lift off the page,

> For all who have sinned without the law will also perish without the law, and all who have sinned under the law will be judged by the law (ESV).

This meant that even those who hadn't heard of Jesus specifically were still under the judgment of God, since they had a "law" written on their hearts. And each of us, without exception, Paul explains, has rebelled against that law. Our only hope, therefore, is the gospel (Rom. 10:14–17). And people can only hear about it through us.

I had read these verses before, but it was as if the importance of the mission suddenly became alive to me. The reality of whole nations of people perishing, having never heard about hope in Jesus, broke me. You see, at most, one third of our world is Christian, and that's if you count *everyone* who claims to be a Christian. That means that *at least* 4.5 billion people remain separated from God right now. And of that 4.5 billion, two billion have no access to the gospel.[3]

These two billion are people created in the image of God, just like you and I are. They have the same needs, wants, hurts, and desires that you and I have. Each one is someone's son or daughter. Many are someone's mom or dad. They know what it feels like to be lonely and afraid. God loves them just as he loves you and me.

And here I had chosen my career without giving hardly any thought to those two billion people.

My mind flooded with the image of what Christ had gone through to save me. I had been hopeless and helpless, had rejected Christ for years, and still he had pursued me. And here they were, hopeless and helpless, and with no way to hear except through my testimony. It just didn't seem right to keep going on about my life, pursuing my own dreams, waiting on God to tell me to do something about it. He had already done something about it. What was I doing?

I was asking God what he wanted from me, but he already had told me what he wanted: "The Lord ... [does not want] anyone to perish, but everyone to come to repentance." (2 Pet. 3:9). I kept talking about "*finding*" God's will, but was it really "lost"? His will is that none perish and that all hear about Jesus. Was my life conformed to that will?

That morning, my prayer for the Spirit's direction changed. Fundamentally. It went from "God, whatever you tell me to do, I'll do," to, "God, here I am. You've done so much to save me. Use my life, Lord, to the greatest extent possible, to bring salvation to others. I give my life now to you as a grateful offering. *Please, send me.*"

And *that* is when the Holy Spirit really began to direct me. Once he had placed in me the heart of his Son, his Spirit directed me specifically in what I was to do.

In order for the Spirit of God to lead *your* heart, he has first to reform it into the image of Jesus. Until that happens, you'll never hear his voice rightly.

Get into that posture of active waiting. In response to the gospel, *seek* to sacrifice, *yearn* to give, *get ready* to offer yourself, and *look* to the Holy Spirit to show you where he wants you to go and what he wants you to do. And I guarantee you that it will have something to do with seeing Jesus' church built up and lost people all over the world saved. I guarantee you it will call forth great sacrifice from you. When Jesus said, "Follow me," he didn't beckon us toward a path of prestige and privilege. He bid us to "come and die."

Not everything that comes from heaven has your name on it. But *something* from heaven does, some portion of the cross is yours, and you must find it and follow it to the fullest.

Take Inventory

Before we talk through how to experience the presence of the Holy Spirit, perhaps we should stop and take inventory. Can I encourage you to get alone with God and write out a prayer of thankfulness to him? Think about where you would be without him. Thank him for the things he has put into your life that you don't deserve, starting with the forgiveness of your sin and an eternal inheritance with him.

Then, write out all the things that you have wanted from life.

Finally, draw a cross over it as a symbol that you are offering it in sacrifice to God, saying, "Not my will, but yours be done."

Then you'll be ready for where the Holy Spirit wants to take you next.

You'll be moved by the winds of worship, and the Spirit will steer you in the pursuit of God's mission on earth.

Do you not know that your bodies are temples of the Holy Spirit, who is in you, whom you have received from God? You are not your own; you were bought at a price.
— *1 Corinthians 6:19–20*

PART 2

EXPERIENCING THE HOLY SPIRIT

And the disciples were filled with joy and with the Holy Spirit.
-- Acts 13:52

CHAPTER 7

Experiencing the Holy Spirit ...

In the Gospel

I would like to learn just one thing from you: Did you receive the Spirit by
the works of the law, or by believing what you heard?   —*Galatians 3:2*

A friend once told me about a Christian singer he knew who rented a recording studio. After an extensive setup and sound check, she began per-
forming her first song. The sound technician thought it sounded great,
but about halfway through the first verse, she stopped abruptly, threw
up her hands, and said, "It's no use. Turn it off! He's not here."

The sound tech said through the studio mike, "Uh ... Who's not
here?"

"*Him*," she said, "the Holy Spirit. His presence—it's missing." She
called a few friends into the studio, and they commenced to laying their
hands on various pieces of equipment, praying for God's presence and
dabbing the equipment with oil.

After a few minutes, she began singing again. About thirty seconds in, she again said: "Stop! He's not here. Let's pray again." Another
fifteen-minute session of walking about the room: anointing, shouting,
muttering incantations. Again she started ... and again she stopped.

And again in came the prayer posse. By this time, the sound tech was getting annoyed. His equipment was getting greasy.

As she began recording for the fourth time, he noticed that the reverb on her monitor was turned off, so he reached down and turned it up, at which point she put her hands in the air and began to say, "Hallelujah, there he is! He is here!" The sound tech simply did not have the heart to say to her, "Uh ... no ma'am. That was the reverb."

Many Christians equate the presence of God with a mysterious, tingly feeling you get when the music crescendos just right at a Christian concert or as the pastor goes on an alliterative roll at the climax of his sermon.

For some, an encounter with the Spirit means getting a "peace that passes all understanding" in your heart that you made the right choice or goose bumps when a spectacular confluence of events convinces you "that just had to be God."

For others, the presence of God is some powerful, psychosomatic manifestation that happens during a good prayer time, often accompanied by falling or dizziness. Toward the beginning of my ministry, I attended a meeting for mission leaders led by a famous Christian leader. At the end of his talk, he invited those who wanted a special manifestation of God's presence to come forward so he could lay his hands on us. I genuinely didn't want to miss out on anything, so I went forward. As the man moved down the row, I noticed that at the end of his prayer he'd give a little shove to each person on their forehead, and they'd crumple to the floor, where they would lie spellbound for several minutes. I whispered to God, "God, I don't want to resist anything you want to do to me. I want more of you. I'm willing for you to humiliate me. If you want to knock my shirt off and tattoo John 3:16 my back, I'm open to it. But I am not letting that man *push* me down."

As this anointed mega-leader prayed for me, I could feel his gentle pressure on my forehead. But it felt to me like his hand, not God's Spirit, so I didn't voluntarily take a dive. His praying got louder, and the pressure of his hand got stronger. I heard him mutter something about "God, you have something special for this one." By this point, I was having to push back on his hand with my head to keep him from pushing me over backward. But it sure felt like the pressure was coming from his hand, not God, so I stood my ground. Eventually he gave up and moved on to the next person, who flopped right on cue. Was I missing something? I went home that night wondering if I had missed a chance to experience the presence of God.

What Is the Presence of God?

What exactly *is* the presence of God? And how do you know when you are experiencing it? And how do we distinguish his movements in us from a charismatic leader pushing us down? How can we tell the difference between the Spirit's stirring in our spirit and, say, indigestion?

What does it sound like, or feel like, when he's speaking to us? What's the difference between general intuition and Spirit-prompted insight ... or between God orchestrating a set of events to communicate something to us and just a "lucky" or "meaningless" coincidence?

These and similar questions will occupy our next several chapters. They are exciting questions, deeply personal, and sometimes baffling. I do not pretend to know all there is to know about them (remember the "mystery" chapter!), but I hope that through careful biblical examination and some really honest personal reflection, I might provide some handles to help you better grab hold of where the Spirit is moving in your life.

I plan to present six distinct ways in which we experience the Spirit's presence:

- The gospel
- The Word of God
- Our giftings
- The church
- Our spirit
- Our circumstances

I believe the gospel is the most important and powerful means by which we experience the Spirit's presence. Surprisingly, it is also the one most often overlooked (at least in our day). So let's start with that one.

The Gospel

Perhaps the most overlooked truth about the Holy Spirit is that his presence is intricately tied to the gospel.

Jesus told us his Spirit would bring to our remembrance all that he had said and done (John 14:26). The Spirit would convict us of sin, righteousness, and judgment, give us faith, and help us see Jesus' beauty (John 16:7–11). The Holy Spirit, as J. I. Packer said, has a floodlight ministry: he illuminates Jesus.[1]

The gospel he illuminates is the announcement that Jesus saved us by doing for us what we could never do for ourselves, living the life we were supposed to have lived, and dying the death we were condemned to die. These saving acts of love are given to all who will receive them as a gift. He substituted himself for us, fully satisfying the divine penalty against our sins so that the Father could fully accept us.

The Spirit of God makes that intelligible to our hearts. God sent the Spirit to illuminate that message and to spread it over all the earth. Whenever he is present, the message of that gospel grows larger. And in order to know the Spirit of God more, the gospel is the place we must continue to look.

In a previous book, *Gospel*, I explained that the gospel is not merely the entry rite into Christianity, but the source of our entire Christian experience.[2] Every blessing in the Christian life flows from faith in the gospel, including the fullness of the Spirit. Fullness of the Spirit and depth in the gospel are inseparable, and one always leads you to the other. The more you grow in your knowledge of the gospel, the more intimate you will become with the Spirit.

Numerous places in the Bible teach this, though sometimes we read right past them. At least I did, for years.

"You Are My Beloved Son"

The Holy Spirit's descent upon Jesus at his baptism gives us a pattern for how we are to seek the fullness of the Spirit. The fullness of the Spirit came simultaneously with the declaration of God's full pleasure in Jesus. God the Father spoke from heaven: "You are my beloved Son; with you I am well pleased" (Luke 3:21–22 ESV). At that moment the Spirit descended on him, like a dove.

In the gospel, the declaration God gave to Jesus that day by the Jordan River becomes ours. Because Jesus took our punishment, we share in his position before the Father (2 Cor. 5:21; Gal. 3:26–27). In Christ, God looks at us and says, "*You* are my beloved son [or daughter]; in you [because of Christ] I am well pleased." *As we believe this,* the Spirit falls on us, as he did on Jesus. As he floods our heart, we feel the truth of that gospel intimately. The more intimate we become with the gospel, the more the Spirit manifests himself to us. The more I embrace that I am his son, the more I am filled with his Spirit.

"Show Me Your Glory"

On Mount Sinai, God put Moses in the cleft of a rock, covered him with his hand, and passed by in front of him. It's hard to imagine being more in the presence of God on earth than that! But note how Moses describes the situation:

> Then the LORD came down in the cloud and stood there with him and proclaimed his name, the LORD. And he passed in front of Moses, proclaiming, "The LORD, the LORD, the compassionate and gracious God, slow to anger, abounding in love and faithfulness, maintaining love to thousands, and forgiving wickedness, rebellion and sin. Yet he does not leave the guilty unpunished...." (Ex. 34:5–7)

As God passed in front of Moses, *he declared his name to him,* describing his character and proclaiming his gracious acts of salvation. The sense of God's presence and the awareness of God's great saving acts went together.

Martyn Lloyd-Jones said that this text pictures how God's presence comes into our lives today.[3] God's Spirit "declares God's name" in our hearts, hiding us within his cross, rehearsing his mercy toward us, and making his holiness, justice, love, and glory come alive.

It's not new knowledge about God that we gain, *per se.* It's often old knowledge becoming more real. Moses already *knew* God's name. But in that moment, he felt it. His face glowed for days as a result.

The Puritan Thomas Goodwin compared this experience to a father walking along the road with a young son when he suddenly picks him up, spins him around, kisses him, and says, "You know that I love you, I will never leave you, and I'm so proud you are my son!" Goodwin asks, "Was the boy any more his son in that moment than he was the moment before?" Legally, no. But in that moment, the son *felt* his sonship in a new way.[4]

So it is with God's presence, Goodwin says. The fullness of the Spirit makes us *feel* the love of the gospel. Salvation goes from being a doctrine we believe to an embrace from our Father. And just as Moses' face glowed from the experience, so our souls radiate with the joy and love of Christ. Paul said that souls radiate, like Moses' face, with the fullness of the Spirit as we gaze, unhindered, into the face of Jesus Christ:

> And we all, with unveiled face, beholding the glory of the Lord, are being transformed into the same image from one degree of glory to another. For this comes from the Lord who is the Spirit. (2 Cor. 3:18 ESV)

As we "behold the glory of the Lord" in the face of Christ (2 Cor. 4:4), the Spirit sets our souls aflame.

When Moses wanted to be in the presence of God, God placed him in the rock and dedicated his name to him. When we want to be in the presence of God, he buries us in the cross and makes his name come alive in our hearts.

"Filled with All the Fullness of God"

After giving the Ephesians a lengthy exposition on the doctrines of the gospel, Paul stops and prays that they

> ... may have strength to comprehend with all the saints what is the breadth and length and height and depth, and to know the love of Christ that surpasses knowledge, that you may be filled with all the fullness of God. (Eph. 3:18–21 ESV)

Did you see the phrase "all the fullness of God"? That's the Holy Spirit. We experience that fullness as we perceive how wide, long, high, and deep the love of Christ is for us. According to Paul, those two things — knowing the love of the gospel and being filled with "all the fullness of God" — are synonymous.

"How Did You Receive the Spirit?"

Paul presented this question to the Galatians, and then he answers for them: You first received the Spirit *by believing the gospel*. "So if you first received the Spirit in that way," Paul says, "isn't that how you will continue to 'receive' him as well" (Gal. 3:1–5, my paraphrase)?

Don't miss that. The way we first received the Spirit is also how we grow "more full" in him. We received the Spirit not by *asking* for him, but by believing the gospel. So if we want to grow in the Spirit, we don't just plead for more of the Spirit—we put renewed faith in the gospel! Fullness of the Spirit, you see, is the *byproduct* of believing the gospel. Prayer for the Spirit is great (Luke 11:13), but faith in the gospel is better.

Recently, I heard a respected theologian remark that the theme of Galatians is "the fullness of the Spirit." His statement surprised me, because evangelicals have usually thought of Galatians as Paul's most concise defense of "justification by faith." This book was, after all, Luther's primary text for the Reformation! But after further study, I had to conclude this theologian was right. Actually, both he *and* the Reformers are right. Justification by faith dominates the first half of Galatians, and the fullness of the Spirit the last, because the former produces the latter. Justification by faith is the "root"; the fullness of the Spirit is the "fruit." *The two are inseparably linked.* Believing the gospel is the *means* by which we release the power of the Spirit into our lives. The life of power in the Spirit we now live in the flesh we live by faith in the finished work of the Son of God (Gal. 2:20).

Paul makes the same point in a different way in the book of Romans. He explains that we gain the power to overcome sin by "reckoning" ourselves crucified with Christ and raised in him. "Reckoning" ourselves dead to sin means believing that God has done what he said he did in the gospel. When we believe that, the power of new life flows into us (Rom. 6:3–5, 11–15). We don't believe we are dead to sin because we see the evidence in our lives, but because God has *declared* it to be so in Christ. As we believe it has been done, God gives us the power of the Spirit to live that way.

"The Fruit of the Spirit"

Paul says in Galatians that love, joy, peace, patience, kindness, goodness, faithfulness, gentleness, and self-control are the *fruit* of the Spirit.

Think about that analogy of "fruit." Fruits on a plant are the natural result of its being alive. When the Spirit is alive in us, his fruit will grow *naturally* in our hearts. The deeper we go into the gospel, Paul says, the larger the Spirit's presence in our heart, and the larger his presence, the more his fruit begins to abound in our lives. We don't produce fruit by working it up with self-discipline and resolve. We simply drive our roots deeply into the gospel and the fruit grows naturally.

Think of how a married couple produces physical "fruit." In the moment of conception, they are not thinking about the mechanics of making the child; they are swept up in love for one another! The "fruit" of that is a child. In the same way, when we get swept up in intimate interaction with Jesus in the gospel, the "fruit" that results is love, joy, peace, patience, kindness, goodness, gentleness and self-control. Spiritual fruit comes not by concentrating on producing those attributes, but by becoming intimately aware of God's full acceptance of us in the gospel.

The Gospel "Magic Eye"

Have you ever seen one of those "magic eye" hidden pictures? At first, it looks like only a meaningless morass of dots ... but if you stare at it long enough, your eyes will refocus and you can see in those dots a space shuttle, or the Statue of Liberty, or a grinning zebra.

The first time I saw one, I stared at it for ten minutes and saw nothing but black and blue dots. Of course, I lied to everyone else: "Oh yeah ... what'd you see? The space shuttle — yeah, I see that too ... look at the detail!" Later, alone, after staring at it for about thirty minutes and crossing my eyes every possible way, my eyes did *something* on their own, and out of that scramble of dots a three-dimensional shape lifted off the page. After that happened, I couldn't not see it whenever I looked at the picture.

The Holy Spirit does something like that in our hearts with the gospel. He makes the gospel come alive, allowing you to truly see it. Doctrines become multi-dimensional. God's words in the Bible become his voice *to you*. This illustrates why the Holy Spirit is a better teacher than even Jesus and confirms why Jesus said having the Holy Spirit in us would be better than having Christ beside us. The Spirit teaches us from the inside out.[5]

Jonathan Edwards compared the Spirit's illumination of the gospel to the experience of tasting honey for someone who had never tasted sweetness. No words can capture the sensation of sweetness bursting alive on the tongue for the first time. Edwards said,

Sometimes, only mentioning a single word caused my heart to burn within me; or only seeing the name of Christ, or the name of some attribute of God. And God has appeared glorious to me.... When I enjoy this sweetness, it seems to carry me above the thoughts of my own estate; it seems at such times a loss that I cannot bear, to take off my eye from the glorious, pleasant object I behold without me, to turn my eye back in upon myself.[6]

Such moments are more than "flashes of insight." They are, as the apostle John explains, communion with God himself.[7] In those moments the Spirit is making the gospel personal to you.

Do you feel that way about the gospel? Do you feel the waves of God's love washing over you as you consider it? Does it make you weep? If not, seek the Spirit!

Chuck Colson, who served as special counsel to President Richard Nixon and went to jail for his involvement in Watergate, came to faith in Christ during his trial. After his release from prison, he went on to found Prison Fellowship, a ministry dedicated to helping prisoners find new life in Christ. I once heard him describe what he called the most remarkable prison he'd ever visited during his more than thirty years of ministry. It was a prison in South America that boasted the lowest recidivism rate in the world, and Colson had gone himself to see the secrets behind its success.

When he arrived, the warden explained that the presence of God in the prison transformed its inmates. One of the prisoners walked Colson down a long hall to the solitary confinement chambers, where the only inhabitant was a metal crucifix.

"He's doing time for the rest of us," the man said.

The only thing stronger than the captivity of sin over our souls is the power of the Holy Spirit released by faith in the cross of Jesus Christ. As we dwell on it, embrace it, and drive it deeper into our lives, the power of new life comes into us.

It's About Relationship

The gospel is an invitation to *relationship*. To truly delve into the doctrines of the gospel is to commune with the God revealed in them by his Spirit. To fail to interact with the Spirit of God in the doctrines is to miss their real purpose.

Do you have this kind of relationship with God? If not, you can begin now.

A relationship with God begins by faith in Jesus' finished work. Jesus paid the full debt for *your* sins when he died on a cross and rose again. If you repent of your sin and receive that finished work as your own, the Spirit of God will make you God's child, immediately, baptizing you into Christ's body (1 Cor. 12:13; Rom. 8:9; Gal. 3:1–3).

And just as we begin by faith in Christ, we grow in that relationship by delving ever more deeply into that glorious sacrifice he made on our behalf. As we've said, we don't grow by going beyond the gospel, but by going deeper into it.

As you grow deeper in your awareness of the grace God has shown you in the gospel, and as you yearn to offer your life as a sacrifice for others as he has offered himself for you, you experience the specific direction of the Holy Spirit for your life. As we discussed in chapter 6, as you develop a gospel-centered outlook on the world, he puts specific passions and gifts for ministry into your heart, showing you what part of the mission is for you. This direction is the *by-product* of going deeper into the gospel. The more alive your heart is in the gospel, the more in touch you'll be with the Spirit's direction for you.

Over the years, I've used this prayer by A. W. Tozer from *The Pursuit of God* to express my desire to know more of God in the gospel. I invite you to pray it, too, as a plea for more of his presence in the Holy Spirit:

> O God, I have tasted Thy goodness, and it has both satisfied me and made me thirsty for more. I am painfully conscious of my need of further grace. I am ashamed of my lack of desire. O God, the Triune God, I want to want Thee; I long to be filled with longing; I thirst to be made more thirsty still.
>
> Show me Thy glory, I pray Thee, that so I may know Thee indeed. Begin in mercy a new work of love within me. Say to my soul, "Rise up, my love, my fair one, and come away." Then give me grace to rise and follow Thee up from this misty lowland where I have wandered so long.[8]

CHAPTER 8

Experiencing the Holy Spirit ...

In the Word of God

All Scripture is God-breathed and is useful for teaching, rebuking, correcting and training in righteousness, so that the servant of God may be thoroughly equipped for every good work.   —2 Timothy 3:16–17

One Sunday, an usher brought to me an offering plate holding a bacon biscuit that a college student had deposited in the morning offering. A little note attached said, "Silver and gold have I none, but such as I have, give I unto thee."

This is what you can expect when you have a church with a large number of college students around.

The other thing you can expect is a lot of questions about how to know the will of God for your life. Students want to know how to know which job God wants them to take; if God wants them to date boy *x* or *y* or stay single and run an orphanage in India; whether to go to medical school or become a musician.

And, of course, students aren't the only ones who ask such questions. All of us enter seasons in which we wonder, *What is God's will for me in this situation?* We fear that if we make the wrong decision, we'll mess

ourselves up for life—like one of those Choose Your Own Adventure®
books in which you make some seemingly arbitrary decision, like who
to sit next to on a bus, that results in marriage to a beautiful princess
on your own island in the Caribbean, while the opposite choice leads to
your slow, painful death by flesh-eating bacteria in a South American
prison. (I can still recall the terror those books put into my heart about
decision making!)

So we start to obsess: *What if I choose the wrong option? What if I go
to college A ... but God planned for me to meet my wife at college B? Does
that mean I'll be single for the rest of my life? And what if I make the right
choice but she makes the wrong one? Can she mess it up for me too?*

And so we peer into our hearts as into a Magic 8-Ball, nearly hyper-
ventilating as we look for the one right "Spirit answer" to various questions. We wait for that "peace that passes all understanding" to show
that God is pleased with our choice. We start to obsess about hunches:
*Was that strange urge I just had the Spirit moving me? Was that sense of
uneasiness in the pit of my stomach the Spirit's disapproval of my choice?* I
once heard a well-known Christian teacher say that any time you have
a "restlessness" in your spirit, you should consider it an indication that
you are getting out of God's will. Really? I am a type-A, overly analyti-
cal person, which means I *always* have a "restlessness in my spirit" about
any decision I make. So how can I know which "restlessness" is from
God and which results from my own hyperactive personality?

Is "peace in your heart" really proof that God wants you to make a
certain decision? I remain often skeptical about that. First, people often
tell me about some colossally stupid decision that, at the time, filled
them with perfect peace. I've done that too. Second, I made some of
the *best* decisions of my life filled with fear and trembling. Third, I see
in Scripture an enemy whose whole goal is precisely to give us "peace"
about spectacularly wretched decisions. (When Satan tempted Eve to
eat the fruit, no doubt he gave her a "peace" about it, even though she
was about to make the biggest mistake of her life.) Fourth (and most
important), I see *nothing* in Scripture telling us to look for peace in our
hearts as proof the Spirit is behind something. If there's a verse that says
such a thing, I don't know what it is. But what about the "peace that
passes all understanding" Paul refers to (Phil. 4:6–7 NKJV)? If you read
the context of those verses, you'll see that "peace" comes from reflecting

on God's fatherly promises to provide for us, not as a warm fuzzy from the Spirit when he's happy about a particular choice. This peace is the result of a trust, not a litmus test for confirming which choice is right.

Maybe you assume that God always reveals his will by "opening doors" for you: That is, when God wants you to do something, he sets up strings of coincidences that make decisions easy. That may be true sometimes, but not every "open door" is from God. Some are from our enemy. Think about Jonah. As he ran from God, the Scripture says there "happened" to be a ship going to Tarshish (Jonah 1:3), a city 180 degrees in the opposite direction of where God had told him to go. Was Jonah to conclude that the coincidence of a ship going to Tarshish was God's new direction for him? (Can't you hear Jonah going up to the ticket window at the harbor: "Do you have any tickets going away from Nineveh?... Oh, you do! *Jehovah Jireh!* It must be the will of God for me to go to Tarshish!")

Clearly, open doors are not *always* reliable guides to what God wants of us. (We'll get more into this in chapter 11.)

The Spirit of God Guides Us Primarily Through His Word

The most reliable guide to the will of God is the Word of God. I'm not sure this is the kind of thing to which you can assign a percentage, but if you could, I'd say 99 percent of the will of God is in the Word. The Spirit primarily guides us to obey God's revealed commands, adopt his values, and become the kind of people he wants us to be.

And, when I say "the Spirit guides us through his Word," I don't mean "Bible lottery," where you flip open your Bible, point to a random verse, and draw some mysterious guidance from it. Such a practice can be really dangerous, like the guy you may have heard about who prayed to know God's will, flipped open his Bible, and randomly pointed to Matthew 27:5: "And Judas went away and hanged himself." Feeling certain he'd made a mistake, he repeated the procedure, and this time his finger fell upon Luke 10:37: "Go and do likewise." Thoroughly rattled now, he urgently hoped for a better result the third time around. But this is what he got: "What you are about to do, do quickly" from John 13:27![1]

Rather, I mean that Scripture spends more time focused on the type of people we should *be* and less on the specifics of where and what we *do*. When you become the kind of person God wants you to be, you will do what he wants you to do. Nearly every time we find the phrase "the will of God" in the Bible, it refers to the shaping of our moral character.

> Be very careful, then, how you live—not as unwise, but as wise, making the most of every opportunity, because the days are evil. Therefore do not be foolish, but understand what *the Lord's will* is [meaning, what he is doing on the earth]. Do not get drunk on wine [meaning, don't spend your days foolishly glutting your pleasures and hiding yourself from what God is doing in the world], which leads to debauchery. Instead, be filled with the Spirit. (Eph. 5:15–18)

> Therefore I urge you, brothers and sisters, in view of God's mercy, to offer your bodies as a living sacrifice, holy and pleasing to God—this is your true and proper worship. Do not conform to the pattern of this world, but be transformed by the renewing of your mind. Then you will be able to test and approve what *God's will* is—his good, pleasing and perfect will. (Rom. 12:1–2)

> It is *God's will* that you should be sanctified. (1 Thess. 4:3)[2]

When we think like God thinks, we'll do what God does. Augustine, a fifth-century Christian saint, summed it up best: The will of God? "Love God and do what you will!"[3]

The book of Proverbs describes the will of God more like "a path" than a door. It's not that college A leads to God's will and college B leads to his wrath. Rather, if we walk in the way of wisdom and avoid the paths of folly, God will direct our steps and establish our lives (Prov. 2:20–22; 3:5–6; 4:26–27).

Paul and Peter both pointed to the sufficiency of God's Word for guiding us in the ways of God: Paul says the Word of God makes us "complete," equipped for *every* good work (and every good work would certainly include where we live and whom we marry); Peter says that the knowledge of Christ (through the Bible) is the power for "all things that pertain to life and godliness."[4] *Every* good work? *All things* that pertain to life and godliness ? Those are pretty tall promises!

Three Kinds of Decisions

But how do we approach those decisions for which the Bible gives us no clear direction? Nothing in Scripture tells us whom exactly to marry, where to go to school, or how many kids to have. Does God leave us on our own in those decisions? Great question.

Philip Jensen and Tony Payne helpfully distinguish between three kinds of decisions we make each day and how God's Word relates to each:[5]

1. Matters of righteousness

These things involve a clearly revealed right and wrong in the Word of God; or, as it is called in Proverbs, the "path of folly" versus the "way of wisdom." It is never the will of God, for example, to cheat in your business, to put yourself in a compromising position where you are likely to feel tempted, to use your money selfishly, or to marry an unbeliever. God's Word clearly tells us not to do these things, and so there's no use even praying about whether to do them. The Spirit has already directed.

2. Matters of good judgment

In these kinds of decisions, we're not dealing with a particular commandment of God, but one decision *is* clearly wiser than another. King Solomon talks in Proverbs, for example, about how to go about choosing your circle of friends, a spouse, or even at what stage in life to build your house. God's Word may not have a specific "command" about whom to marry, but godly wisdom gleaned from the Bible can still inform your choice.

3. Matters of triviality

These issues involve matters of such little consequence that you shouldn't waste a great deal of time and energy on them. But here's where our fears from the Choose Your Own Adventure® books come in. Can't small coincidences have massive effects? For example, have you ever heard of the "butterfly effect"? Mathematician Edward Lorenz once demonstrated that an extra flap of a butterfly's wing, in just the right place at just the right time, could lead to a series of chain reactions that produce a hurricane several hundred miles away.

And so we think, "What if some small decision out of the will of God messes up my whole life?" As in, "I stayed in the car on my phone for an extra thirty seconds, listening to my friend gossip, which was wrong, and that made me miss special boy *z*, whom I was supposed to meet on the sidewalk because he noticed my Jesus Loves Me bracelet. And now I will be single the rest of my life!"

But if that is true, where would this kind of thinking stop? Christian philosopher Peter Kreeft says, "If God has 'one right choice' in everything you do, then you can't draw any line. That means that God wants you to know which room to clean first, the kitchen or the bedroom, and which dish to pick up first, the plate or the saucer."[6]

Some decisions are "trivial" and should be treated as such. God just wants you to make what seems like the best choice and move on without fear. God remains in charge of all the butterflies, and neither small nor large things will keep him from providing for us or guiding us to the people and places he wants us to go. We should make decisions based on the best wisdom available to us at the time, and then trust God with all the butterflies. So, if you want to know which grocery store God wants you to go to, don't wait for a warm feeling; find out which one has the best deals.

A Promise to Cling To

The greatest part of all this is that God attaches a truly amazing promise to decisions made in line with the Scriptures:

> In all your ways acknowledge him, and he shall direct your paths.
> (Prov. 3:6 NKJV)

If I am acknowledging him in all my ways, he promises to work behind the scenes to "direct my paths." Much of this direction happens without my knowledge or my "conscious cooperation," as Jensen and Payne call it — it's just what God does in the background as I obey his revealed will in the Bible.[7]

I read those verses like a contract. If I do my part ("in all my ways acknowledge him," which means availing myself of every means he has given me for discerning his purposes), then he will do his part ("direct my paths").

Much of the stress we feel about discerning the will of God comes from assuming we are responsible for both sides of this contract. But we are not! We are responsible only for our side. I actually drew a wall in my Bible between those phrases to remind myself that I have a side and God has a side. Most of my stress comes from meandering over to God's side of the wall! I see that wall and hear God saying, "Hey, get back on your side of the wall."

I've found further comfort over the years in a rather insulting analogy God uses for me over 200 times in Scripture: he's my shepherd; I'm his sheep. Bad news: Sheep are idiots. They rarely make good decisions. They walk with their heads low to the ground and have notoriously bad eyesight, so they rarely see more than four or five feet ahead of them. Left to themselves, they walk headlong off of cliffs, drown in rivers, or fall down and become "cast" (unable to turn over off of their own backs, like a cockroach).

Thus, if a sheep is going to get to where it needs to be, it won't be because of his acuity as a sheep, but because of the competency and compassion of his shepherd. Therefore, what seems to be an insulting analogy turns out to be actually rather comforting. We have an *uber-competent* and endlessly compassionate shepherd, who has promised to get us where we need to go, not because of our ability to follow him, but because of his commitment to lead us.

That's why Solomon said, "Trust in *the LORD* with all your heart, and lean not on your own understanding" (Prov. 3:5 NKJV). In other words, don't lean on your abilities to figure out the will of God. *Lean on his willingness* to guide you. God, you see, lost confidence in our decision-making ability back in the garden of Eden. There he determined that if we were ever going to get to the places he wanted us to go, it would be because of his leadership and not our "followership."

So, relax. The majority of God's guidance happens as the Good Shepherd guides us behind the scenes. God calls for us to pursue his will as expressed in his Word and to trust him to guide in the details. We don't have to obsess about various coincidences or every holy hunch. When God wants to give us special instruction in the application of his Word, he'll make it reasonably clear what he wants us to do, just as he did in Acts—for example, when the Spirit of God forbade Paul and Silas to carry the gospel into Asia, then specifically the province of

Bithynia (Acts 16:7). Unless he breaks in with clear direction, we should follow the paths of godly wisdom, make the wisest decisions we can, and trust that God is guiding behind the scenes.

So when we come to a place where we have no clear instruction from God, we should do exactly what Paul and Silas did in Acts 16—obey the objectives laid out in God's Word as best we know how (in their case, testifying to the gospel among unreached peoples). When it was time, the Spirit broke in with special direction. They remained open to these "interruptions" of the Spirit, but they did not depend on them for day-to-day decisions.

Nearly three hundred years ago John Newton gave this same counsel to a friend. Notice that while he urges his friend to trust the Spirit's guidance, he puts the focus on obedience to the Word (and not some weird, superstitious manipulation of the Word, either—just adherence to its plain meaning):

> The word of God is not to be used as a lottery: nor is it designed to instruct us by shreds and scraps, which detached from their proper places, have no determinate import; but it is to furnish us with just principles, right apprehensions to regulate our judgments and affections, and thereby to influence and direct our conduct ... *By treasuring up the doctrines, precepts, promises, examples, and exhortations of Scripture, in their minds ... [believers] grow into a habitual frame of spiritual wisdom, and acquire a gracious taste, which enables them to judge of right and wrong with a degree of readiness and certainty, as a musical ear judges of sounds....*
>
> And the Lord, whom they serve, does not disappoint their expectations [for specific divine guidance]. He leads them by a right way, preserves them from a thousand snares, and satisfies them that he is and will be their guide even unto death.[8]

Jesus is the Great Shepherd. Just think about that for a while. We can trust that the God who cares more for us than we do for ourselves, and who knows when even one hair falls from our heads, will do his part to lead us in his paths for his great name's sake. He's not up in heaven hamstrung by our inability to interpret various hunches and strings of coincidences. He gave us the Bible, and promises to direct our paths as we acknowledge him in it. When we need him to point us somewhere specific, he'll break in and make that plain.

my finding my
app

"But how," you ask, "can we perceive more of those 'special' Spirit-movements or interruptions in our day-to-day lives? How do we know we're following the Spirit in that special part of the mission he has just for us?"

That's what we'll consider next. And the answer is not as mystical as you might think.

CHAPTER 9

Experiencing the Holy Spirit ...

In Our Giftings

For this reason I remind you to fan into flame the gift of God, which is in you ...
—*2 Timothy 1:6*

Where the Holy Ghost implants divine life in the soul, there is a precious deposit which none of the refinements of education can equal. The thief on the cross excels Caesar on his throne; Lazarus among the dogs is better than Cicero among the senators; and the most unlettered Christian is in the sight of God superior to Plato.
—*Charles Spurgeon*

I love the scene in C. S. Lewis's *The Lion, the Witch and the Wardrobe* in which "Father Christmas" gives each of the four displaced children a mysterious gift. Though they don't realize it at the time, these gifts will prove essential in the coming battle they are to have with the White Witch and her minions. For example, in the heat of that battle, Lucy realizes that her gift, a healing ointment, has been given to her to bind up the wounded in battle. Peter realizes his sword has been given to lead an assault on the White Witch. In those moments they perceived what Aslan (the lion representing Jesus) wanted from them in the battle by looking at their *gifts*.

In the same way, we come to know more about what God wants from us by reflecting on the gifts he has given to us. Do you know your specific spiritual giftings? Knowing these is *essential*, you see, to understanding what the Spirit wants from your life. I would go so far as to say that you cannot really walk with the Spirit until you are familiar with the gifts he has sovereignly given you for service in his kingdom.

"All Believers Are *Anointed*"

"Anointed" is a word Christians throw around to mean a person has a special endowment of the Holy Spirit's power. Paul tells us in 1 Corinthians, however, that this "anointing" does not belong to a sacred few, but is the birthright of every believer.[1] If you have the Spirit of God, you are "anointed."

God's Spirit bestows upon each believer *pneumatika* (1 Cor. 12:1–4; 14:1). We typically translate that word as "spiritual gifts," but it literally means "spirituals." It's kind of a weird word, implying something like a "spiritual manifestation" or a "spiritual experience." (It doesn't translate well into English.) God gives to us, and to others through us, *experiences* with the Spirit through the *pneumatika* he distributes to each of us. Through these *pneumatika* the Spirit himself touches people, cares for them, ministers to them, and speaks to them.

Paul captures this in his analogy of the church as a body. In my body, my head works through each of my members to accomplish its desires. If my brain wants to alleviate an itch in my left elbow, it doesn't send down a magic bolt of brainpower to my left elbow for relief. Rather, it sends a message to the fingers on my right hand: "Hey, your brother, 'left elbow,' itches. Go and take care of that." Does the fact that my fingers do the work lessen the fact that it is my brain's will being expressed? Of course not. My brain works through my fingers. Apart from the brain, the fingers can't do anything. In feeling the touch of my fingers, my elbow is experiencing the will of my mind.

In the same way, God works on earth through his body, the church. He empowers his church as his voice, his heart, and his hands. We don't work *for* him as much as he works *through* us. Christ is the "head" of his body, literally acting through his members to do his work.

If you are a believer, you have *pneumatika*. In Romans 12:6 Paul calls them "grace gifts" (*charismata*) and says God has placed a few specific ones in your heart for his purposes. Through them, God *himself* works through you. *So you can know more about what God wants from you, specifically, by getting to know your gift(s).*

How You Can Discover Your Spiritual Gifts

In three primary passages (1 Cor. 12–14, Rom. 12, and Eph. 4) Paul lists out various spiritual gifts. None of the lists are identical, and each contains a few the others leave out. This shows us that spiritual gifts are not so much a defined set of functions as much as they are various manifestations of God using us in the lives of others. We are not to list out these gifts on a spreadsheet and assume they comprise the full scope of all that God empowers his people to do. Each list simply gives examples of how God works through his people, identifying the most significant ways God is at work in the church. In this chapter we will not discuss all the gifts Paul mentions, but rather five guiding principles to help you discover the *pneumatika* in your life:

1. A spiritual gift bestows an unusual effectiveness in a responsibility given to all believers.

Most spiritual gifts are assigned somewhere as duties to all believers. For example, God commands all believers to serve, evangelize, prophesy, pray for healing, intercede for others, trust God for provision, be generous, exhort one another, and so on. But some believers are particularly effective in those things. This unusual effectiveness is the sign of a spiritual gifting.

2. We discover our spiritual gifts as we actively pursue those responsibilities.

As we obey the commands God has given to all believers, God reveals to us, through our own experiences in obedience and by the testimony of others who observe us, where we are the *most* effective for him.

The Spirit of God called out Paul and Barnabas, for example, to a special gifting of evangelism and directed the church to send them out into the nations as their ambassadors (Acts 13:1–3). That happened as they were evangelizing their neighbors in Antioch. It was out of this obedience God called them to their special task. Think of it like a baseball player getting called up into the major leagues. You're playing the same game—you just get called up to a higher level. As we faithfully execute our duties, others recognize an unusual ability given to us, and God uses their observation to call us up into the major leagues of a spiritual gift. By "major league" I am not referring exclusively to full-time ministry, either. God gives *each* of us a major-league role in his kingdom.

As we learned earlier, God steers pedaling bicycles. He's the rudder for moving ships. If you and I will get moving in obedience, he will steer us into our special giftings.

For example, I discovered I had the gift of exhortation and teaching by leading some of my friends to Christ and discipling them in high school. I was literally sitting on the front porch of my childhood home, explaining to a friend how to set up a quiet time, when I first had the thought, "I really enjoy teaching people how to do this." In college, I began to lead small groups of new believers, teaching them how to pray, understand Christian doctrine, and share their faith. Eventually those small groups turned into larger ones. I never really had a "Damascus Road" experience in which God called me to ministry by saying, "Thou hast the gifts of exhortation and teaching." I discovered I had those things simply by obeying the command to make disciples. As I "obeyed" his general commands to all believers, God made his specific will for my life clear.

Sometimes, however, the Holy Spirit does reveal a spiritual gift through a special, unexpected, prophetic word, as he did with Timothy: A group of elders laid their hands on Timothy and one of them declared that he would become a great teacher, even though he was young and timid. Evidently this caught Timothy totally by surprise (2 Tim. 1:6).

This kind of thing has happened to me at least twice. A pastor I'd just met once told me about a leadership assignment that he believed the Holy Spirit had given to me, one for which I felt totally unprepared. But I've seen the fulfillment of the words he spoke. (Some of the details he gave me were quite specific.) In seminary, our president told me about a calling God had on my life to bring the gospel to Muslims, which again took me a little by surprise. But it also has come to pass.

3. A spiritual gift usually reveals itself in the confluence of what we are passionate about, what we're good at, and the affirmation of others.

I have found the following diagram helpful[2]:

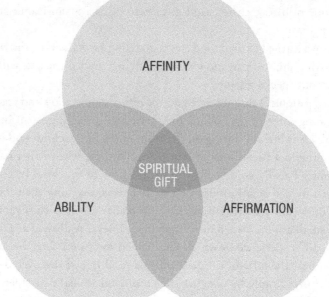

The circle labeled "ability" refers to what you are naturally good at; "affinity" to what you feel passionate about; and "affirmation" to ways people have testified that God has used you. Where all three circles converge is typically an indication of a spiritual gift.

Often, spiritual gifts coincide with natural abilities you already have. God takes a natural talent and "supercharges" it for his purposes. For example, my gift of exhortation coincides with a natural ability I have for coaching, public speaking, and persuasion. Evidently, Paul was a great thinker and leader *before* he became a Christian, having been selected to apprentice under the highly respected Jewish leader Gamaliel (Acts 22:3). His special calling as an apostle and teacher coincided with his natural abilities to think and lead and write.

There are exceptions, of course. Sometimes, God gives spiritual gifts that have little to do with natural abilities, in part to highlight that power in ministry comes from God, not from our talents. For example, I know a young woman in our church who is terribly shy around people, yet God has given her an unusual ability in evangelism. It makes no sense. But watching how effectively she brings other people to Jesus directs your attention away from her abilities to the God who is using her. On the flip side, I know some great orators who just can't preach God's Word effectively, even though they know and understand it well. It kind of baffles me. I also know selfish, materialistic people who, upon their conversion, became the most generous, giving people in our church. (Think Zacchaeus; he went from unscrupulous tax collector to a guy who joyfully gave half his income to the poor!) I know of several great preachers who had terrible stage fright when God called them to preach. As one saying goes, "Sometimes God calls those he's gifted; other times he gifts those he's called!"

In *The Purpose Driven Life,* Rick Warren uses a tool similar to our three circles. We discover the Holy Spirit's plan for us, Rick says, by discovering our "S.H.A.P.E.":[3]

- S = Spiritual Gifts. Learning the scope of spiritual gifts God gives to his body, as outlined in Romans 12, 1 Corinthians 12 and 14, and Ephesians 4.
- H = Heart. Discovering what God has made you particularly passionate about.
- A = Abilities. Reflecting on what natural talent God has given you. (This includes everything from teaching, hospitality, administration, business, to art.)
- P = Personality. Where your personality best suits you to serve.
- E = Experiences. Unusual things God has done in your life that give you insight into particular aspects of his character.

Let's talk about that last one—"Experiences"—for a minute, because our three circles didn't discuss it.

4. Spiritual giftings arise out of the unique ways God has written our life stories.

God sends each of us through particular experiences to teach us things about himself that he will use in us to reveal to others. Jesus said to Paul on the Damascus Road, for example,

"Now get up and stand on your feet. I have appeared to you to appoint you as a servant and as a witness of what you have seen and will see of me." (Acts 26:16)

Paul was special, of course. He was an apostle, which means Jesus showed things to Paul that were new and specific—things that would be written down with authority in the book that tells us what God wants us to know, doctrinally speaking, about Jesus. Our insights and experiences will never rise to that level. But God does give us individual experiences (analogous to Paul's) that enrich our understanding of him and enrich others as we share them. Jesus is like a bazillion-sided diamond. No one person can see and experience the whole thing. So God allows various members of his body to see and experience different dimensions of his beauty, and as we share these things with others in the body, we all end up with a fuller picture of Jesus than any of us could have obtained alone. That's part of the beauty, by the way, of being in a local, Spirit-filled church. You see so much more of Jesus than you can alone.

Paul told us that God had allowed him to go through a great time of pain so that he could "comfort those in any trouble with the comfort we ourselves receive from God" (2 Cor. 1:4). Paul knew that part of God's purpose in his pain was to show him something about God that he could later use to comfort those who are confronting similar circumstances.

Charles Spurgeon, Britain's nineteenth-century "prince of preachers," saw his gout and depression—so severe, he said, that at times he could barely move—as specially given to him by God for the benefit of the church. He said, "I would go into the deeps a hundred times to cheer a downcast spirit, that I might know how to speak a word in season to the weary." His pain became the Spirit's gateway into new insights into Jesus' beauty, which he could then share with others. Having benefited personally from Spurgeon's writing on suffering, I am grateful.

My friend Hannah has a driving passion to see the gospel brought to broken women. While she has not experienced the same brokenness many of those women have, she sees how God has written her life story so as to prepare her for this assignment—through the divorce of her parents, through Afghanistan, through her college major, and even through her singleness. God has given her an unusual effectiveness with those women. They trust her. and confide in her. When other girls her age were hanging out at the mall, she was reaching out to girls at the local strip club. Her passion to see broken women reached for Christ is an unmistakable gifting. She chose a place where many troubled women live and went to live and work there.

I know that God has called me to lead a church that specializes in discipling parents to disciple children. My parents stumbled into a church nearly forty years ago, when I was two years old, and because this church was focused on discipling new believers, not merely counting converts, I grew up in the home of two dynamic, growing believers. That made an eternal difference for me, and now through me for my kids. Of all the things our church could focus on, I *know* God wants us to specialize in equipping parents to disciple their children. That passion came from how God wrote my life story.

God writes *each* of our life stories in unique ways so that we can testify about him to others. There's just so much of Jesus to see; no one can contain him all. No one can embody every ministry he desires to perform on earth. This must have been on John's mind when he concluded his Gospel with the words:

> Jesus did many other things as well. If every one of them were written down, I suppose that even the whole world would not have room for the books that would be written. (John 21:25)

Each of us is a book, written by the Holy Spirit about Jesus, for others to read.

What can you learn about how the Spirit of God wants to use you by looking at *your* life story?

5. The Spirit of God works in our (so-called) secular vocations.

An often-overlooked dimension of the Spirit's guidance is how God uses our "secular vocations" as part of his plan for us in the world. We tend to reduce the Spirit's empowerment to church stuff, things like preaching, leading worship, or taking meals to shut-ins. And those are all great things. The Scripture, however, presents the Spirit at work also in our natural, "secular" giftings, too, using them for his purposes in the world. These vocational abilities are not the same thing as *charismata*, but are still ways the Spirit works in and through us.

In fact, the very word "vocation" comes from the Latin word *voca,* which means "to call." Our vocational abilities are part of our calling. So if we want to know his specific plan for us, we should think about "secular" skills too.

In Exodus 31, for example, we find a brief description of two very important, although largely unknown, Old Testament characters named Bezalel and Oholiab. These two artists, one filled with the Spirit of God and another appointed by God as a helper, showed that fullness by the excellent way they made artistic designs, cut stones, and worked with wood (Ex. 31:1 – 5).

Martin Luther observed that when the Lord answers our prayer "for daily bread," he does so in a variety of ways. He gives the farmer the skill and ability to plant the seed, grow and harvest the grain. He equips someone to build the road on which we transport the grain, and someone who will drive the vehicle that carries it. He equips the engineer who designs the plant that processes the grain, the store owner who packages the bread for purchase, and the advertiser who alerts us to its availability. Occasionally God has dropped bread directly from heaven, Luther says, but he typically provides it in "natural" ways. Thus, God answers our prayer for daily bread by a multiplicity of vocational endowments. These vocations are the "masks" God wears, Luther says, in meeting our needs.[4] Discovering your vocational abilities is part of learning how the Spirit wants to use you on earth.

Perhaps you feel something deeply satisfying, even divine, in some kind of "secular" work. In the 1981 movie *Chariots of Fire,* Eric Liddell, a committed Christian who believed God had called him to serve as a missionary in China, takes several years "off" to train to run in the 1924 Olympics. When questioned why he would "waste time" running when there were so many in China needing to hear the gospel, Liddell responds, "I believe God made me for a purpose, but he also made me fast. And when I run, I feel his pleasure."[5] God glorified himself, not only in how Eric witnessed, but also in how he ran.

I know doctors, businessmen, lawyers, forest rangers, artists, nurses, and waitresses who feel that same sense of satisfaction — something akin to the "pleasure of God" — when they work. This is because the Spirit of God is *in* their work, just as he was with Bezalel and Oholiab, expressing his creative work of the tabernacle through them. God is *using* them in their work. The Spirit of God works through all of his people as they engage their abilities to arbitrate a case, build a wall, paint a picture, treat a body, or tweak an assembly line.

This means that not every person filled with God's Spirit goes into so-called "full-time ministry." Far from it! God may have included a number of "secular" skills in your design—such as dentistry, carpentry, or parenting. In stewarding those vocations and giftings, God cares for the world through you. Psalm 127 tells us that *the Lord* is at work in the watchman watching over the city and in the carpenter building the house.[6] So you can also get to know the Spirit's will for your life by getting to know the specific vocational abilities with which he has equipped you.

Work Strategically for His Glory

Stewarding our Spirit-given "vocations" means we must also think, however, about God's larger purposes in a fallen world when we choose our vocations and where we pursue them. God's command in Genesis 2 to care for the earth has been coupled for the New Testament believer with the command in Matthew 28:19 to make disciples of all nations. Our secular giftings can help us spread his gospel. So at our church we say: "Whatever you are good at, do it well for the glory of God—and do it somewhere strategic for the mission of God."

A very talented young man from our church recently landed a dream job in a prestigious field in a leading company. After developing his career for a few years in Durham, North Carolina, he volunteered to expand his company's market to a section of the Middle East where we had just sent a church-planting team. He now works in the Middle East with a dual purpose: he does his work well to the glory of God (to the benefit of his investors and the local people); and he does it in the Middle East as a witness in the mission of God. He did not abandon his career for so-called full-time ministry; he chose to pursue his career in a place of strategic need. He believes he is called as both a disciple-maker and a businessman, and the best place for him to pursue both simultaneously is on a church-planting team in the Middle East.

Have you ever thought about how God might use your career in his mission?

Where to Begin?

We've talked in this chapter about discovering your spiritual gifts in the general sense, and I've tried to give you some ways to reflect on where the Spirit is at work in your life. If you want to get down to more specifics, I'd suggest you pursue the following:

First, study all the relevant Bible passages on spiritual gifts: 1 Corinthians 12–14; Romans 12:3–6; and Ephesians 4:4–16.

Second, check out some of the great books written on the gifts, like Sam Storms' *The Beginner's Guide to Spiritual Gifts*.[7]

Some people like "spiritual gift tests" that help them pinpoint their gifts, usually through a Myers-Briggs-style, multiple-choice test. I suppose those might do some good, but I'll warn you, a lot of the ones that turn up in an Internet search can be a little hokey and sometimes very misleading. (Full disclosure: I'm a little cynical on these because after my wife and I got engaged, she took one of those tests and her #1 gift came back as "Celibacy." True story.)

Let me suggest that you take a few minutes to fill out the Venn diagram I presented earlier (see copy below). Write in your answers to the items below around each circle:

- *Ability*: What are you particularly good at?
- *Affinity*: What are you really passionate about in the body of Christ or the mission of God?
- *Need*: Can you think of a time when people told you that God used you in their lives? What had you done?

When you find something that appears in all three circles, you probably are onto one of your spiritual gifts.

Finally, I encourage you just to get alone with God and ask him to reveal the gifts of his Spirit in your heart. Write out the acronym S.H.A.P.E. and fill out the sections. Take a journal and draw yourself a spiritual map, a kind of timeline through the high and low points of your life where God has been at work in you. Think back about your most significant, defining experiences, whether joyous or painful. Weren't these used by a sovereign God to shape you and equip you? Can't you see how even the pain has given you special insight into his grace—grace that can be shared with others? What he lets you go *through* indicates what he is calling you *to*.

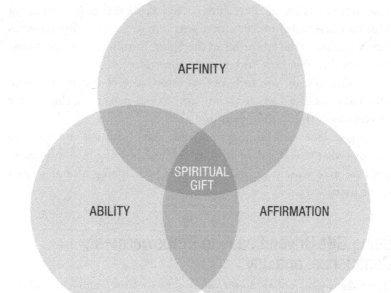

Years ago, when I took a spiritual retreat reflecting on such questions, the Spirit of God helped me see that he had consistently placed a series of "high-water" marks in my life around two areas: (a) defending the faith with college students, and (b) and international missions.

The first book that someone placed in my hands after I became a Christian was the biography of Adoniram Judson. It seemed random at the time, but now I can see it was God planting that idea of international missions into my head from the beginning, something like when he told Paul on the road to Damascus that he would be an apostle to the Gentiles.

I remember being spellbound in college by a video called *EE-TAOW* about an African village hearing the gospel for the first time. It made me yearn to see lost nations worship. I've already told you about my experience of feeling the crushing lostness of the world, like a suffocating weight on my heart, during my junior year in college. Over and over again, like a repeating record, the Spirit of God has opened my eyes to the lostness of the world and let me experience *his* joy of seeing lost nations worship. His Spirit continues to move in me for international missions in a more potent way than he does all the other aspects of his mission. Even as I write these things, I feel a renewed excitement about what God has called me to, a new yearning to get to it! I perceive in these experiences the footprints of the Spirit, forming a line that points me in the direction he is taking me in the future.

I would love for you to have that same sense of excitement about what God has called *you* to. It will come from perceiving the specific movements of the Spirit in your life.

So get alone with God, grab a Bible and a journal, and begin to map out what God has done in your past and is doing in your present. You can often sense plans for your future by mapping his movements in the past.

Being Gift-Driven Leads to Empowerment, Confidence, and Joy

If you knew God had *appointed* you to do something, and had *anointed* you for it, and was *working* in you to accomplish it, wouldn't that produce an enormous amount of confidence?

"Guilt-driven" motivation produces frustration and burnout. Being "gift-driven" produces empowerment, confidence, and joy.

As I explained earlier, throughout my life I have struggled with both "gift-envy" (envy over gifts God has given to others but not to me) and "non-gift guilt" (feelings of guilt about what I'm not gifted to do). But in Romans 12:6–8 Paul tells us plainly,

> We have different gifts, according to the grace given to each of us. If your gift is prophesying, then prophesy in accordance with your faith; if it is serving, then serve; if it is teaching, then teach; if it is to encourage, then give encouragement; if it is giving, then give generously; if it is to lead, do it diligently; if it is to show mercy, do it cheerfully.

In other words, each of us has particular assignments that God gave to us. My role in his kingdom is to execute those gifts faithfully. In doing so, I am part of a body that is doing all the wonderful things Jesus is doing on earth. I may never personally take care of orphans in Uganda, but in using my gifts faithfully, I am part of a body that is.

This is not, of course, to excuse a callous heart toward things that don't interest you. I should pray for and support those who are doing things I am not called to, and I should always be open to God revealing to me new ways he can use me to bless others. But the focus of my life needs to be built on using whatever gifts God has given me in the places that need them most.

Do you want to walk with the Spirit? Do you want to experience the exhilaration of being used by divine power? Then discover and pursue your spiritual gifts.

The Greatest Discovery of Your Life

My greatest joy as a pastor is seeing people come alive in their spiritual gifts. If there ever has been someone I knew who had the spiritual gift of faith and intercession, Curtis was he. Curtis was an older gentleman in our church who had worked for more than thirty years in the Veterans Affairs hospital. One day, in his late fifties, he listened to a message by Jim Cymbala of the Brooklyn Tabernacle on how God answers prayer. Curtis confessed he'd *never* seen God *clearly* answer a prayer in his life, so he set aside five minutes a day to pray for others. That grew to ten minutes, then half an hour, then eventually an hour and a half each day. He developed a large email chain in our church that involved hundreds of people praying around the clock for one another's needs. At every stage of our church's growth, he bathed our steps in prayer. He spoke prophetic vision into my life, and into the future of our church.

Curtis has gone on to be with Jesus, but he remains for our church an example of the extraordinary accomplishments God brings about through those who pursue his mission in step with the Spirit.

So I ask again: Do you want to walk with the Spirit? Pursue your spiritual gifts, because spiritual gifts are the manifestation of the Spirit's power and presence in you.

CHAPTER 10

Experiencing the Holy Spirit ...
In the Church

Now to each one the manifestation of the Spirit is given for the common good ... he distributes them to each one, just as he determines. Just as a body, though one, has many parts, but all its many parts form one body, so it is with Christ. — *1 Corinthians 12:7 – 12*

While [the church was] worshiping the Lord and fasting, the Holy Spirit said, "Set apart for me Barnabas and Saul for the work to which I have called them." — *Acts 13:2*

Earlier I mentioned Olympic runner Eric Liddell, whose story is so elegantly told in the 1981 British movie *Chariots of Fire*. The movie is not completely accurate in its depiction of Liddell, however. The movie depicts Eric as an eloquent, gifted speaker. In reality, Liddell hated public speaking. As a Christian and an Olympian he often got called upon to address crowds, but he felt terribly shy in front of audiences. Furthermore, he felt conflicted about even *being* an Olympic runner; his mother, father, and siblings all served as missionaries in China, and he struggled with feelings of guilt for not being there. As a result, he was reluctant to appear in public to talk about his athletic exploits. Shy people talking about things they feel ashamed of before large crowds is never a good recipe for oratorical success.

When he accepted his first preaching invitation in 1923 to address a group of young people eager to hear from the national star, he immediately began to regret it. The very next morning, however, he received a letter from his believing sister, Jenny, in which she pointed him to Isaiah 41:10 (KJV): "Fear thou not; for I am with thee: be not dismayed; for I am thy God: I will strengthen thee; yea, I will help thee; yea, I will uphold thee with the right hand of my righteousness." Biographer Eric Metaxas writes, "Eric felt that those words were God's way of speaking directly to him. Sometime later, he said that 'those words helped me make my decision, and since then, I have endeavored to do the work of the Master.'"[1]

The Spirit of God empowers members of his church to speak words of insight and direction directly into our lives, to apply various promises to us, and to call us to special acts of obedience. Sometimes it is simply to help us apply general biblical wisdom to our situation; other times he gives us specific counsel and direction. The New Testament often calls this "the gift of prophecy."

Use of this gift fills the pages of Acts. The Holy Spirit appears fifty-nine times in Acts, and in thirty-six of those appearances, we see him speaking through someone. Empowering prophetic speech is *the* primary thing the Spirit does in Acts.[2]

Let's unpack that some more. What exactly is the gift of prophecy?

The gift of prophetic speech takes two primary forms: preaching, and words of wisdom and knowledge.

Preaching as Prophecy

The act of proclaiming and applying God's Word to people in particular situations is the *primary* form of prophecy. Scripture is, of course, *always* God's Word; but through the gift of prophecy, God empowers his church to speak that word in a timely way that addresses the situation of the moment. When it happens, you have the sense that God has not just spoken in the Bible, but is speaking *to you*.

In 1 Corinthians 14:20–25, Paul imagines a church assembly in which every member is proclaiming the Word of God to each other and testifying to the power of the gospel in their lives through the empower-ment of the Spirit of God. An unbeliever comes in, and five powerful things happen to him through their Spirit-prompted prophetic speech:

1. *He is "convicted by all."* What the congregation members proclaim about the gospel convinces him that the gospel is true and that he is guilty before God. In this, we are seeing the fulfillment of Jesus' promise that the Spirit would convict unbelievers of sin, righteousness, and judgment (John 16:7–9).

2. *He is "judged [that is, called to account] by all."* His sin becomes *personal* to him. His feeling about himself goes from a general "well, of course, I've made some mistakes" feeling to the knowledge that he has personally broken God's law, blasphemed God's name, rebelled against God's authority, and that he will stand accountable.

3. *The secrets of his heart are disclosed.* He feels completely exposed before the penetrating eye of God. I love how Thabiti Anyabwile puts it: "The unbeliever leaves church and says to his friends, 'Come meet a congregation that told me every-thing I ever did.' "[3]

4. *He "falls on his face and worships God."* Conviction turns into humility, and humility turns into an awe of the God who knows even how many hairs we have on our heads.

5. *He declares, "God is really among you."* Now he *knows* God is real, because he has experienced the penetration of his search-ing eye. God is no longer an abstract reality, but a living God dwelling among his people, speaking *to him* through them.[4]

These are the five results, Paul says, of the Spirit of God filling the mouths of his congregation with his Word. What exactly are they pro-claiming? The same thing the Spirit put into the mouths of believers at Pentecost and the same thing that God declared to Moses when he invited Moses into his presence: the gospel—the glories of God, the purity of his law, the severity of his judgments, and the greatness of his mercies (Acts 2:11–12; Ex. 34:5–7). Theologian J. I. Packer said,

Ordinarily, and certainly sometimes if not every time, a prophetic "revelation" (1 Cor. 14:26, 30) is a God-prompted application of truth that in general terms had been revealed already, rather than a disclosure of divine thoughts and intentions not previously known and not otherwise knowable.

(This kind of) prophecy has been and remains a reality whenever and wherever Bible truth is genuinely preached — that is, spelled out and applied, whether from a pulpit or more informally.[5]

Hearing the Spirit of God speak to us the Word of God through the people of God ought to be our experience every time we gather.

As a pastor, I depend on this gift heavily as I proclaim God's Word. I do not want to merely explain a body of doctrine deposited to the church two thousand years ago. I want to proclaim a God alive, present, at work among his people, and ready to encounter all who will believe. I want the Spirit to convict of sin, righteousness, and judgment.

Have you ever felt like a sermon was speaking right to you? That God addressed you through the teacher, applying his Word to your situation, exposing you, giving you understanding, or guiding you? If so, then you have experienced a manifestation of the gift of prophecy.[6]

Words of Wisdom and Words of Knowledge

The second form of prophetic speech Paul calls "words of wisdom" and "words of knowledge" (1 Cor. 12:8 NKJV). Though he never defines for us what those terms mean, Acts gives us enough examples that I think we can figure it out.

A "word of wisdom" is likely at work in Acts 15 as the council of church leaders in Jerusalem navigated a controversy dividing the early church. God gave them wisdom about a *particular* situation for which they did not have a specific chapter and verse. Their wisdom *included* the application of biblical principles, but also went beyond it. They sensed what the Spirit of God wanted in *that* situation.

God uses his church to speak wisdom into your life, guiding you more fully into the paths of wisdom. Important decisions made in isolation usually end in disaster. I have people frequently sit in my office and tell me about a colossally dumb decision, and I say, "Did you talk to others before you did that?"

They'll say, "No, but I prayed about it."

"Great!" I say, "but then you cut yourself off from how God wanted to answer your prayer—the counsel of the church?"

God guides us in the paths of wisdom by means of the church. Sometimes through supernatural insights; sometimes through just good advice and wise counsel.

"Words of knowledge" are likely supernatural revelations about situations or people that we have no way of knowing about on our own. Jesus knew in the Spirit that the Samaritan woman at the well had five former husbands. When he revealed this information about her, she said, "Sir, I perceive you are a prophet!" (John 4:16–19). His supernatural knowledge of her situation was "prophetic."

Through a word of knowledge, God places information into the mouth of one of his children, giving specific insight into the secrets of an unbeliever's heart, which convinces the individual God is really present in the one speaking. The person realizes there is no way this person could know such things apart from God revealing them.

When my wife entered college, she was not walking with God. One weekend she reluctantly agreed to go to a Christian ministry retreat with a group of friends. She went for the social aspects, completely uninterested in the ministry ones. So she tried her best to tune out the speakers. At the end of one talk, the subject of which she can't even remember, the speaker asked all attenders to pair up and pray for one another. Veronica was sitting next to a young woman she had never met, and when the girl asked what she could pray for, Veronica wanted to crawl into a hole. Veronica had not paid attention to the first word of the speaker's talk. But as this young woman prayed for Veronica—a young woman who knew almost nothing about her—she began to call out with great specificity Veronica's fears, questions, and sins. And she then began to pray the love of God into her life.

Veronica left the meeting immediately, deeply disturbed. She felt exposed and ashamed. But also deeply broken and sure that she had been in the presence of God. That night, alone with God, she repented of her sin and re-embraced Christ's offering of forgiveness. The young woman who prayed for her that night had no idea what she was praying. God had given this young woman, I believe, "words of knowledge" about Veronica that God used to make his Word come alive in her heart.

This is the gift of prophecy.

Prophetic speech, Gary Tyra says, was one of the "secrets" of the early church's incredible evangelistic success in their highly pluralistic, antagonistic environment, much like ours today. He says,

> The kind of missional ministry that does the best job of mitigating religious relativism is prophetic in nature, that is, it involves Spirit-inspired words and works, prophetic speech and actions. Despite the fact that the church was birthed into such a religious relativistic environment, the testimony is that for all its imperfections the faithful Spirit of mission was able to use the church to turn the world-upside down. And this happened in large part through their utilization of the Spirit-gift of prophetic speech.[7]

Have you ever had the strong impression to pray something specific for someone, not sure quite where it came from? Or a strong impulse that you needed to warn someone or remind them of a certain promise of Scripture? This very well might be the spirit of prophecy at work within you.

"Words of Prophecy" Don't Compete with "the Written Word"

Don't confuse this kind of "prophetic revelation" with Scripture. As we discussed in chapter 2, Scripture is a class of revelation set apart. The apostles and the prophets held up the Scriptures (literally, "the writings") as the *very words of God,* given by direct and full inspiration of the Holy Spirit, unable to be broken.[8] When the Scriptures speak, God speaks. We can neither add to them nor take away from them. They stand alone as the complete, inerrant Word of God.

Yet when we read Acts and the Epistles, we can see that the Holy Spirit said a number of things through early believers that never quite made it into the Bible. In 1 Corinthians 14:25 Paul talks about believers speaking words from the Holy Spirit that revealed the secrets of others' hearts. None of those "secrets" were recorded for us. And though the gift of prophecy was very active in the church at Corinth, Paul still said, "Did the Word of God originate with you" (1 Cor. 14:36)? Even though they spoke words to each other from the Holy Spirit, Paul pointed to another class of revelation, "the Word of God." So not every-thing the Holy Spirit said in the early church was deemed as "the Word of God," or Scripture. Thus, when we speak words from the Holy Spirit to one another, we understand that we are not speaking on the level of Scripture.

Even in the early days of the apostles, Scripture possessed a much greater authority than "prophecies." Paul said to the Corinthians, for example, "If anyone thinks they are a prophet or otherwise gifted by the Spirit, let them acknowledge that *what I am writing* to you is the Lord's command" (1 Cor. 14:37). Paul set his writings above prophecies, mak-ing them *the criteria* by which prophets were to be judged (and not vice versa!). The Corinthian prophets were not to "judge" the Scriptures, Paul said; the Scriptures judged *them*.

Paul encouraged believers to "weigh" prophecies given by other believ-ers (1 Cor. 14:29). In his first letter to the Thessalonians, he said, "Do not treat prophecies with contempt but test them all; hold on to what is good" (5:20–21).[9] Paul would *never* say such a thing about the Scriptures. About his writing, Paul said things like, "I am speaking as an apostle, so you shut up and listen. If you know God, you'll recognize what I am writing is the Word of God" (1 Cor. 14:37 — clearly, my paraphrase).

In fact, God gave another spiritual gift complementary to the pro-phetic gift called "the discernment of spirits" to help the church deter-mine which things the Lord was saying and which he was not (1 Cor. 12:8–10 NRSV; cf. 14:29). Application of "the gift of discernment" is never applied to the Scriptures themselves. (No one had the right to say, "Paul, the Spirit showed me that what Moses said in Deuteronomy 6 is inaccurate," "This parable of Jesus is unhelpful," or "You've lost your mind in your instructions about women in the church." In the same way, no one today can take one of Paul's commands and "through the Spirit" discard or alter it.)

Furthermore, as we noted earlier, sometimes the "prophecies" by the church can be "off" in a few details and still contain the voice of the Spirit. The early church prophet Agabus, for example, told Paul, "through the Spirit," that Jews would bind Paul and deliver him to the Gentiles (Acts 21:10–11). Wayne Grudem points out that this proph-ecy was *mostly* correct, though to be exact it was the Romans, not the Jews, who bound Paul. And the Jews did not want to *deliver* Paul to the

Romans, but rather kill him themselves. Grudem says, "The prediction was not far off, but it had inaccuracies in detail that would have called into question the validity of any Old Testament prophet.... This is exactly the kind of fallible prophecy that would fit the definition of New Testament congregational prophecy—'reporting in one's own words something God has spontaneously brought to mind.' "[10]

Such fallibility does not occur in the Scriptures. God said that anyone who claimed to speak in his name and gave predictions that did not come true should be stoned (Deut. 18:20–22). If Micah, for example, had prophesied that the Messiah would be born in Bethany rather than Bethlehem (5:2), he would be in error and considered, by Deuteronomy standards, a false prophet. Scripture is infallible; contemporary believers speaking prophetically are not.

But how can we say the Spirit of God is speaking through someone and yet allow for error? Is God revealing wrong? Is it possible to perceive God speaking in his church and still reserve judgment on what's being said? Well, Paul commands us to do that very thing (1 Thess. 5:19–21)! Paul himself chose not to heed the warning given by Agabus, even though he knew the information he was hearing was at least partially given by the Spirit (Acts 21:14). Clearly, he did not classify the Spirit-prompted warning from Agabus as infallible Scripture!

God, of course, can never be wrong, and when he revealed himself in the Scriptures he guaranteed that the writers would get his revelation exactly right.[11] But evidently, when he speaks through his church in the gift of prophecy, he does not guarantee that we will get all his movements, impressions, and instructions exactly right. We must "test" what is being said.

Theologian Vern Poythress wrote an article many years ago that really helped me get my mind around this.[12] He explained that the Holy Spirit speaks in his church today in a way "analogous," but not identical, to how he spoke through the apostles. Through the apostles, the Holy Spirit gave the very words of God, infallible and unbreakable. Sooner would heaven and earth pass away than one jot or tittle of that Word fail. Yet he *never* gives that same guarantee to what he says through the church in the gift of prophecy. Prophetic words in Acts, therefore, were constantly evaluated. And so we should exercise discernment in words we give and receive today.

141

Poythress points to a number of church leaders throughout history who spoke words they believed were "from the Holy Spirit," though they never gave these words the weight of Scripture. These leaders include Martin Luther, John Wycliffe, John Hus, Charles Spurgeon, and Peter Marshall. (In case you're unfamiliar with those names, they were all old-time theologians on the conservative side, not modern-day, coiffed-hair, fund-raising TV evangelists driving church vans with flames roaring down the side. I use them as my examples to show you that the idea that the Holy Spirit speaks in his church is not a recent phenomenon coinciding with the televangelist movement! Spurgeon was notorious for calling out specific sins from the pulpit that he believed the Spirit was revealing to him as he preached—in one famous story he tells a man in the balcony that he had a pair of stolen gloves in his pocket.)

Scripture even records the Holy Spirit speaking "prophecies" through unsaved people without their knowledge or intention, as he did through Caiaphas the High Priest, who prophesied "that one man should die for the people" (John 11:50–51 ESV). The apostle John recognized that the Spirit of God had spoken through Caiaphas even though Caiaphas was not a believer.

Scripture is in a class all by itself, but the Spirit of God is still moving and speaking in the church. His movements never contradict Scripture, nor do they add to its message. But the Spirit's presence in the church today guides his people in the application of his message and the execution of their mission.

We May Not Have Thrown Out Just the Bathwater, But the Institution of Bathing Altogether

The gift of prophecy scares a lot of Christians because they have seen how easily it can be abused in the church. "Start allowing this," they say, "and the next thing you know, you'll have a man on stage telling the church that God wants those present to give him a million dollars."

I understand that fear. I've seen a lot of abuse of this gift firsthand. We must be cautious, however, of throwing out the proverbial baby with the bath water and thereby discarding a gift God gave to his church for its good. The church in Acts depended on this gift for guidance in the mission. I don't think we have become so much more competent in our generation that we no longer need what they relied on so desperately! Are we less in need of the Spirit's guidance than those early Christians?

Many Christians have not only thrown out the baby with the bathwater, but have thrown out the institution of bathing altogether. They seem completely unaware, even opposed to, a Spirit alive and at work, dynamically, in his church. But doing so cuts us off from one of the primary sources of our evangelistic power and ministry support!

Lesslie Newbigin points out that the early church was, by our standards, poorly staffed, poorly resourced, poorly equipped, and in an extremely hostile, emphatically pluralistic culture; yet they experienced dizzying success. The secret of their power? The dynamic operation of the Holy Spirit in their midst, he says. Most often, he observed, New Testament preaching happened as a response to people gathering to ask the question, "What is going on among you Christians?" as a result of the works of the Holy Spirit.[13] This kind of ministry cut through the mind-numbing confusion of the religious relativism of the Roman Empire. Despite all the challenges posed by the pagan culture, the poor state of the church, and even her incessant moral problems, the Spirit-filled church of Acts "turned the world upside down" with the gospel, largely through the gift of prophecy.[14]

Peter's first sermon explained that prophecy was a mark of the new age of the Spirit. He seems to have expected *every* believer to participate in it.

> "I will pour out my Spirit on all people. Your sons and daughters will prophesy." (Acts 2:17)

Peter's first use of this gift led to three thousand converts (Acts 2:41).[15] Can we really afford to neglect this gift today?

Justin, a young man in my church, told me a story recently about an Indian woman he observed sitting by herself in a city park. He had never seen her before, but had the inexplicable urge to go tell her that though her brother had recently died, God loved her and would never forsake her. He told me that this kind of thing *never* happens to him, but this impression was so strong ... still, he just couldn't bring himself to go up to her to say it! What if he was wrong? So he demurred. Several hours later, he ran into the same woman at a Starbucks in another part of the city, and he considered this to be God gently giving him another chance. So he held his breath, walked up to her, and said, "Ma'am, we've never met, and I'm not sure why I feel this way ... but I had the sense that God wanted me to tell you ..." and he gave her the message.

Justin said that when he finished, she stared at him with wide eyes for several, terribly long seconds. Then she dropped her head and began to cry. She said, "How did you know? I thought no one in this city knew. Actually ... he was not really my brother, but my cousin, but he grew up in my house and I always thought of him as my brother. I even introduced him to others that way. He died last week." She was Hindu and had just moved away from her family in India to the United States. Justin told her that he could only guess that God gave him that message so she would know that God cared for her and had a plan for her and her family. Eventually, through further conversation, the lady came to profess Christ as her Savior.

There are two kinds of prophecy at work in this story: Justin knowing something about this woman, like Jesus knew about the Samaritan woman; and Justin's presentation of Christ as the only hope for eternal life. The second is by far the most important kind, but the first helped open the door for the presentation of the second.

Have you ever thought what possibilities might await if you yielded yourself to be the mouthpiece of the Spirit?

If You're Still Having Trouble

If you still have trouble with the idea that God speaks by his Spirit through his church, just consider:

- Do you believe God is active now in his church, leading and guiding us through his Spirit?
- Do you believe he sometimes places thoughts and burdens into our minds as we pray?
- Have you ever said something to someone that God really used, even though you had no idea he was doing so? Or has God used someone's words in your life that way?

I've never met a Christian who has walked with God for any length of time who would answer a categorical "no" to all those questions. You may not have known exactly what to *call* those experiences, but I believe these are what the apostles called "words of knowledge" and "words of wisdom"—God, alive and active, speaking to and through his church.

Ground Rules for Giving Words

Maybe at this point you feel pretty nervous about where all this could lead in your life. It's understandable—more havoc has been wreaked upon the world following the words, "God just told me ..." than any other phrase. So, I can identify with your anxiety, even commend it. Let me therefore suggest a few "ground rules" for when you think you have been given a "word from the Holy Spirit" that does not come directly from the pages of Scripture. And then I'll give you a few rules for interpreting what someone says to you.

1. ***Never claim the authority of God on your words, even if you feel convinced the Holy Spirit might be speaking through you.***

Prophetic speech in our day never carries the authority or certainty of Scripture, no matter whom it is from. Never. So unless you have a verse reference to back up your words, don't say emphatically, "God says ..." Rather, say something like this: "I believe God might have put this on my heart to say ..." Words of prophecy should always be given with a lot of humility and a bit of tentativeness. Because, you see, when you claim the authority of God, you put the other person in a terrible position; he must either fully heed your word or feel like he is rebelling against God. Or think you're a quack. Paul makes it clear that *all* prophecies are subject to "testing," including our own.

2. ***Prophetic speech is strongest when tied to actual Scripture.***

While you can't always be sure that what's in your heart is from God, you can be sure Scripture is. Often the Spirit places commands and promises from his Word in your heart to communicate to others. When you pass Scripture on to others, you can be sure that what you are saying is from God, even if your timing and application are not!

3. ***The gift of prophecy has a purpose: building up the church and guiding in mission. Use it only for those things.***

Paul says prophecy is for the "upbuilding, encouragement, and consolation" of people (1 Cor. 14:3 ESV) and, as I've shown throughout this book, for guidance in mission. The ministry of the Holy Spirit is not given for personal empowerment or selfish gain. Several years ago, a Christian leader said on his TV network that a nine-hundred-foot Jesus told him that unless viewers raised eight million dollars, God would kill him. I have a hard time seeing that as "upbuilding" the body. When you get the sense that someone is using "Spirit direction" to enrich their status or authority, you have a reason to be skeptical.

Ground Rules for Receiving Words

1. *It's okay to be a little skeptical.*

Paul tells us to test the prophecies, which means to be, *by nature*, a little skeptical. At the same time, he tells us not to *despise* prophecies (1 Thess. 5:20 – 21). In other words, don't believe someone just because he or she claims to have heard from God, but neither should you let your skepticism keep you from receiving what God might want to say to you through a member of his body.

2. *Ask, "Does this word contradict what God has said in the Scriptures?"*

If someone says to me, "God told me to divorce my wife because I'm in love with another woman," I say, "Really? God *told* you that his Word in Matthew 5:32 doesn't apply to you? I'm sorry; I'm going to need to see that in writing, with a notarized signature by another member of the Trinity." Words from the Spirit *always* line up with existing Scriptures. The Scriptures are the first place you "test" the prophecy.

3. *Ask, "Does the word accord with what I know God is doing in my life?"*

Does this word line up with other things you see God doing in your heart? (For example, if you're a girl and some guy claims that God has put on his heart that you are supposed to marry him, yet you feel no attraction to that person, you can safely assume that word is not from God.) Does the word resonate with what you've been sensing, speaking clarity into questions you've had? Does it line up with your giftings and passions? Do others in the church corroborate it?

I've been given some "words" which clearly did not line up with my experience. One weekend while in seminary, I accompanied a friend who had accepted an opportunity to preach at a small, country church in South Carolina. The piano player got sick that Sunday, and so when my friend got up to do the call to worship, he told the crowd that I played the piano beautifully and asked if I could lead the songs. The crowd clapped its approval of his request, a gracious response, but it ignored one particularly relevant fact: I do not play the piano, and I am not a good singer.

Actually, I could *sort of* play two songs—one, the old praise chorus "Alleluia," which has only three repeating chords; and the other, "Faithfully," by Journey, which I had learned to pound out in high school to impress the ladies. This was my entire repertoire, and my friend knew it. But we had made a pact that if either of us ever played a joke involving the other, we'd follow it through to the end. Probably not the wisest thing we ever did, but we had sealed it with a pinky-swear, and I didn't want to have my pinky broken.

So I dutifully walked up to the piano and pounded out the chords to "Alleluia," trying to sing loud enough for the congregation to follow and (internally) swearing a swift and devastating revenge on my friend. After his message, however, my friend asked if I'd come *back* up to play the invitation hymn, which was ... you guessed it, "Alleluia." (I didn't have the nerve to play Journey's "Faithfully" in church.)

After the service ended, the pastor's wife came up and (with a very serious look on her face) said, "Boys, God impressed something on my heart this morning which I have to speak over you." She looked first at my friend and said, "God says to you, young man, that you are to be the next Billy Graham. You will preach to untold millions of people." Then she looked at me and said, "And you will be his traveling concert pianist. The beauty of your music will draw in the crowds, and your friend will lead them to Christ. Let me see your hands so that I can pray over them."

She could not have been sweeter or more sincere. But I am pretty sure she did not convey the voice of God to me. I keep rhythm about as well as a bag of popping popcorn, and my hands are more like meat cleavers than finely tuned instruments. And no one—not one person—has ever told me my music has blessed them spiritually. Made them laugh, yes. Gave them a headache, yes. Made them long for Jesus' return, definitely. Spiritually enriched them, no.

Her word, though sincere, did not resonate with other things I saw God doing in my life. So I do not feel bound in the Spirit to pursue a career as a traveling concert pianist.

4. *Ask, "Does this word glorify God or the one giving it?"*

Believing someone is speaking from God to you gives them extraordinary influence in your life, so be careful lest you allow yourself to be manipulated. The Spirit came to glorify Jesus and propel Jesus' mission. Spirit words will always line up within those two objectives. He did not come to glorify a "prophet" or advance someone's personal agenda.[16] So when the word does not line up with Jesus' mission, you can safely assume the word is not from God.

Do You Come to Church Prepared to Be Used by the Spirit?

When you gather with your church or your small group, do you do so with the expectation that God may have words—gospel promises, warnings, and exhortations—for you to give others in the church, or that he may have such words for others to give to you? Do you come ready to speak in the Spirit and listen for the Spirit? Paul instructed the believers in Corinth to come to church prepared to do just that. Paul envisions a gathering of believers in which many are given a word, or a hymn of praise, for others (1 Cor. 14:26). You see, God intends *all* of us to be his vessels in the church, not just pastors and leaders.

A New Testament "church service" consists of three things: the Word of God, the people of God, and the Spirit of God. The Spirit of God puts the Word of God in the mouths of the people of God. And when that happens, Paul says, believers are built up and even unbelievers recognize that God is alive and at work in his church.

If you ask my wife to describe the most powerful experience she's ever had in our church, she likely won't mention one of my messages. Make no mistake, she loves my messages, takes copious notes on what I say, and tells me often how God uses my teaching in her life. But if you asked her about her most powerful moment in God's presence, she'd probably bring up a recent prayer time in which she and one of her friends met together after church to talk and ended up praying Scripture over each other. As Veronica's friend prayed over her, she began to apply God's promises to her secret fears, questions, and doubts.

Veronica knew the Holy Spirit was communicating God's goodness and his promises to her and her situations in a special way.

This kind of supernatural experience doesn't happen every week, she says, but the Spirit of God seems to give them with precious timing. In those moments, she feels like she's done more than gained new spiritual insight; she has met with God.

And isn't that what we should most crave when we come to church?

CHAPTER 11

Experiencing the Holy Spirit ...

In Our Spirit

"It seemed good to the Holy Spirit, and to us ..." —*Acts 15:28*

There is no question but that God's people can look for and expect
"leadings," "guidance," indications of what they are meant to do ... Men
have been told by the Holy Spirit to do something; they knew it was the
Holy Spirit speaking to them; and it transpired that it obviously was his
leading. It seems clear to me that if we deny such a possibility we are
again guilty of quenching the Spirit. —*Martyn Lloyd-Jones*

As a junior in high school, I once took an "unauthorized" road trip on a
Saturday evening to a ski resort several hours away from my home. My
friends and I raced home that next morning to try to get to church on
time so that no one would know we had been gone. One friend drove
while the rest of us slept. Then he decided to take a nap too. Unfortunately, he also kept his position in the driver's seat.

The car, set on cruise control at 62 miles per hour, barreled off the
side of the road and into a twenty-foot ravine, landing upside down.
How any of us survived I'm not quite sure. The crash mangled the car,
crushing it in several places. And yet every one of us walked out of the
wreck without a scratch.

Just moments before the accident, I woke up and shifted from the left backseat to the right. The spot where my head had previously lain got completely crushed in the accident, while the roof over my new seat remained untouched. And here's the strangest detail of the story: As we were drifting off the road toward the ravine, we had hit a discarded mattress lying on the roadside that threw us into a tailspin, which slowed our speed dramatically. Without that mattress, we would have rocketed into the ravine at more than 60 miles per hour. I have no idea why someone deposited a mattress at that particular spot. Seriously. What are the odds?

Of course, after we got home, I had to tell my parents what had happened. As I related the details, my mom asked what time this had all gone down. I told her, "5:21," because when I got jolted awake by the car landing upside down, the inverted digital numbers were the first thing I saw. She told me that she had been awakened at 5:00 that morning with an inexplicable urge to pray for me. She prayed for about thirty minutes — for God to work in my life, to get my attention regarding where I was going in life, to protect me, and to perfect his will in me. At 5:30, she went back to sleep.

I tell you this story for two reasons:

1. To demonstrate how God can move in our spirit to pray for others.
2. To request that if God ever wakes you up at 5 a.m. with a strong desire to pray for me, you go along with it.

Often, when God wants to do something in the world, he moves in us to do it. He moves in our spirits through desires, convictions, and revelatory insights.

He accomplishes his purposes through us, the members of his body.

"But It Makes Me Nervous"

I admit that discussing how to "hear from God" in my own spirit, like hearing from him through others, makes me nervous. How do you know the difference between a special burden and ... say, excess emotion that comes from too little sleep?

I've tried for several years to glean everything I can on this from

Scripture, to reflect honestly on my own experiences, and to listen cautiously to other Spirit-filled believers as they recounted how God moved in their lives. The following is what I have concluded.

First, as I noted in chapter 2, being led by the Spirit is not an exact science. We shouldn't think of this process like a formula in which we punch in variables and pull out an answer; and we should always approach this subject with an extreme amount of humility. Furthermore, as we learned in the last chapter, we should remain cautious about hearing or delivering messages unless the message has chapter and verse attached to it. Yet, I do believe God moves and speaks in our spirits (I can't read Acts and conclude otherwise). We must hold our perception of his leadership tenuously, remain open to godly counsel, and always subject our convictions to Scripture.

But before I tell you what I believe the Bible says about what hearing from God in your spirit sounds like, let me tell you about a time I evidently got it wrong—hopefully as an encouragement for you to approach this whole process with a great degree of humility.

After my wife and I had three kids, we sought God about whether to have any more. At three kids, I considered my quiver full. At no point in the week did I feel like I needed more to do or another mouth to feed. But we also knew that rearing godly children is among the greatest ministries you can have (Ps. 127:1–4), so we thought, *Well, why not have one more—for Jesus?* God had also touched our hearts regarding orphan care, and so we prayed about whether we should adopt. We set aside a day, April 28, 2009, for a time of prayer and fasting.

At the end of that day, we both felt that God might be leading us to pursue an international adoption. But when Veronica woke up the next morning, she felt sick . . . she took the test and sure enough, she was *pregnant*. I don't think I've ever had a prayer answered that quickly and definitively. While we sought God about what to do next, the answer had been (unbeknownst to us) growing inside of Veronica for nearly six weeks.

But what about the "sense" that our next child would come through international adoption? Perhaps that's something we should pursue later, but clearly it was not God's will for us at that moment, as I had sensed. We began to support others pursuing adoption, but we have put any plans to adopt on hold for a while, maybe permanently.

I would encourage you to hold loosely what you think God is saying to you. God simply did not outline for us a definitive way to know with *absolutely certainty* that he is moving in our spirits about something. I've searched every passage in the Bible related to that topic, looking for that definitive answer. But there is none. So when it comes to those things not spelled out by Scripture, stop short of any semblance of absolute certainty.

That said, let me suggest four ways I have experienced God speaking in my spirit that I believe are validated by Scripture.

1. Particular Burdens as I Pray

The prophet Habakkuk said, "I will stand at my watch and station myself on the ramparts; I will look to see what he will say to me" (Hab. 2:1).

Prayer is supposed to be two-way interaction. Prayer is not just informing God about things we need his help with. He already knows everything and doesn't need us to be his news-ticker reel for our lives. Prayer is relationship in which we pour out our requests to God and experience his guidance in how we pray.

I've heard it said that prayer works like a laser beam. You create a laser by stacking light waves on top of one another, channeling all the photons in the same direction. A handful of photons going in different directions yields only a soft, incandescent glow, but when you stack and concentrate the light waves, they release a power that can cut through steel. In prayer, you stack the "wave" of your faith with the "wave" of the Spirit's prompting, releasing the laser beam of God's power. Our greatest power in prayer, you see, occurs when our prayers are prompted by the Word of God and the Spirit of God. Prayers that *start* in heaven are heard by heaven. So we should look to the Word of God and the Holy Spirit to inform and guide us as we pray.

Paul promised the Spirit would help us as we prayed, and he often talked himself about praying "in the Spirit." John Piper asks, "To what exactly does Paul refer to by prayer in the Spirit?"

> It seems clear to me that speaking "in the Spirit" means speaking under the guidance of the Spirit, or energized and helped by the Spirit. That's why no one can say "Jesus be accursed" when speaking "in the Spirit." And no one can say, "Jesus is Lord" (and mean it) unless he is speaking "in the Spirit."

So I take it that praying "in the Spirit" means praying under the guidance and with the help and energy of the Spirit. *The Spirit is shaping our prayers and helping us pray.*[1]

What does this experience *feel* like? Quite often, the Spirit does it in the background, acquainting us with situations he wants us to pray about. We may not have a special "feeling" as we pray, but God's sovereignty has arranged our circumstances so that we pray about the things he wants us to pray about.

At other times, God does seem to press a particular burden on our hearts, or bring very clearly to our minds verses of Scripture for a situation. I don't automatically assume that whatever pops into my mind as I pray is the voice of God. However, I will often jot down verses or thoughts he brings to mind as I pray and later ask the Spirit to confirm whether he's put these things in my heart by bringing them back to mind again. Sometimes I will share these verses or burdens with the person for whom I am praying, and on numerous occasions, the individual has told me how timely and helpful that word of encouragement was.

I have encouraged our church to develop the habit of "listening prayer." Ask God to bring to your mind verses and special burdens as you pray and *listen* for how he might do so. Is that just New Age mysticism? Not necessarily. Prayer ought to be more of a communion with the living Father *in and through his written Word* than a mere recital of our needs.

I have written out a prayer list for each of my four kids. I try to remain very sensitive to verses of Scripture that the Spirit drops into my heart as I pray for them. Not long ago, God gave me a specific verse to pray over my oldest daughter about the fear of God and the praise of men. One afternoon, I told her what God had given me to pray for her. She usually listens to my counsel, but these words seemed to resonate in her in an especially powerful way. God used the words of Proverbs 29:25, which I believe he gave me to give to her, to speak to her about a specific situation at just the right time.

The more Scripture you know, the more illumination the Holy Spirit can give regarding his will for various situations. God has never brought to my mind a Scripture I did not already know. Memorizing Scripture is like stocking myself with ammunition for the Spirit to fire as I pray—promises I can claim or warnings I can heed. The Bible contains more than three thousand promises, and I want to know all of them, so the Holy Spirit can flood my mind with them whenever he wants! God did not give us the Bible simply to read through, you see, but to *pray* through as well.

As we've learned repeatedly throughout this book, being led by the Spirit of God depends upon being filled with the Word of God. The Word is the Spirit's primary weapon. Paul even called the Word of God "the sword of the *Spirit*" (Eph. 6:17). The Holy Spirit cannot wield the weapon if you have not sheathed it to your side.

Charles Spurgeon described his experience praying "in the Spirit" this way:

> He [the Spirit] guides us in prayer; thus, he helps our infirmities. But the blessed Spirit does more than this; he will often direct the mind to the special subject of prayer. He dwells within us as our Counselor and points out to us what it is we should seek at the hands of God. We do not know why it is so, but we sometimes find our minds carried as by a strong undercurrent into a particular line of prayer for some definite purpose. It is not merely that our judgment leads us in that direction, though usually the Spirit of God acts upon us by enlightening our judgment, but we often feel an unaccountable and irresistible desire rising within our hearts.
>
> He will guide you both negatively and positively. Negatively, he will forbid you to pray for certain things, just as Paul "tried to enter Bithynia, but the Spirit of Jesus would not allow [him] to" (Acts 16:7). On the other hand, he will cause you to hear a cry within your soul that will guide your petitions, even as he made Paul to hear the cry from Macedonia, saying, "Come over to Macedonia and help us" (v. 9).[2]

Now just to be clear, I'm not talking about hearing from God on a constant basis about everything for which you're praying. Quite often I don't feel *anything* when I pray, and during those times, I trust the Spirit is guiding my prayer in the background. But occasionally, the Spirit does "break in" with a particular burden or focus. I want to encourage you to be open to considering whether particular burdens in your spirit are from the Holy Spirit.

2. Special Insights into People and Situations

Recently, I was praying for a couple in my small group when I sensed God impressing upon me that he had something really special for their son, who was ten years old. They had only recently come to faith in Jesus, and they often worried about the bad habits they may have sown into him. As I prayed for them, I felt a certainty that God's hand was upon him, that God was working in his life, and that God wanted me to communicate to them that they should follow him closely and trust him because he was doing something special with their son. As I prayed for them, 1 Chronicles 28:9 – 10 kept coming to mind, God's promise to bless Solomon if he followed God closely. I told them that I believed God wanted them to be assured that he had brought them to salvation just when he wanted, and that he had already provided for their children. I told them that the future of their family was in his merciful hands. The relief on their face told me everything. I believe the Holy Spirit was communicating to them through me. And in the past year I've seen God's hand work mightily on this kid.

I don't sense things like this every time I pray, but I sensed it this time, and so I told them what I perceived in my spirit. I am eager to see what God does with it. Here's why:

When I was four years old, a pastor told my parents something very similar about me. He said to them one day after a church service, "God has something special for this one," and he placed his hand on my head. I remember it. Four-year-olds don't typically do much that would make you think God has set them apart for anything, and I was no exception. I was not remarkable; I never gathered the religious teachers at my feet to learn from my wisdom. In fact, for many years after that, I walked away from God. Yet this pastor perceived the Spirit's purpose for me and called it out. My parents prayed this word back to God during those times I wandered and rejoiced in it later when he brought me back to himself and called me into his service.

Praying "with the help of the Spirit" means asking God how to pray more specifically about certain situations. Don't write off this kind of prophetic praying to a fringe sect of mystical Christianity. Throughout history, Christian believers of all stripes have reported God moving in their hearts this way:

Reformed theologian R. C. Sproul, for example, said that early on in his ministry, he had this sudden thought: "Go throughout the world and preach the gospel to every living creature.... Take Vesta [his future wife] with you."[3]

Cotton Mather, an early American Puritan theologian with heavy influence on Jonathan Edwards, said that God sometimes gives a general faith to believers to trust the promises of God, and sometimes a "special" faith during prayer that assures them of what he's going to do in a particular situation:

> In addition to 'general' faith in Christ, there is a *particular faith* that is granted to believers *now* and *then*, under the *energy* of some *superior cause*, a strong *Impression* made upon his mind, which dissolves him in a flood of tears, and assures him, "You *shall have the petition which you desire of God.* " The impression is born upon his mind, with as clear a light, and as full a force, as if it were from heaven *angelically* ... these are instances of the *prophetic spirit* upon believers.[4]

Sometimes God gives us foreknowledge about situations for which he wants us to get prepared. The Holy Spirit told the apostle Paul, for example, that danger awaited the ship on which he was sailing, which helped prepare him to minister to the passengers when it happened. In Acts 11:28, the prophet Agabus warned the church that a famine would soon devastate the whole Roman world, which allowed the church to get prepared to minister during it. Very similar things happened to the Reformer Martin Luther and Presbyterian theologian John Flavel.[5] Time and experience confirmed that the "impression" upon their hearts really was from God. (In case you wonder why I am using a lot of older theologians as my examples, I am trying again to show that the experience of God speaking in the Spirit is not something invented by modern-day TV evangelists, but has been the experience of believers of just about every faithful tradition *throughout* church history.)

Here's a difficult verse many Christians have trouble with: Jesus told his disciples that if they had faith, they could move mountains. Does that mean that I can go up to any old mountain any time I want and say, "Hmm ... I don't feel like going over you. Get out of my way, mountain!" No. The Spirit fills us at certain times with faith for *certain* mountains. Adding the wave of your faith to the wave of his will releases the laser of his power. And then those mountains he wants out of the way move.

3. Holy Ambitions

The Spirit of God sometimes works in us by stoking the fires of a particular, holy ambition for a specific ministry or need. You feel the fire of passion for God to see something happen on your school campus, in your family, or in your generation. It won't go away and grows to a fever temperature inside of you. It's less of a "word" from God than it is a "holy discontent" with a situation, a broken heart over injustice and pain, or a burning passion to see God glorified.

We see this occur repeatedly in Scripture. As far as we can tell, God never *told* David that he wanted him to fight Goliath. (We find no "holy huddle" with David and God in which God said, "Okay, David, go see your brothers, and there will be a giant there, and he will say this ... and then you get five rocks, and then ...") David simply found himself in a place with a defiant giant, the pagan's taunts caused him to burn with holy zeal, and he assumed God wanted him to fight. Furthermore, even after David agrees to go and fight, God gives David no verbal assurance that he will defeat Goliath. David simply believed God wanted him to battle the giant and trusted God with the outcome. Was the urge to fight from God? It seems hard to doubt that on this side of that battle!

In the same way, God never told Shadrach, Meshach, and Abednego that he would deliver them from the fiery furnace when they challenged King Nebuchadnezzar's command to worship the golden statue. In fact, we see them going into that encounter with a curious mixture of certainty and uncertainty:

> "The God we serve is able to deliver us from [the burning fiery furnace], and *he will deliver us* from Your Majesty's hand." (Dan. 3:17, emphasis mine)

That sounds like certainty! But they also say,

> "But even if he does not, we want you to know, Your Majesty, that we will not serve your gods or worship the image of gold you have set up." (Dan. 3:18)

"But if not ..."? That doesn't sound nearly as certain!

We often feel that mixture of certainty and uncertainty when the Spirit of God pushes us into a venture in his name. It's a holy ambition.

We feel "certain" the impulse is from him. But we've been given no clear verbal direction on how things will turn out.

Here's another one: I can't find anywhere in Acts where God *tells* Paul to go to Rome to preach the gospel. Acts 19:21 (ESV) tells us that Paul "resolved in the spirit" to go to Rome, but I'm not totally sure what that phrase means; and based on the commentaries, neither is anyone else. It seems to mean that Paul had a yearning to go to Rome that he perceived to be the impulse of the Spirit. Paul called it *his* "ambition" (Rom.15:20–21 ESV). Later, God directly affirms it through a vision (Acts 23:11), but it seems to have *begun* as a yearning in Paul. Paul redirected his whole life around it, calling it his life's "race" (Acts 20:24).

In another place, Acts records *Paul's* spirit being "provoked within him" when he saw how thoroughly Athens had given itself to idols (Acts 17:16 ESV). He proceeded to preach one of the most famous sermons ever given, a spontaneous sermon that has become the basis for Christian apologetic approaches. Can anyone doubt that this provocation in Paul's spirit was caused by the Holy Spirit? In saying that Paul did this because "*his* spirit" was provoked within him, Luke did not mean to imply that this was Paul's work instead of the Holy Spirit's; rather, he meant that the Holy Spirit used Paul's own spirit to indicate to the apostle what God wanted him to do. The two spirits were united, after all!

Provocations in *my* spirit are often provocations *from* God's Spirit. Because our spirit has been united to God's, unscrambling where ours stops and his begins can be difficult, if not impossible! When we let the Holy Spirit have his way in us, our emotions become melded to his. So as Paul burned with holy zeal to go to Rome, he began to speak with near certainty about *God* wanting him to do it.

Or consider the story of Jonathan, King David's best friend. Jonathan and his armor bearer took on an entire garrison of Philistine soldiers (1 Sam. 14:1–6). Most intriguing to me is how Jonathan invited his armor bearer to join him:

> "Come, let's go over to the outpost of those uncircumcised men. Perhaps the LORD will act in our behalf. Nothing can hinder the LORD from saving, whether by many or by few." (1 Sam. 14:6)

Uhhh ... Perhaps? If I were the armor bearer, I'd probably have said, "I'm sorry, bro, but if you are inviting me to take on an entire, fortified garrison of trained Philistine soldiers, then I'm going to need more than your *'perhaps.'* "

It is clear, on this side of the battle, that it was indeed the Holy Spirit prompting Jonathan's holy zeal. God gave to Jonathan and his armor bearer a great victory on that day (1 Sam. 14:11–15). But in the moment, all Jonathan had was holy ambition.

Let me tell one story from my life. As I've mentioned, I spent two years living as a missionary in Southeast Asia. Shortly after I left, the worst tsunami on record swept onto the island, killing more than 100,000 people. When I returned and stood at the very spot where the tsunami had come ashore, I sensed God telling me that he would send a wave of salvation through that same area, and that our church was to labor and pray toward that end. We've tried to obey. Currently our church has over two hundred of its members serving overseas on church planting teams, most within Muslim unreached people groups. Our "holy ambition" is to send out five thousand. We are going, by God's grace, to see that wave of salvation.

Not every ambition in our heart comes from God, but God certainly uses holy, burning desires like these as a compass to point true north for our lives, to show us where he wants *us* to go and how he wants *us* specifically to be involved in his mission. Do you have a "holy discontent" about something right now?

For example, are you disturbed about any of these things?

- An unreached people group with no access to the gospel or a people group that is resistant to the gospel
- A ministry in your church that needs development (Hey—maybe instead of complaining about it, you should realize God is calling you to lead it!)
- A career field with little Christian influence or witness
- The suffering of the poor, the immigrant, the homeless, the minority, the addicted, the mentally ill, the sick, the grieving, the unemployed, the incarcerated, the widowed, the elderly, the hungry, or the ignored and the shunned
- The evils of injustice, corruption, sexual exploitation, ignorance, destruction, waste, and greed
- The millions of babies murdered each year in the name of freedom of choice and thousands of children orphaned or in foster care

- A school that is failing from lack of resources and parental support
- The many kids in your community growing up without knowledge of the Bible
- The broken, lost, or hurting among children, teens, singles, couples, families, or senior adults

Might this not be God calling *you* to get involved in one or more of those things? You—and your church—are not called to be involved equally in *everything* on this list, but you will be called and empowered individually and as a body to tackle *certain* issues. Are you actively looking for those places where God is calling you to work?

Perhaps your "holy discontent" will not lead to a lifelong calling. As far as we know, Goliath is the only giant David ever killed personally. Sometimes God moves us to be involved in situations for a particular season.

The whole mission belongs to the whole church, but God calls different churches and different individuals to *specialize* in particular aspects of the mission. I (and the elders of our church) burn with a holy passion to see 1,000 churches planted out of our church; to see 5,000 missionaries raised up from our church and sent out; to baptize 50,000 people in the Raleigh-Durham area; to help start more than a hundred community organizations to minister to broken parts of our city; to see God bring a gospel awakening to a Muslim nation. He's also put onto my heart a particular guy in my neighborhood I believe he's leading me to reach out to and a local college campus he's calling me to get more involved with. These are areas of deep, holy discontent for me. So I'm going to keep charging up those hills until God tells me to stop. Perhaps the Lord will act on my behalf.

4. Dreams and Visions

God spoke throughout the book of Acts in dreams and visions. Nothing in Scripture indicates that he has entirely stopped speaking in these ways. We may have reason to believe they do not happen as often as they once did, and to be really skeptical of many claiming to have those dreams, but that's not to say they have ceased happening altogether.[6]

Just to be honest, I've never personally been given a revelatory dream, but I know firsthand of too many of them to sweep them away as the nocturnal musings of people with overactive REMs. Here's just one:

I had lived in Southeast Asia a few months when I received a phone call from a man I had never met. Mahmud explained that he had had a very disturbing dream, and he believed that I was supposed to help him interpret it. In his dream, he wandered aimlessly in an endless field. This field, he told me, seemed to symbolize his life. He felt alone, without purpose, true companionship, or direction. Yet after walking for what seemed like days, he heard a voice behind him call his name. There he saw a man who, in his words, "was dressed in shining white clothing. I could not look on his face, because it shone like the sun." This heavenly man reached into the sash of his robe and pulled out a copy of the Gospel and tried to place it in Mahmud's hands. "This," the man said to Mahmud, calling him by name, "will get you out of this field."

Mahmud refused. Mahmud was a faithful Muslim and he had no desire to possess or even read anything Christian. He woke up in a cold sweat, heart beating quickly, feeling very afraid. He said he felt as if he had rejected a prophet and did not know what to do.

When he fell asleep the second night, he found himself again in the field. Again, the "man" appeared, offering Mahmud another copy of the Gospel. And again Mahmud refused. The third night when Mahmud went to sleep, the man was there, waiting on him. "This, and only this," he said to Mahmud, "will get you out of this field." With trembling hand, Mahmud took the Gospel from the man.

Mahmud then said to me, "My friend tells me that you are an expert in the Gospel. Can you interpret my dream for me?" No joke. That is what he said.

"Mahmud," I replied, "I don't believe in visions and dreams. They ceased with the Apostles."

Just kidding. For the next two hours, I explained the gospel to him. Though he still had questions, he didn't doubt the answers I offered. After all, he'd been instructed by a divine messenger to listen. When he said "yes" to the gospel, I asked if he knew what such commitment might cost him. "Mahmud," I said, "You might lose your job. You might get kicked out of your family. This commitment to Christ might even cost you your life."

I'll never forget what he said next. He smiled and answered, "Of course, I know all that. That is why it took me over a month to come talk with you, because I knew that if I became a follower of Jesus, it might cost me everything ... but I know that was Jesus speaking to me in that dream. And I'll go anywhere with him. If it costs me everything, I'm ready."

I do think God might do this more in places where there is little to no access to the Word of God, but I find no biblical reason to doubt that God, whenever he so chooses, can still speak to us too through dreams and visions.

Although the Bible most clearly spells out for us God's will, his Spirit also moves in our spirits by giving us particular burdens, special insights, holy ambitions, and, yes, supernatural dreams. As we follow *them* (holding them tenuously, submitted to his Word and others in his church), we follow *him*.

Be Cautious, But Not Cynical

As I've said, it's okay to be a little skeptical, not believing everyone who says they have been given a special insight from the Holy Spirit (or even believing everything you personally feel!). To be honest, I probably don't believe 60 percent of the "miracles," "visions," or "God told me" reports that I hear! Is that bad to admit? Well, it is what it is. But don't let that caution turn into cynicism. Sixty years ago, Martyn Lloyd-Jones said,

> There is no question but that God's people can look for and expect "leadings," "guidance," indications of what they are meant to do.... Men have been told by the Holy Spirit to do something; they knew it was the Holy Spirit speaking to them; and it transpired that it obviously was his leading. It seems clear to me that if we deny such a possibility we are again guilty of quenching the Spirit.[7]

That's from a really, conservative, Reformed British pastor whose church was filled with Victorian ladies and gentlemen who sung hymns each week with a pipe organ and never lifted a hand in worship.

Then, speaking of those who prefer to critique and mock everyone who claims to hear from the Spirit, Dr. Lloyd-Jones said:

God have mercy upon them! God have mercy upon them! It is better to be too credulous than to be carnal and to be smug and dead.[8]

That's good advice for any Bible-loving Christian to heed today. Don't discard the Spirit just because you see some abuse him.

With God, Not *for* God

The Christian life is something you do *with* God, not *for* God. He works through you. That's a theme we return to again and again. Jesus did not merely issue an assignment; he invites us into a relationship. Christian prayer, therefore, ought to be a two-way, not one-way, conversation; less a presentation of a catalog of needs and more a dialogue with a Person. Instead of merely praying *to* God, we ought to pray *with* God, *in* the Holy Spirit.

Get your mind around this: While not every missional need in the world is your responsibility, God has particular, special assignments just for you. His Spirit wants to lead you into those and calls you to be faithful to what he has assigned *you* (1 Cor. 12:11; 4:2). *"Follow me,"* Jesus said.

Do you know what those specific things are? Are you *following him* by pursuing *them*?

Go find *your* calling. In which direction does the Spirit's compass point true north *for you*? Tell *that* mountain to move, and then put your hiking boots on and go toward it!

CHAPTER 12

Experiencing the Holy Spirit ...
In Our Circumstances

Paul and his companions traveled throughout the region of Phrygia and Galatia, having been kept by the Holy Spirit from preaching the word in the province of Asia.   *—Acts 16:6*

Every honest Christian I know admits there are times when God does exactly the opposite of what you expected him to do. You felt sure God was leading you one way, but a door unexpectedly closed in your face. You thought God was about to give you some blessing, one you had already made plans to put to good use, when at the last minute, he withheld it. The job went to someone else. The sickness got worse. The girl said no. The home loan fell through. The visa was denied.

I once heard a prominent Christian leader confess that when he was in his early fifties, he felt convinced that God was telling him he had only one year left to live and to get his life's work done. He obeyed, publishing his *magnum opus* within the year. More than twenty years later, he's still alive and well.[1] Does that mean he's a kook? Well, he's not alone in that experience: the patriarch Isaac spoke in Genesis 27 like he expected to die at any moment too (Gen. 27:2–4). Usually when people in the Bible speak that way, they expire pretty quickly! Isaac, however, lived on for several decades, reaching the age of 180 (Gen. 35:28–29)!

What should you conclude when God throws you a curveball? That God changed his mind? That you messed it up? That this idea about God moving in your spirit is imaginery?

Hold Your Interpretations Loosely

At the risk of belaboring this point: Such experiences should teach us to hold our perception of what the Holy Spirit is "telling us" loosely.

Even some of the *holiest* "ambitions" we feel certain God is moving us to undertake don't pan out exactly like we expect—but that doesn't mean God wasn't in them! Jim Elliot believed God gave him a vision of seeing the Auca Indians of Ecuador embrace the gospel. He and his four companions got speared to death before making a single convert. Had they heard wrongly?

Elisabeth Elliot, Jim's widow, recounts how this tragedy led to the eventual conversion of the whole tribe. Furthermore, Jim's example of commitment to the Great Commission has inspired thousands of young adults to go to the mission field, many to that same area. God did indeed inspire Jim's ambition, even if it didn't play out exactly like Jim had expected.

Maybe you've felt "led" to make a certain decision, only to see things not work out as expected. My friend Mike, for example, moved to North Carolina, believing God had led him to move closer to his girlfriend so they could marry and move back to Texas. The relationship dissolved, however, shortly after he arrived. Yet, while in North Carolina, Mike discovered a new spiritual gift that set him on a whole new life's course. Now he leads one of the most exciting ministries at our church. Mike says God probably did it that way because only the love of a girl could get a native Texan to leave his homeland. Either way, God clarified his will for Mike through his sovereign control of circumstances.

Another friend, Chris, a worship pastor, was going through an extraordinarily difficult time in the church he was serving when another church asked him to consider moving there. When he went to visit this church, he immediately was filled with new vision for that work. And it was located in the town he'd grown up in. As he was driving back from his visit, he believed the Spirit of God was saying to him, *"I am sending you back to the place of your heritage to help bring salvation there."* He began to make plans to leave. Two weeks later, however, the search committee called and told him they were going in a different direction. Chris felt devastated and confused.

Shortly after that expereince, however, God brought a new, young pastor to Chris's church. This pastor had a strong connection to Chris's heritage: this pastor was led to Christ as a young boy by Chris's grandfather, and Chris had known this pastor when he was only three years old! Chris now serves with that pastor today, sensing, he says, that the greatest days of his ministry are ahead.

(That young pastor, by the way, was me.)

Chris says the only way he can interpret what happened in that chapter of his life is that God countermanded his desire and "would not allow him to go there," just as he did with Paul and Silas when they were seeking to go into Asia (Acts 16:7 – 9). Paul and Silas were excited about ministry in Asia, full of dreams and vision they believed were from the Holy Spirit. It *seemed* right. It *felt* right. But they were not to experience the fulfillment of those desires in the way they assumed. God had a different plan — and a greater one, it turns out.

God Uses Our Circumstances to Guide Us

God often leads us by his sovereign control of our circumstances. He opens certain doors and closes others. Sometimes we experience his direction by following those opportunities. We see this happen repeatedly throughout Scripture.

Mordecai told Queen Esther she should risk her life by appearing before her egomaniac, emotionally unstable husband and appealing for clemency on behalf of the Jews. His rationale: "Who knows whether you have not come to the kingdom for such a time as this?" (Est. 4:14 ESV). In other words, "It seems that God has put you in this place and at this time with this opportunity for this purpose." Mordecai seems to discern what God wanted by reflecting on God's sovereign direction of their circumstances. At no point did either Esther or Mordecai get audible direction from God. Scholars point out, in fact, that God's name is never mentioned in the book of Esther. Might this be designed to teach us, among other things, that even when we don't see other signs of his activity, we can trust that God continues to direct our circumstances? God has us where we are for a reason.

Luke tells us that he wrote his Gospel and the book of Acts because it seemed to him as if he had a unique perspective on the events and could report them from a good perspective (Luke 1:3). In other words, the circumstances of Luke's life made him an ideal reporter for these events. Notice what Luke doesn't say: "The Spirit commanded me in a dream to write these books." Was the Spirit of God behind Luke's assumption that he was in a good place to write out the events? Well ... God put Luke's two books into the canon, so I'd say yes. But Luke does not *say* he commenced the writing of Luke and Acts because he heard God "command" him to. Circumstances simply indicated to Luke that he could make a helpful contribution to the early Christian movement. *Later*, the apostles recognized the Spirit had been behind Luke's idea, but Luke pursued it because circumstances provided the opportunity.

Here's another one: In Acts 8:1, the Holy Spirit scattered the existing church into the world through a severe persecution. No dream or vision, no laying on of hands, no bold instruction by an apostle ... simply external forces moving believers into the places God wanted them. They rightfully concluded, however, that the Spirit of God was in those circumstances, putting them into places to do his work (Acts 1:8; 8:1–4).

As we've seen before, Paul often interpreted open doors as invitations by God to preach the gospel and closed doors as God's direction to go elsewhere. In 1 Corinthians 16:8–9, for example, he explained to the Corinthians that he would stay in Ephesus a little longer than planned because "a great door for effective work has opened to me." No "Spirit voice"; just an open door.[2] And we've already noticed how in Acts 16, Paul perceived God was leading him to enter Macedonia only after several unsuccessful attempts to enter Asia.

Jesus himself followed this divine, circumstantial leadership. At one point he explained that he simply joined in whatever work he saw the Father already doing (John 5:19). In other words, sometimes he determined where God wanted him to work by where he saw the Spirit already working. His encounter with the woman at the well provides a perfect example; their sovereign meeting and the thirstiness in her heart all revealed to Jesus that the Father had prepared her for an encounter with the Messiah (John 4:24-26).

We ought therefore to look for the Spirit's leadership, in our circumstances. When God promises to "direct our paths" as we acknowledge him in all of our ways, that certainly includes controlling what happens around us! For the believer, nothing is random. He works *all* things according to the counsel of his will (Eph. 1:11).

But here again, we should always hold our interpretation of those circumstances loosely, and always, of course, subject to Scripture. Consider the following principles as you seek to interpret the Spirit's guidance through your circumstances.

The Presence of Obstacles Doesn't Always Mean a "Closed Door"

Often, we assume that difficulty automatically indicates that God is not "in" a particular venture. But in 1 Corinthians 16:8–9 Paul said:

> I will stay in Ephesus until Pentecost, for a wide door for effective work has opened to me, and there are many adversaries. (ESV)

He doesn't say, "Well, I thought a wide door for effective work had opened, *but* there are many adversaries ... so clearly this is not the will of God." Instead, he says, "God opened this door, *and* there are many adversaries; so pray for me to overcome them." Likewise, in Acts 20, he says that the Holy Spirit had told him to go to Jerusalem, but then revealed to him that only "imprisonments and afflictions" awaited him. Paul perceived these difficulties to be *part* of the will of God for him, not indications he was out of it. Because we have an enemy who works around the clock to try and thwart the purposes of God, and because God often uses difficulties to test and deepen our faith, the presence of adversaries more likely indicates that we are *in* God's will than out of it.

Many of God's sweetest blessings are obtained only by persevering through difficulties. "Knock," Jesus said, "and the door will be opened to you." When you knock on a door, you don't hit the door once and then just stand there. You hit *repeatedly*. When you seek God's blessing, you keep pressing through stubborn obstacles and difficulties. You knock once, then again and again. So don't let difficultly in your path make you automatically assume you're out of God's will.

An Open Door Doesn't Always Indicate *It Is* God's Will

In the same way, open doors don't always mean God is behind something. As we observed earlier, Satan himself "opened the door" for Eve to partake of the forbidden fruit. Jonah "happened" upon a ship sailing for Tarshish as he ran from God. We have an enemy who works 24/7 to open up the *wrong* doors for us, and then give us "peace" about going through them!

Every open door should be viewed through the lens of Scripture and in the counsel of godly wisdom. Over the years, I have had people tell me that the Spirit of God was leading them to leave their spouse, move in with their boyfriend, or not pay their taxes. When I ask how they know that, they point to circumstantial evidence — it feels right; it's the only way we can afford to live; I really need the money to pay my tithes, etc. You can absolutely be sure these things are not from God. God doesn't issue "recall notices" on parts of his Word. Doors that *God* wants us to go through are always consistent with his Word.

We Can't Always Explain What God Is Doing

One of the first mistakes I made as a new Christian was thinking that given just a little time and distance I could always explain the good things God was up to in my bad situations. Sometimes, of course, we can: You didn't get into the school of your choice, but the school you attended led to a relationship that changed your life for the better. It is very unwise, however, to think that because you can see *some* of what he is doing in your life, you can therefore see *all* of it. Moses warned the Israelites that many of God's ways remain "secret" to us:

> The secret things belong to the LORD our God, but the things revealed belong to us and to our children forever, that we may follow all the words of this law. (Deut. 29:29)

This drives us type-A folks crazy. I feel like I am entitled to see God's purposes in everything. God, however, never invited me to be a co-God with him. This means that some of the reasons for what he does in my life may well remain a mystery to me for all of my days.

Job had to learn this lesson the hard way. For thirty-five chapters, he built a case against God, demanding to know the reasons why the Almighty allowed his health to deteriorate, his fortune to crumble, and his children to die. And for thirty-five chapters, God says nothing. When the Lord finally does speak to Job, he doesn't even explain himself, but only says, "Job, have you ever created a universe? Oh ... No? Then why don't you shut up and let me run mine, and quit acting like you are my peer and in a place to evaluate my decisions" (Job 38:1 – 40:2). That's one of the primary points of the book of Job: Some of the reasons for why God does what he does will remain a mystery to us in this life. Turns out Job's troubles had more to do with God glorifying himself before Satan and the heavenly hosts than anything Job had done or not done. God had his reasons, but Job couldn't see them, and we won't always be able to see God's reason for our troubles, either.

Following the Spirit Means More than Just Reacting to Circumstances

Several years ago, Henry Blackaby wrote *Experiencing God,* one of the bestselling Bible studies of all time. I went through it in college, and it had a profound impact on me. Blackaby shows that following God means "perceiving where God is at work and joining him in it." Believers are not out working for God, he says, as much as God is working through them. Blackaby stacks up example after example of believers in the Bible responding to God in this way.

It was a life-transforming realization for me: I find out what God is doing and join him in it, not do it *for* him. The Holy Spirit works through me; I do not work *for* him.

Unfortunately, many took *Experiencing God* to mean that believers should only go to work in circumstances where they *see* God at work, rather than proactively *bringing* God's work to places where it has yet to become visible.

This is not, of course, what Blackaby meant. Blackaby was himself a pioneer missionary, and the whole focus of pioneer missions is taking the work of God into places where it is not yet manifest. The apostle Paul strove to take Christ "where he'd never been named," not because he saw God already at work in those places, but because God was moving in his spirit to begin a work there (Gen. 12:3; Matt. 24:14; Acts 16:8; 26:16). Even then, however, God is taking the initiative—by moving in Paul's spirit—and inviting Paul to *join* him (see also Acts 13:1–4). And when Paul got to these new places, he found evidence that God's Spirit had gone before him and prepared people (as you can see in how God had prepared Lydia, the slave girl, and the Philippian jailor in Philippi [Acts 16:11–34]). This is a pattern for effective ministry.

Paul always worked with the Spirit, never for him. As Richard Blackaby (Henry's son) recently told me, too many well-meaning Christian organizations today are attempting to work for God and then asking for his blessing, rather than seeking to work with the Holy Spirit, where the blessing is "pre-built-in."

God Works Through Even Sinful Choices in Accomplishing His Will

What if your difficult circumstances result from the sinful choices of others, choices clearly outside of God's will? Are you doomed to suffer the effects of their sin? What if your difficult choices result from *your own* dumb choices? Are you doomed to be outside of God's will forever?

When you think about it, Romans 8:28 is a really expansive promise:

> All things work together for good to them that love God, to them who are the called according to his purpose. (KJV)

What does "all" include? "All" is a complex Greek word that means: "all." ALL = *Everything* with *nothing* left out.

Would that include the cruel and unfair things others have done to you? The Old Testament story of Joseph answers unequivocally. Absolutely. Joseph ended up in a terrible situation because of some really sinful decisions by his brothers. Instead of growing up to become a successful businessman in his hometown, he spent his best years languishing in an Egyptian prison. And yet God used those dreadful circumstances to put Joseph in a unique position to rescue his family, which had been God's intention all along. Near the end of his life, Joseph said of his brothers' sinful choices, "You intended to harm me, but God intended it for good" (Gen. 50:20).

According to Romans 8:28, God called us for *his purpose,* and he's a really powerful God, so he marshals "all" things in our lives for that purpose. Even what others intend for evil on you. God was at work accomplishing his perfect will, Peter explained, in even humankind's most sinful choice, the crucifixion of Jesus. Think about it! Never has something been, in one sense, more evil, and more "out" of the will of God. And yet that evil action perfectly accomplished God's will (Acts 4:27–28). He overrode mankind's most wicked action for good. The same is true of the evil others have thrust upon you. It's not that *God* was doing those things to you, just that he overrides them for good.

Does this "all" include your own stupid decisions? It has to! Otherwise "all" would not be "all," it would be "most." In the great mystery of grace, God commandeers even our stupid decisions to accomplish his purposes in us.

Think about it again: the most radically stupid decision humans ever made was to crucify Jesus, and yet God used *that* as our salvation. This is one of the greatest miracles of God's providential grace. He works even in our stupidity and our sin for his glory and the world's salvation. This doesn't excuse our wrong or sinful decisions, or exempt us from the painful consequences of such decisions; it just means that even our own stupidity can't get beyond the "all" of God's grace and purpose.

My wife loves to tell how she and I first met. It all happened, she says, because she sinned against her parents. When she applied to college, both the University of Virginia and Virginia Tech accepted her application. She leaned toward Virginia Tech because her father and numerous other family members had gone there (and in those circles, if you're connected to one, you avoid the other). But the night before she turned in her acceptance letter to Virginia Tech, she and her parents had a ferocious argument. To spite them, she went to UVA.

At UVA, she met a friend who invited her on a Christian retreat where God got a hold of her life, a story I've already shared with you. And through those new, Christian relationships at UVA, she got the opportunity to serve as a camp counselor at a small Christian camp in

North Carolina, a camp where I happened to be the speaker that summer. And now here we are, in ministry together, with four wonderful kids and a very blessed life. She believes she is right where God wants her, but the path here included a rather silly decision made in sinful reaction to an argument with her parents.

But all things work together for good to those who are called according to his purpose. This verse doesn't *excuse* our sins, but it does redeem them. This, I think, is really good news. God's love is so great, his control so complete, and his purposes so fixed, that *nobody* can mess it up.

Not even you.

You may be reeling from a stupid, sinful decision right now. And you may be wondering, *Well, is this it? Am I finished?* Paul would tell you, "No way! No one — not even your sinful self — can put you outside of God's ability to guide you back into his blessing." At this very moment, regardless of how you got to where you are, you can surrender to God, and immediately he will rewrite the painful story of your life with his beautiful pen of redemption. You are one simple decision away from being able to say, *"All things in my life have worked together for good."*

God's Work in Your Past Hints at His Plans for Your Future

Earlier in this book I encouraged you to map out the high-water points of God's work in your life because, like the apostle Paul, you can usually tell a little about where God is taking you in the future based on what he's done in your past. When you draw that map, clear patterns of the Spirit's work begin to emerge.

Reflecting often on what God has done in your circumstances is one of the best ways, outside of Scripture, to perceive what God is doing in you now. Socrates famously said, "The unexamined life is not worth living." This makes even more sense for those whose lives are directed by the loving, sovereign Spirit of God! Examine your life often, looking for patterns in how God has revealed himself in you. What particular kinds of grace have you encountered? What parts of God's character have you experienced personally?

As Mordecai said to Esther, "Who knows if perhaps you were made queen for just such a time as this?" (Est. 4:14 NLT). Who knows if perhaps you lost your job … or had to move … or made a boneheaded decision … or got stabbed in the back … and ended up where you are now, *for just such a time as this?*

Trust the Shepherd

At the end of the day, we must trust that the God who cares more for us than we do for ourselves will lead us in his paths for his great name's sake, just as he has promised.

God has more invested in your life than even you do. He purchased you with his blood, the universe's most precious commodity, worth infinitely more than anything you or I have ever spent on ourselves. I *love* that thought. He's saved me for his purposes, which are far more important than my own; at the cost of his blood, which is far more than anything I have invested in myself.

> In seeking to follow the Spirit, never let go of the wonderful promise of Proverbs 3:5 – 6:
>> Trust in the LORD with all your heart, and lean not on your own understanding. In all your ways acknowledge him, and he shall direct your paths. (NKJV)

Acknowledging him in all your ways means availing yourself of every means of guidance he has put at your disposal. That means looking for him in:

- His Word
- The gifts he has placed in you
- The holy ambitions he has placed in your spirit
- The counsel of your church
- His sovereign arrangement of your circumstances

God uses *all* of these things to guide us. He guides most clearly through his Word, and that's the only one you can be absolutely certain about, so let that one anchor all the others. Beyond that, hold the others loosely, and in tension with one another. Sometimes you'll think God is putting something in your spirit, but he overrules through your circumstances. Or vice versa.

Mark Driscoll, a well-known American pastor with a thriving

ministry in Seattle, Washington, says that when he was nineteen years old and a brand new Christian, he heard the Holy Spirit tell him very clearly that he should "marry Grace, train men, and plant churches." He did all three of those things. He founded the Acts 29 Network, one of the most successful church-planting networks in the country.

I have another friend, Dr. Tom Elliff, who served until recently as president of the International Mission Board (IMB) of the Southern Baptist Convention. Tom had a much different experience than Mark. As a young man, he and his wife Jeannie sensed a clear call by the Holy Spirit to take the gospel overseas. They believed God wanted them to spend their whole lives among unreached peoples in Africa. Nine months after arriving in Zimbabwe, however, they got into a serious car crash that left their daughter, Beth, with severe injuries. Her injuries forced them to return home, leaving Tom and Jeannie confused about what God really wanted from them. Had they been wrong in what they had sensed?

Tom became a pastor and grew one the most vibrant churches in America. During that time, he mobilized scores of people for the mission field, including two of his four children and (so far!) the first of his grandchildren. In 2011, God called him to serve as president of the largest mission-sending agency in the world, the IMB. Because he has served as both pastor and missionary, he can bridge the gap between churches and their missionaries. I've heard him called "a pastor to missionaries and a missionary to pastors."

None of this would have occurred had God not redirected Tom through an unusual and unforeseen set of circumstances that in many ways contradicted the "voice" he and Jeannie thought they had heard. Recently, Tom told me in a letter,

> Looking back (I will soon be seventy and have been ministering the gospel now for over fifty-one years) we are constantly taken with the fact that, through those years, God has sovereignly rolled together each set of previous experiences in preparation for his next assignment. We sense that he has led us all the way.

Was it really God who placed into Tom's heart that passion and calling for overseas missions? If you had asked that question shortly after the accident, Tom and Jeannie may have felt tempted to conclude "no." But from this vantage point, the answer is obvious: God was in both the passion he gave them *and* the circumstances he used to guide them in the application of that passion. The road has been confusing, if not exasperating.

But that's how it often works. Hearing from God means balancing what God puts in your heart with how he guides you through other means, and trusting him all the way.

And sometimes you won't perceive any activity of God—in your spirit, your circumstances, or from the counsel of friends. You'll feel like you are left to make some crucial decision on your own. But still, there's no need to stress. He is the good shepherd. He never slumbers nor sleeps. And not one hair of your head falls to the ground without his knowing.

But that raises another question! How can we walk with the Holy Spirit when the heavens seem silent and he "feels" miles away?

PART 3

SEEKING THE HOLY SPIRIT

"If you then, though you are evil, know how to give good
   gifts to your children,
how much more will your Father in heaven give the Holy
   Spirit to those who ask him!"   — *Luke 11:13*

CHAPTER 13

When You Can't Feel God

Then Jesus was led by the Spirit into the wilderness to be tempted by the devil. After fasting forty days and forty nights, he was hungry.

—Matthew 4:1 – 2

"If the LORD is with us,... where are all his wonderful deeds that our fathers recounted to us?"   *—Judges 6:13 ESV*

By his Spirit, God is alive and active in his church. Nevertheless, if you think that walking with Jesus means an endless series of miracles, burning bushes, still, small voices, warm fuzzies, and sensations of peace that pass all understanding, then you are going to be disappointed.

Many of the greatest (and most honest) saints have confessed that they had to walk through many valleys with *no* sense of God's presence, sometimes nearly going deaf from the heavenly silence. C. S. Lewis wrote that during one of the most painful times of his life, he cried out to God and got

... a door slammed in [my] face, and a sound of bolting and double bolting on the inside. After that, silence. You may as well turn away. The longer you wait, the more emphatic the silence will become.[1]

He confessed that this heavenly silence made him doubt whether there was even a God at all:

There are no lights in the windows. It might be an empty house. Was it ever inhabited? It seemed so once ... Why is God so present a commander in our time of prosperity and so very absent a help in time of trouble?[2]

Somehow, these honest words seldom make it into anyone's list of favorite C. S. Lewis quotes.

Have you ever felt this way?

I once told a group of interns at our church that if they ever had days when they couldn't feel God's closeness, experiencing regular waves of his pleasure and mercy wash over their souls, that was proof they weren't really saved. You should have seen the looks on their faces. I realized they hadn't gotten what I thought to be a rather obvious joke. If that were true, none of us could be sure of our salvation! *Every* believer has times in which they feel as though God is distant. Or absent altogether.

Many Christians assume that silence from heaven means something has gone wrong, that the inability to "feel" God's Spirit means God has turned his face away. But this is not what God's Word tells us. His apparent silence is, in fact, an important part of how he works in our lives and grows us up into the men and women of faith he wants us to be.

An Ancient, Recurring Story

The greatest saints in the Bible often felt the absence of God. No less than the prophet Isaiah himself cried out in despair, "God where are your dramatic, awe-inspiring works of God in *my* day?" He had heard of "times past" when God would "rend the heavens and come down," when people "quaked in God's presence." But where was that God *now*, Isaiah asked? He cries out in dismay, "You have hidden your face from us" (Isa. 64:1–7). The psalmist Asaph says plainly, "We are given no signs from God; no prophets are left, and none of us knows how long this will be" (Ps. 74:9). And Gideon, right before God used him to destroy an entire Midianite army with only three hundred men, said to an angelic messenger,

> "If the LORD is *really* with us ... where are all his wonderful deeds like the ones our fathers recounted to us?" (Judg. 6:13, my paraphrase)

The experience of feeling like God is absent or silent, you see, is anything but new. So why does God leave us feeling that way sometimes? And what are we to do during those times?

White Space

When God calls someone to follow him, he frequently sends them through times in the "wilderness." Right after God first put into Moses a vision to see Israel led out of slavery, he exiled him into the wilderness for forty years to herd sheep. Only after a long, silent, four decades, did God finally appear to him in the burning bush with the command to go. Can you imagine what kind of despairing, "God, where are you?" conversations Moses must have had with God during those forty silent years?

Or consider the story of David. After being anointed as future king of Israel by Samuel, what was David's next move? Did he...

> ... go straight to the palace to try on robes?
> ... immediately confront Goliath?
> ... get billed as one of the "sexiest men alive" in *Israelites Today* magazine?

None of the above. First Samuel 16 tells us he went straight back to the pasture to tend the sheep. When David encounters Goliath, he's in between sheep-care and crackers-and-cheese runs for his brothers (17:15). Samuel had anointed David as king in 16:13. This means David went from being named "future king" and "man after God's own heart" by the most famous prophet alive to "field hand shoveling sheep dung" and "Cheeze-It boy" for his big brothers.

Right after the conclusion of the last verse in the story of David's anointing (16:13), my Bible has a white space, and the author moves on to something else happening at a different place in Israel. In that white space is where David went back to the pasture. The space between the call of God and the fulfillment of the dream. Nothing is written there, for David or for us, and I'm sure it felt terribly confusing for David.

Are you in a white space right now? White spaces are typically the hardest parts of life to endure: The white space of silence; the white space of singleness; the white space of sickness; the white space of finishing out a prison sentence; the white space of unfulfilled promises and unmet expectations.

How many times must Joseph—sold by his brothers into slavery, falsely accused of adultery with his master's wife, overlooked for parole by the magistrates—have called out to God, "*Where are you?*"

After Jesus called Paul to be his apostle on the Damascus Road, Paul wandered in the desert for three years and suffered obscurity for another fourteen (Gal. 1:17–19; 2:1). Paul endured *seventeen years* in the background before he was appointed by the church as a missionary (Acts 13:2)!

After Mary became pregnant with the Messiah, God waited for several months to tell her fiancé, Joseph, about the miraculous conception. Why did God wait? During that delay, Joseph (naturally) assumed she had cheated on him (I mean, what else could you assume?). This means that for several months, Mary had to go through the humiliation of pregnancy *alone* with everyone, even her beloved fiancé, assuming she was a cheater. God chose to do it that way. Why? Why did he wait so long to tell Joseph? *Why the "white space"?*

Why does God sometimes leave *us* feeling alone, deserted, humiliated, abandoned—like we are in darkness, like he doesn't care—as though he's abandoned us altogether? Why is the only sound we hear at those times the echo of a door slammed in our faces?

I don't know the full answer, but I know that part of it has to do with the fact that he wants us to walk by faith, not by sight; and walking by faith means sometimes pressing on when we can't feel or see him.

Martin Luther, who struggled with intense seasons of feeling like God had abandoned him, said:

> Faith in Christ is far from simple and easy because he is an astounding king, who, instead of defending his people, (apparently) deserts them. Whom he would save he must first make a despairing sinner. Whom he would make wise he must first turn into a fool. Whom

he would make alive, he must first kill. Whom he would bring to honor, he must first bring to dishonor. He is a strange king who is nearest when he is (apparently) far.[3]

God sanctifies us by humbling us. He works his salvation out in us by taking us through the valley of the cross, which often means *feeling* alone and abandoned. This may be why God didn't tell Joseph his plans for Mary at first; he wanted Mary to *feel* the shame of the cross. Moses had to endure the wilderness of isolation. Paul had to learn to suffer (Acts 9:15; 2 Cor. 11:24–27). In reality, we most certainly are *not* alone during these dark times, but walking by faith means believing that we are not alone even when we can't feel the warmth of God's presence.

Another reason God often leads us through dark, silent valleys is that he wants to purify our hearts. *Why* do we want to be close to God? Is it because of what he gives us, or is it simply because we want *him*? What is more valuable to us: God or his blessings? Sometimes God withholds *everything* from us except his promises in order to make us ask ourselves, "Is this—his promise—enough for me?" You can never know that Jesus is all that you *need*, you see, until he's all that you *have*.

So let me ask you a very important question, one that the survival of your faith depends on. *Can you walk by faith in God's promises alone, even when you can't see or feel anything?* Can you delay gratification, even the gratification of "feeling" the Spirit?

If not, you'll never make it. The righteous, Paul says, can only live by *faith*.

God Does His Best Work in Our Darkest Hours

Just because God *feels* absent doesn't mean that he actually is. Just because you can't track his footprints doesn't mean he's not walking beside you.

In Scripture we see that God often does his best work in our darkest hours. Even though Joseph felt alone during his betrayal, abandonment, and extended time in prison, the writer of Genesis says over and over again, "But the LORD was with Joseph" (Genesis 39:2, 21, 23). God was there, even in the betrayals and the darkness, and he was hard at work. Down in the dank well where his brothers had thrown him, Joseph learned that God saves even out of desperate circumstances. While a

185

slave in Potiphar's house, he learned that God had equipped him to manage a large household. In prison, Joseph learned the organizational skills he'd need to save a whole nation from starvation. Through it all, God worked in him the patience and compassion to forgive his brothers. And in his trials Joseph gave to us a picture of Someone much more important who one day would be falsely accused, abused, and killed because of our betrayal, yet rise to the throne to save us all. God allowed Joseph's suffering to prefigure Jesus' cross for us.

It was in the wilderness that God taught Moses the all-surpassing value of his kingdom.

It was in the pasture that God imparted to David the skills necessary to fight Goliath and taught him the joy of knowing the Lord as his own shepherd.

> But David said to Saul, "Your servant has been keeping his father's sheep. When a lion or a bear came and carried off a sheep from the flock, I went after it, struck it and rescued the sheep from its mouth. When it turned on me, I seized it by its hair, struck it and killed it. Your servant has killed both the lion and the bear; this uncircumcised Philistine will be like one of them." (1 Sam. 17:34–36)

It was in the desert that God taught Paul "to live is Christ" and "to die is gain" (Phil. 1:21).

God *uses* the wilderness. The pasture is his laboratory. When he puts you into a white space, don't assume he's forgotten you. In the pasture, he's commencing some of his best work.

Don't waste your white space.

During my seminary years, my best friend, Bruce, and I built for ourselves a little preaching circuit. Each week we preached in churches, youth groups, campus clubs, sports-team chapels, and rest homes and on street corners. We made business cards. We skipped class a lot, feeling justified because we were doing God's work and saving the world.

The president of our seminary called Bruce into his office one day. There, on his desk, sat a little, plastic sand pail, filled with sand and a shovel. Bruce said "What is that?" The president said, "For the next week, everywhere you go, you are going to take this pail with you. Set it on top of your desk during class. Sleep with it beside your bed. Take it into the shower with you, and carry it with you in the stores you shop in. If I catch you without it even one time, in the next seven days, I will suspend your classes for the semester."

A dumbfounded Bruce asked, "Uhhh ... *Why?*"

The president replied, "Because you are so busy trying to save the world that you are skimping on your preparation. You think the world depends on you. But when God calls his servants, he routinely puts them in the wilderness to learn first. He did it with Moses, David, and Paul. Learning what God is teaching you in the wilderness is the most important part of your training, and I don't want you to miss it because you are too busy thinking God needs you. So for the next week, anytime someone asks you what this is for, explain to them that if the desert wilderness was important for Moses, David, or Paul, it's important for me, too."

God does his most important work in the "wilderness" of our lives, the places away from Goliath, away from the crowds, away from the warm fuzzies.

Don't waste your white space.

Not much may occur in the white space that seems worth writing down in a book, but a lot is being written *into you.* During these fallow, wilderness times, we often worry that somehow fortune has passed us by, we've missed our chance, and our future is ruined. We wonder if God has "set us on the shelf" and moved on to some more promising candidate. That's what I have often thought. But God did not have Jesus die for you so that he could waste you. He has plans that neither you nor I know anything about. And they would blow your mind if you got even a glimpse of them (Jer. 29:11–13; 1 Cor. 2:9).

You May Feel Alone, But You Are Not. Not Ever.

If you are a believer, that feeling of being alone is always an illusion. In fact, it's a *divinely designed illusion* — designed to strengthen your faith. Martin Luther described it this way:

> Like a child trying to push against the hand of a parent, the parent gives only enough resistance to test the resolve of the child, so God resists us in prayer, to see our resolve in his goodness.[4]

Here's how I know you're not alone. Right before Jesus died, Jesus experienced true aloneness, true abandonment — and he did it so that you would never have to experience it.

Jesus knew he was about to go through the greatest trial of his life and he wanted to spend a few precious minutes alone with his Father beforehand. So he went to his favorite spot to commune with God—the garden of Gethsemane. But as he prayed for God's presence in that garden, for the first time in his life he was met with utter silence. Twice he asked God for comfort; twice he received no answer. The gospel of Mark says he was overcome with a sense of horror (14:33). Scholars say the word for "horror" indicates the kind of the feeling you'd have if you came home one evening to find your family murdered, mutilated, and hung up on the wall. It felt so overwhelming that Jesus almost died from it (14:34).

The feeling of aloneness so crushed him that Jesus began to sweat great drops of blood, a condition doctors call "hematidrosis," when you are under such strain that the capillaries in your face literally burst.

A friend of mine had spent the afternoon at the pool with his family, and when they all got into the car to go home, he noticed his three year old was missing. He raced back to the pool and found, to his horror, his three-year old son lying unconscious at the bottom of a pool. He snatched him out, began CPR, and managed to revive him. They rushed him to the emergency room, where they ran a series of tests on him and kept him overnight for observation. The following morning, my friend noticed small, purple blotches, like dozens of tiny bruises, all over his son's face. He asked the doctor about them, and the doctor said that right before his son lost consciousness at the bottom of the pool, he had evidently been screaming so forcefully for his father that the capillaries in his face burst.

And here is Jesus—who spoke the worlds into existence, who walked on top of angry waves, calmed the fiercest storms, cast out the vilest demons, healed the gravest diseases and brought life back to the dead—so horrified at something that his capillaries burst, his soul overwhelmed "to the point of death."

What had he seen?

Aloneness. Utter and total aloneness. He had come to the garden to commune with the Father and found instead an eternal coffin gaping open before him. The crucifixion, you see, started long before the nails pierced Jesus' hands. In the garden, God already had begun to turn his face away.

"My God, My God, why have you forsaken me?"

New Testament scholar William L. Lane says, "This is the horror of one who lived wholly for the Father, who came to be with his Father for a brief interlude before his death and found hell rather than heaven open before him."[5]

Why is this good news? The essence of the cross was substitution. Jesus faced our aloneness—the utter abandonment we had brought upon ourselves through our sin—so that you and I would never have to. The Father turned his face away from his Son so that the Father would never have to turn his face away from us.

So when we feel abandoned—that's all it is, a feeling. A lying, deceptive feeling. It has to be. Jesus faced the full measure of our aloneness in our place and put it away forever. By his death, he reconciled us to God, so that we can know he will never leave us or forsake us. In some strange way we can never hope to comprehend, he *was* abandoned ... for us.

The Father turned his face away from his Son so we could boldly approach the throne of grace with confidence. Because of Gethsemane, we can know he feels our every pain, hears our every petition, and never takes his affectionate eye off of us. We are literally "engraved on the palms of his hands" (Isa. 49:16). Because Jesus prayed, "My God, my God, why have you forsaken me?" we can cry with confidence, *"Abba,* Father" (that is, "My Daddy")!

So When You Feel Alone ...

So what do you do when you *feel* alone?

Simply: walk by faith, not by sight. You must re-believe the gospel, that God has removed the full extent of the curse—all that could ever separate you from him—and has given you Christ's complete righteousness in its place. You must re-believe that in his finished work you couldn't be closer to him than you are right now, regardless of how you *feel*. And you must reclaim the promises of God, *almost all of which* are made to us for times in which God appears distant.

Here is a life-saving spiritual lesson: What you "feel" is not usually a good indicator of what really is. I've heard that people who survive getting overrun by a snow avalanche often lose all bearings as to which way is up, and often will try to dig themselves out in the wrong direction. That happens to us in a time of aloneness. We "feel" like we are not close to God, but that feeling is not telling us the truth. God's Word tells us what reality is, not our emotions. Emotions come out of our belief system; they should not be the basis for it. Our emotions, you see, do not have minds. They cannot think for themselves. We have to think *for* them, *telling* them what is real. Feelings should be reoriented around God's reality, not our perception of reality around feelings. And the best presentation of reality is found in God's Word. Therefore, we must believe our way into our feelings, not feel our way into our beliefs.

Many Christians go through long seasons in which they feel disconnected from God, doubting whether or not they are even saved. In a short book I wrote called *Stop Asking Jesus into Your Heart: How to Know for Sure You Are Saved*, I explored the source of those doubts. We must train our feelings, I explained, to follow faith in God's Word. Feeling arises from faith, and faith is built upon fact. When we reverse that order, allowing feelings to determine faith and fact for us, spiritual disaster occurs.

The gospel *declares to us* that God has made himself close to us in Christ, holding us even tighter than a mother holds a newborn child (Isa. 49:15). When our feelings tell us that is not true, we must defy those feelings with faith in God's promise.

I have a Christian friend who went through such a horribly dark time that eventually he came to believe he couldn't possibly be saved, or even hope to be in the future. In his anxiety and depression, he reasoned that he had deceived himself for years about really walking with Jesus. Every time my friend thought about God—the same God whom for years he had depended on—he felt condemned. But God's promise, he learned, was greater than his heart's lying testimony (1 John 3:20). So he labeled his feelings the liar and God's Word the truth. Renewed faith in God's promises, not renewed feelings, lifted him out of his pit of despair.

So when you can't "feel" God, be assured, he's there. The cross assures you that he is. He will never leave you nor forsake you. Nothing can ever separate you from his love. He has united himself, through his Spirit, inextricably to you. And just as with David, and Esther, and Moses, and Joseph, and Paul, he is likely doing his best work in you in those dark times.

When I served as a missionary in Southeast Asia, I went through one of the darkest spiritual seasons of my life. I was seeing no fruit, no conversions. Conflict plagued our team. My prayer times with God felt perfunctory at best, drudging at worst. A few missionaries I knew had been thrown into a prison close by. I regretted ever coming to the field. I even asked my supervisor if I could get a transfer, and when he said "no," I contemplated quitting.

"Where is God? Where is his blessing? Was this call an illusion?" I asked myself.

Looking back now, I see how much God was teaching me during that time. He revealed to me, for example, that the bravado with which I had carried myself (I had proudly boasted before audiences, "I'd gladly die for Jesus!") was just that—bravado, built on the crumbling foundation of my flesh. God revealed how much more concerned I was about my "success" in ministry than about my faithfulness to him. He showed me I loved my life more than I loved seeing people saved, and that I cared more about being highly regarded by others than I did knowing and loving him.

These are lessons I desperately needed to learn (and still need to re-learn!), but no sermon could have taught them to me. I had to walk through the dark valleys with Jesus, unsure at times if he were even there, before those hidden areas of unbelief could be brought to light and healed by Jesus. Looking back, I see now that I've come to know God more in the pastures, and wildernesses, and white spaces, and valleys than I have on the mountaintops.

I've spent most of my life hating those white spaces, trying desperately to get out of them into the next section of writing. But in those times—those sometimes very silent and dark times—the Holy Spirit has done his *best* writing in me.

And he's doing the same in you.

CHAPTER 14

Revival: When the Holy Spirit Moves in Power

Sometimes I leave Christian events wondering if we resemble the prophets of Baal in I Kings 18 more than Elijah, the prophet of God.... We can have a great time singing and dancing ourselves into a frenzy.... But at the end of it, fire doesn't come down from heaven. People leave talking about the people who led rather than the power of God. —*Francis Chan*

See, darkness covers the earth and thick darkness is over the peoples, but the LORD rises upon you and his glory appears over you.
—*Isaiah 60:2*

The most effective sermon ever delivered came via the mouth of a hypocrite.

Jonah has to qualify as worst prophet *ever*. He hated the people he was preaching to. No teary, "O, God, please open their eyes," or "But for the grace of God, there go I" prayers. He wanted nothing more than for God to destroy the Ninevites. He had gone there only because

God threatened to kill him if he didn't, putting him into the belly of a fish for three days just to show him that he was serious. So Jonah went to save his own skin, but he hoped the Ninevites wouldn't listen to his sermon, and he ran out right after his preaching tour to get a front-row seat to see God go Sodom and Gomorrah on the city.

Not only was Jonah an unlikely preacher to cause revival, but the Ninevites were an unlikely people to receive one too. They hated the Israelites, being big fans of their own god, Ishtar. They reveled in cruelty, perfecting techniques of torture and subjugation. For example, they would take enemy soldiers whom they had captured and bury them up to their necks in the hot sand, cut off their eyelids so they could not blink, and nail their tongues to the ground. Then they would put Bee Gee's songs on repeat and blare them all through the night. (Okay, so I made that last part up, but the rest is true.) Point is, they weren't exactly "noble savages" who stared up at the stars each night and yearned to know the God of love and justice.[1]

Furthermore, Jonah does not seem to have preached a very compelling sermon. As we can tell, it consisted of only eight words, with no alliterated points, no illustrations, no catchy one-liners, no testimonies from professional athletes, and no practical "next steps."

And yet the entire city repented. *Every single living being,* Jonah records, from the king to the cows. (Yes, Jonah recorded that even the cows put on the garments of repentance and mooed out their lamentation).

How did this happen?

Somehow, as those eight words left Jonah's mouth, the Spirit of God made them come alive in the hearts of the Ninevites. At the preaching of Jonah, the spiritually dead Ninevites became white-hot worshipers of the living God.

Stories of God moving in this way fill the pages of Christian history. When and how it comes, we can't exactly predict — the moving of the Spirit is, as Jesus said, mysterious like the wind — but when it comes, more happens in a few moments than we can typically accomplish in a few lifetimes.

Two Kinds of Gospel Work

The writer of Psalm 126 yearns for that kind of awakening in his own land of Israel:

Restore our fortunes, LORD, like streams in the Negev! Those who sow with tears will reap with songs of joy! Those who go out weeping, carrying seed to sow, shall return with songs of joy, carrying sheaves with them. (vv. 4–6, emphasis mine)

Derek Kidner points out that in these three verses, the psalmist has identified two ways in which God works in the hearts of his people.[2] In verses five and six, the writer talks about "sowing in tears." Israel had many desert regions, and the psalmist is imagining soil so arid that seeds planted needed to be watered individually, with tears. Imagine how many hours of exhausting patience and excruciating labor that would take!

God often works this way through us. We patiently plant the seeds of God's Word in the hearts of those around us, water them with our tears, and fertilize them with our faith. Disciple-making can be laborious, painstaking work. Some of the greatest missionaries in history labored faithfully for years with almost nothing to show for it! I had never worked harder in ministry than when I served as a missionary in Southeast Asia, but at the end of two years of long, faithful labor, I had only a couple of converts, and both were wavering. What was wrong? Was I in sin? Honestly, I don't think so. As Psalm 126 says, some gospel labor is just like that. It is long, laborious, and costly.

But God works another way, too.

The psalmist says, "Restore ... *like streams in the Negev.*" The Negev was a desert-like region in Israel with little vegetation. Occasionally, however, torrential rains swept the plains, and streams overflowed the land. When the waters receded, it left a moist and supple soil over which greenery spread like a carpet.

The psalmist imagines God doing this among the hearts of his people. This is what happened in Nineveh. God did more in a moment through a shoddy sermon than a thousand missionaries could have done in two generations.

Yearning for an outpouring like this didn't negate the psalmist's responsibility to plant the seeds and patiently water them with tears. But it does give him a hope that he refuses to relinquish, a hope that God will again send his Spirit into his land, like a flood.

We should never give up that hope for our day, either. Martyn Lloyd-Jones said:

[We] can fight and sweat and pray and write and do all things, but ... [we are] impotent, and cannot stem the tide. We persist in thinking that we can set the situation right. We start a new society, we write a book, we organize a campaign, and we are convinced that we are going to hold back the tide. But we cannot.[3]

But then, Lloyd-Jones says, we remember the promise: "When the enemy comes in like a flood, it is the Lord who will raise, and does raise the banner."[4]

Lloyd-Jones here quotes from Isaiah 59:19, using imagery from ancient warcraft. Advancing forces raised a flag to signal when the army should move forward. When in retreat—when the enemy army rushed in and pushed your army backwards—you lowered your flag. But when you regained momentum and began again to advance, you raised back up the standard. Isaiah looks forward to times when God would so empower his people to succeed in their mission that they raise their standard—no longer on the defensive, but advancing quickly against the enemy. How does that happen? Lloyd-Jones continues:

And so we throw ourselves upon the mercy of God. It is not so much an organized prayer emphasis as it is an act of desperation. And then, and only then, does the power of the Holy Spirit come flooding upon us and into us. And he does in a moment what incremental organization can hardly accomplish in half a century.[5]

I love that last phrase. "He does *in a moment* what incremental organization can hardly accomplish in half a century." I feel my heart flooding again with new hope even as I write it down.

Jonathan Edwards, who oversaw the largest religious awakening among Western peoples in modern history (called "the first Great Awakening," in eighteenth-century America), said that at the beginning, a few sermons were preached, a few mission efforts were organized, and a few converts were made. "But then," he said,

God in so remarkable a manner took the work into his own hands, and did as much in a day or two that, under normal circumstances took the entire Christian community, using every means at their disposal, with the blessing of God, more than a year to accomplish.[6]

He's talking about the streams in the Negev.

Again, when we don't experience that kind of outpouring, we must still faithfully labor in the field, diligently planting the seeds one at a time and watering each with our tears. Tim Keller says a revival is "the intensification of the normal operations of the Holy Spirit (conviction of sin, regeneration and sanctification, assurance of salvation) through the ordinary means of grace (preaching the Word, prayer, etc.)."[7] In an awakening, the Spirit of God does not typically do a "new" thing; he simply pours great power upon the "normal" things faithful Christians are already doing. Prayers become more intense; worship becomes more joyous; repentance becomes more sorrowful; and the preached Word yields greater effect. The Spirit of God multiplies the effectiveness of our "normal" work of seed-planting, bringing a bountiful harvest. And he does more in a moment than we can accomplish in a lifetime.

The Lord's Arm Is Not Shortened

Do you believe God is willing to send such an outpouring today? The prophet Isaiah said,

> The arm of the LORD is not too short to save, nor his ear too dull to hear. (Isa. 59:1)

"The Lord's arm is not too short." That means God is no less powerful to save today than he was in the past. The same Spirit who moved in Nineveh and in the Great Awakening still fills the church today. The same power that brought Jesus back from the dead still animates our preaching. People are not "more spiritually dead" today than they were in the days of Jonah or the days of the Great Awakening. There are no degrees of deadness, or any such thing as "mostly dead" (apologies to *The Princess Bride*). *Every* conversion to Christ requires the same, glorious miracle of resurrection, and God has not lost his ability to raise the dead. We've simply lost *confidence* that he *will* do it on a large scale.

"Nor his ear too dull." This means that God is not less compassionate today than he was when he turned the murderous, cruel, idol-worshiping Ninevites into humble God-seekers, or when his Spirit swept through Jerusalem, gathering the same people who had crucified him into his first church. God *delights* in showing great mercy—always has, always will. He is slow to anger, abounding in mercy. He still looks

at the crowd and has "compassion for them because they are weary and scattered, like sheep without a shepherd" (Matt. 9:36).

Isaiah continues,

> Your iniquities have separated you from your God. (Isa. 59:2)

It is *we*, Isaiah says, who have changed, not God. Our sins keep us from God's power, not God's willingness. And might the primary sin of the church be refusing to believe that God *really* does not desire that any should perish, and that all should come to repentance? Is there any sin greater than unbelief? Have we blasphemed God by being unwilling to believe he is as merciful as the cross *tells us* that he is?

Intercessory Faith

At our church, we teach a concept called "intercessory faith." Intercessory faith means believing in the willingness of God to save on behalf of someone else. For many Christians, "intercession" implies dutifully recounting to God all the things we need God's help on, as if God needed us to keep him abreast of what's happening around the world. But intercession involves more than information sharing. Jesus calls us not just to tell him about someone else's problems, but to believe in his compassion and power on behalf of those problems. Intercessory faith perceives God's willingness to pour out his power into a situation and then asks him to do it.

> And he did not do many miracles [in Nazareth] because of their lack of faith. (Matt. 13:58)

Doesn't this verse imply that Jesus would have done miracles—indeed, wanted to do them—but there was simply no one there who believed in his willingness to do so?

Could the same thing be said of your family, your community, or your church? What if the lack of divine activity in those places had nothing to do with "unwillingness" in God's heart, but unbelief in yours?

I never want that to be said of my community. I've asked for the streams of the Negev to pour into my family and to pour in and through our church. As I mentioned, I have asked God to let us baptize 50,000 people in the Raleigh-Durham area, to plant more than a thousand churches, to start at least 100 community-blessing organizations out of our church. I've asked God to enable us to send out at least five thousand people on church-planting teams. You might call that overly ambitious; I call it taking Matthew 13:58 seriously.

John Piper recently told our church, in a message he preached to us, that God wanted to use us, the Summit Church, to bring awakening to several cities around the world. Scripture prophesies, he said, that in the last days, human hearts will grow increasingly dark and the world will become increasingly hostile to the gospel. Even so, there can be, and will be, exceptions. He prophesied Isaiah 25:3 to us: "Cities of ruthless nations will fear you" (ESV). A thick, dark cloud of unbelief, he said, is settling in above the whole earth, blocking the sun of God's glory from view. But the faith of the Summit Church can bore up through that cloud, penetrating the glacier of unbelief like a blowtorch, allowing God's glory to shine upon our city and into those other "ruthless cities" into which we have sent our people. The Spirit of God will then pour forth into our cities like rain, fertilizing the ground and calling forth a harvest of salvation.

In other words, God placed us here to call forth those *streams in the Negev* for our lands.

The First Time I Experienced Those Streams

I was in college the first time I experienced a real outpouring of these streams of revival. A good friend and I were disturbed by the utter disregard for the gospel and the numbing complacency of believers at our university. We believed God wanted to do something about it.

So we started a Monday night Bible study. The format was simple: we'd sing a few worship songs and someone would preach the gospel. Each Sunday before, we met for an extended time of prayer. We'd walk the campus or hole up in our dorm rooms and pray until we sensed God had heard us.

The streams of revival began to flow, slowly at first, but then like a flood. Our small Bible study grew to about eighty. One night, a friend and mentor, Alvin Reid, shared how he believed secret sin in our group grieved the Spirit of God and quenched his activity on campus. He then, rather abruptly, asked if any of us had something to confess. He asked it two or three times and then just stared at us. Honestly, it was an awkward moment. For about thirty seconds no one moved, and I was about to stand up, thank him for his challenge, and dismiss us in prayer, when one of our worship leaders cut me off: "Wait," he said. "It's me. I am obsessed about what people think about me. I am a different person behind closed doors than I am in front of you, and I know that displeases God. I have grieved the Spirit of God, and I am the reason God is not moving more on our campus." He began to weep.

What the Spirit of God did next is hard to describe. It seemed that every person felt a spotlight illuminating his or her soul. The Spirit of God showed me how eaten up with pride I was and how much more I cared about my own glory than God's. Far from being a God-centered leader, I was trying to steal God's glory, attempting to re-direct the attention of Christ's bride away from Christ and onto me. I stood, confessed my sin, and asked others to pray for me.

For the next several hours, an avalanche of repentance poured out of our little community. One freshman said, "I've been at school for three months, and I've yet to tell my suitemate about Jesus. That has to be sin. I haven't spoken to him yet because I've been afraid of what he might say back to me. If you'll pray for me, I'm going to go tell him about Jesus right now." He left the group, led his suitemate to Christ that night, and actually brought him back and introduced him to us before we let out for the evening.

Students continued there in the presence of God until about 2:00 a.m. We only broke up then because several students wanted to start a bonfire and rid themselves of pornography and other things they felt displeased God. People were serious about seeing God come onto our campus.

And he did.

To this day, I have not experienced so mighty a movement of God as I did in the eighteen months that followed that night. More than once, students knocked on my door in the middle of the night, asking how they could be saved. I know of some still serving on overseas mission fields today who experienced the call of God during those months. We had meetings in which hundreds showed up to hear the gospel, many giving their lives to Christ. I still run into people who tell me that they came to Christ during that season on our university campus.

The streams in the Negev.

Again, "Revival is the intensification of the normal operations of the Holy Spirit."[8] We weren't doing anything new or out of the ordinary. We simply started a Bible study and prayed. We planted gospel seeds and watered them with faith and tears. And then the Spirit of God came in and so blessed our efforts that we accomplished more in a few weeks than had happened on that campus in all our previous years.

God *wants* to send us those streams. How do I know? Because they flow from his cross. There Jesus shed his blood to provide a fountain of mercy that flows toward the nations to all who will receive it. Can we really overestimate his compassion for the world? He walked through the horrors of Gethsemane so that he could provide salvation for the peoples of the earth, and then commanded us:

- "Ask me, and I will make the nations your inheritance." (Ps. 2:8)
- "Ask the Lord of the harvest, therefore, to send out workers into his harvest field." (Matt. 9:38)
- "But you will receive power when the Holy Spirit comes on you; and you will be my witnesses in Jerusalem, and in all Judea and Samaria, and to the ends of the earth." (Acts 1:8)
- "All authority has been given to me in heaven and on earth. Go therefore and make disciples of all the nations." (Matt. 28:18–19)

He's shown us his intention to do *"many mighty works."* Now we just have to believe.

Ask, and Then Pursue "Normal" Means of Ministry

As we ask with extraordinary faith, we then pursue the "ordinary" means of grace. What are those "ordinary" means?

1. Repenting of sin

Throughout history, repentance of sin has always accompanied revival. For example, one historian records this pivotal incident that sparked the massive, country-transforming revivals in Korea of the early twentieth century:

> One of the Korean men — Mr. Kang — stood up, trembling, and said in barely more than a whisper, "I have something to confess. I have, for weeks, harbored an intense hatred in my heart for Mr.

Lee, our friend and missionary. I confess before God and before you, and I repent." The room fell silent. Did this man just publicly admit to hating the host of the conference? Every eye turned to Mr. Lee, to see how he would respond to this surprising admission. Mr. Lee was taken aback, and could not hide his own surprise. But he quickly answered, "Mr. Kang, I forgive you." What followed was a scene that reporters later called "a poignant sense of mental anguish due to conviction of sin." Men began to confess hidden sins, to weep over their sins, and to pray for forgiveness. The meeting, which was scheduled for a few hours, stretched on until five the next morning.[9]

Unconfessed, secret, or willful sin deeply grieves the Holy Spirit of God, and where it is cherished, the Spirit will not be present. Nothing quenches the fire of the Holy Spirit faster than unconfessed sin (Eph. 4:30-32; 1 Thess. 5:19).

True revival is not noisy; at least, not at first. It usually begins in a hushed awe. Believers get convicted about sin and the seriousness of God's holiness. Weeping is heard before shouts.

Again, let me repeat this: *Nothing* repels the Spirit of God faster than willful, unconfessed sin. Sin put Jesus, whom the Holy Spirit cherishes, on the cross, and that Spirit cannot dwell where people treat lightly what destroyed God's Son. Sin extinguishes the presence of the Holy Spirit like water does a flame. Timothy Keller says that when he reconnects with college students who have lost their faith, he usually asks, "So whom are you sleeping with?" Nine out of ten times, he says, he will see a flush of embarrassment cross their face and they'll stutter, "Uhh ... what does that have to do with anything?" Everything, he says. Willful sin makes the presence of God imperceptible to us.[10]

John Newton said in heaven, our sense of the presence of God will be constant because there will be no sin, unbelief, or spiritual dullness to obstruct or abate it.[11] But on earth, still trapped in sinful flesh, we experience that presence only sporadically. And when we sin willfully, we destroy our capacity to experience it at all.[12] Yet, God is merciful. When we repent, he restores our sight.

2. Preaching the gospel faithfully
God's means for removing the veil of unbelief and planting seeds of faith is the preached gospel. Sometimes, when we are preaching the

gospel and few are listening, we are tempted to "supplement" the gospel with lights, music, humor, or celebrity. There is nothing wrong with those things in and of themselves, but they can't replace the power of the gospel. Anything that distracts us from the preached gospel cuts off our access to God's power. We might still have huge audiences, but that's different than experiencing God's power.[13] So if we're in a season where the harvest simply is not coming, the *last thing* we should do is abandon the only thing that can produce faith. We must continue planting the seed of his word, watering them with our tears, and yearning for the streams in the Negev.

I love how Martin Luther described his role in the Reformation:

> I simply taught, preached, and wrote God's Word; otherwise I did nothing. And while I slept ... the Word did everything.[14]

3. Saturating *yourself* in the gospel continually

Israel's periods of spiritual decline were characterized by a "spiritual forgetting" (Deut. 4:9; 8:14; Josh. 4:20–24). God brought awakening by "renewing" his people in the stories of his mercy (Rom. 12:2). Israel did not need to learn new things; rather, they needed to have new eyes for the things they already knew. So, Ezekiel prays for "hearts of flesh" to replace stony ones (Ezek. 11:19).

Awakening involves believers "remembering" the great grace and glory of God, and feeling the weightiness of these things all over again. *Personal* revival comes from taking yourself deeper into your own gospel experience.[15] As you "remember" again your salvation, you grow in grace (2 Peter 1:4–9).[16]

4. Persisting in prayer

If you want to see revival, pray, pray, pray, and then pray some more. James Fraser, long-time missionary to China, said, "I used to think that prayer should have the first place and teaching the second. I now feel it would be truer to give prayer the first, second, and third places and teaching the fourth."[17] Jonathan Edwards noted that "extraordinary prayer" characterized the Great Awakening.

There is no awakening apart from prayer.

That's what the next chapter is about, so I'll leave it there for now.

A Final Word

The key to a new movement of the Spirit of God is not found in a new technique, but in the "old" paths of gospel proclamation, earnest prayer, and yearning for the Spirit. Sometimes we will hear how God is using some new discipleship method, preaching, or worship style to awaken others elsewhere; and we assume the key lies in that new method. Don't be deceived. Faith in God's mercy, not a new program, is the catalyst for releasing the Spirit. It was not the open-air preaching of the Great Awakening, the new music style of the charismatic renewal, or the cluster groups of the Brazilian revival that supplied the power of awakening. Don't set the cart before the horse. New techniques originate from the Spirit's movement; they are not the source.

As a friend of mine says, if you're excited about what God is doing elsewhere, don't mimic the miracle, imitate the faith. C. S. Lewis was fond of saying, "You never get into Narnia the same way twice." As you wait for the outpouring of revival, be faithful to pursue the "ordinary" means of grace: planting the gospel seeds one by one, and watering them with your faith and tears.

Before that now-famous revival in Korea, American missionaries had been working faithfully for twenty-three years with little to no fruit. And they almost left in frustration right before it broke out. In 1906, just months before Mr. Kang made his confession in Pyongyang, international relations became so strained that the American missionaries were making plans to leave. They had labored for nearly a generation with very little fruit, and the possibility of war threatened to undo what little progress they had made. Yet, after seeking God in prayer, they decided to stay and preach the gospel for a little while longer. Little did they know how momentous that decision to keep pressing on would be.

Following that first all-night prayer service of January 14, 1907, the Korean Christians gathered again the next night, confessing their sins publicly and praying loudly throughout the night. (By the way, if you've ever known any Korean Christians, you know that one of the things that characterizes their worship is loud, corporate prayer in which the whole congregation, not just the pastor, prays. We have a whole Korean community in our church. I always try to sit close to them in prayer meetings!) They gathered again the following day, and the day after that. This went on for more than a week, until the growing sense of the Spirit's presence grew so strong that the missionaries were unsure what to do next. They had never seen anything like it.

Soon, the revival spread beyond those prayer services. Over the next weeks, believers sought out those whom they had wronged, some even going door to door to ask for forgiveness. New believers were added by the hundreds. Revival spread to the nearby college; within two months, *90 percent* of this college's students had professed faith in Christ. Villagers, hearing about the events in Pyongyang, flocked to the city, some of them walking two hundred miles to see what this "new" God was doing. Many were converted, and they carried the fire of this revival back to their villages.

In one year, 50,000 people came to faith in Christ in Korea, a place where previously there had been only a handful of believers. Churches sprouted up by the thousands. From there, the movement has spread to the surrounding Asian nations.

What happened in Korea did not occur as a product of a perfect method or clever marketing. The key is not in their loud, spontaneous praying (though that is an awesome experience to be a part of!). Koreans experienced revival through the "normal" means of obedience: repenting of sin, praying persistently, and saturating both themselves and others in the gospel. And God used those tears of repentance to begin a flood of salvation.[18]

O Lord, may it be so again in our day!

We won't find it by mimicking the Korean miracle, but by imitating the Koreans' faith. God gives the Spirit to all who simply will ask.

So that's where we'll turn next: what does it mean to "pray for the Spirit"?

CHAPTER 15

You Have Not Because You Ask Not

The one concern of the devil is to keep the saints from prayer. He fears nothing from prayerless studies, prayerless work, prayerless religion. He laughs at our toil, mocks at our wisdom, but trembles when we pray ... Prayer turns ordinary mortals into men of power ... It brings fire. It brings rain. It brings life. It brings God. There is no power like that of prevailing prayer. —*Samuel Chadwick*

If the Holy Spirit was withdrawn from the church today, 95 percent of what we do would go on and no one would know the difference. If the Holy Spirit had been withdrawn from the New Testament church, 95 percent of what they did would stop, and everybody would know the difference. —*A. W. Tozer*

In 1857 a local Christian mission hired a young pastor named Jeremiah Lanphier to share the gospel with people living in Manhattan's lower side. Lanphier jumped into his assignment with zeal, but quickly became discouraged and frustrated. It seemed that no one in this fast-paced city had any time for God. Feeling he had nowhere else to turn, he began to pray.

As he prayed, Lanphier began to experience an unusual sense of God's presence. One day, he put out a sign and invited people just to come in and pray with him—no preaching, no sermon, only prayer.

The first Wednesday, six people showed up. The second Wednesday, twenty. The third Wednesday, forty, and then somebody said, "Let's do this every day." Two months later, the whole auditorium filled up every day at noon with hundreds of people praying. Similar prayer meetings began to spring up all over the city.

Soon the entire downtown area—almost every theater and every church—filled up at the noon hour with men and women crying out for God's presence to fall on the city. Reporters estimated that 10,000 people were praying every day in lower Manhattan for revival. Several churches began holding evangelistic services in the evening (notice the order—prayer meetings first; evangelistic meetings second). In a nine-month period, 50,000 people came to Christ in Manhattan, at a time in history when the population of New York City did not exceed 800,000.[1]

Do you long for this kind of thing to take place in your city? I do. How badly I yearn for this in Raleigh-Durham and in each of the unreached people groups where we have sent our missionaries to live!

God has one means for seeking it: persistent, faith-filled prayer. Let's consider another staggering promise Jesus gave about the Holy Spirit.

Fathers Don't Give Serpents to Sons

Jesus presented the Father's willingness to pour out the power of the Spirit in the most promising of terms. Sometimes when I read his words, they sound so promising I think I must be interpreting them wrongly. Surely the promise cannot be this straightforward. But it is, plain and simple.

> "Which of you fathers," he said, "if your son asks for a fish, will give him a snake instead?" (Luke 11:11)

Do you know any parent whose kid asks for a fruit snack and they say, "Sure, close your eyes and hold out your hand," and then places in their hand a scorpion?

Jesus said that if we, being "evil" parents, would not do that with our children, then how much more would the eternally good heavenly Father freely give the Holy Spirit to those who ask? Won't the greatest Father in the universe, Jesus asks, give his children what they most need, whenever they ask?

(Don't miss, by the way, the fact that Jesus' entire teaching about prayer in Luke 11 centers around the request for the power of the Holy Spirit. We see this in Jesus' conclusion to the teaching: " … how much more will your Father in heaven give the Holy Spirit to those who ask him!" [v. 13].)

The power of the Holy Spirit is what we, his children, most need. And the Father is glad to give it.

I've always thought it a little odd, by the way, that Jesus chose this moment to refer to us as "evil." Was that just a gratuitous insult he threw in to remind us of our depravity? Not at all. Jesus is trying to help us grasp the willingness of God to give the Holy Spirit. Most of us, you see, think of ourselves as being our *most* loving when we interact with our children. Even then, Jesus says, compared to the heavenly Father we are evil. Our compassion for our children cannot compare in the slightest to his compassion for us.

We *so* need the power of the Holy Spirit, and he is *so* willing to pour it out. We just have to ask.

Keep Asking

Let's back up a little in this teaching of Jesus. He gave his disciples this promise in response to an earnest request to teach them to pray (Luke 11:1). Evidently, you see, Jesus' disciples had noticed that prayer was the source of his power. They didn't say, "Lord, teach us to do miracles" or "Lord, teach us how to preach." They said, "Teach us to pray."

In response, Jesus tells a rather odd little story about a man who had unexpected visitors late one night. Because his visitors were hungry, the man went over to a neighbor's house to borrow some loaves of bread. His friend was already in bed, asleep, because that's what normal people do at midnight, especially since people in those days went to bed when the sun went down (thus making midnight the actual middle of the night.) Furthermore, families slept together, so to oblige this request this man would have to wake up everyone in the house. And on top of all *that*, the man asked for three full loaves of bread, which was enough to feed a family of six for a week! In other words, *this importunate neighbor had made a ridiculously excessive request at a most inopportune time.*

Yet, Jesus says, "because of his shameless audacity, he will surely get up and give him as much as he needs" (Luke 11:8 ESV). The neighbor hands over the loaves of bread, not because the man is his friend (in fact, after this event, he probably wasn't his friend!), but *because of his shameless audacity in asking.*

Won't your heavenly Father then, Jesus reasons, who *never* sleeps, and who loves you like precious children (not a begrudging neighbor!), give you *the one thing* you desperately need to do his work?

Jesus goes on,

> "So I say to you: Ask and it will be given to you; seek and you will find; knock and the door will be opened to you. For everyone who asks receives; the one who seeks finds; and to the one who knocks, the door will be opened." (Luke 11:9 – 10)

In the Greek, "ask," "seek," and "knock" are all in the imperfect tense, which means he is referring to something you do repeatedly. It's not enough to ask once. The outpouring of the Holy Spirit will come, he says, when we *persist* in asking. As I pointed out earlier, when you knock on a door, you don't knock once and then quit. (If my wife and I hear a single thump at midnight, we assume that one of our kids has fallen out of the bunk bed, not that someone is knocking!) You keep knocking until someone comes.

That's how prayer for the Holy Spirit works, Jesus says. We must ask repeatedly until God opens heaven's door and pours out the streams of the Negev.

"But why?" you ask. "If it is God's will to send the Spirit, then why not give his power the *first* time we ask?"

Umm … to be honest, I don't know. But that's *clearly* what Jesus teaches here, isn't it?

Charles Spurgeon said that some of the best fruits on God's tree are on sturdy boughs that require more than one shake to get them. God gives some things only when we persist in asking. Ask, and then ask again.

Honestly, this teaching seems so counterintuitive to me that if Jesus had merely given it once, I might feel tempted to write it off as an enigmatic parable. That's probably why Luke records Jesus teaching this exact same thing twice. In Luke 18:1–5, Jesus again teaches us on persisting in prayer, only this time via a different (and even more extreme!) parable.

> Then Jesus told his disciples a parable to show them that they should always pray and not give up. He said: "In a certain town there was a judge who neither feared God nor cared what people thought. And there was a widow in that town who kept coming to him with the plea, 'Grant me justice against my adversary.' For some time he refused. But finally he said to himself, 'Even though I don't fear God or care what people think, yet because this widow keeps bothering me, I will see that she gets justice, so that she won't eventually come and attack me!'"

I'm really glad Jesus told this parable, not me. First, comparing God to a cranky, old, unjust judge? Who but Jesus could get away with such an analogy? And "wearing God down" through persistent, incessant, even annoying, requests? Isn't that sacrilegious, even rude, to God?

Evidently not.

The point is not to *compare* God to an unjust judge, but to *contrast* him with one. If even an unrighteous, selfish judge will grant answers because of persistent asking, Jesus reasons, why wouldn't God, who cares about his children as a tender Father, give us that one thing we need (the power of the Holy Spirit) when we come to him persistently?

What if we aren't experiencing God's power in our communities, in our churches, or in our families—simply because we are not persistent in asking? Sometimes I visualize myself in this parable Jesus told in Luke 11. I am standing outside of God's window saying, "God, I know you're there, and I know you can hear me! I am your child. I need this power. My family needs this power. My church needs this power. I am not leaving until you give it to me."

The Persistent Prayer of the Early Church

As I explained before, Luke wrote both his gospel and the book of Acts to fit together like hand in glove. In his gospel, Luke presents to us the exact shape of the divine hand (in the life and teachings of Jesus); in Acts, we see that hand filling and animating the church. We see this with this teaching on persistent prayer for the Holy Spirit. What Jesus taught about the Spirit in the Gospel we see lived out and applied in the book of Acts.

Immediately after Jesus ascends to heaven, the early church remains in the upper room for ten days. We don't know everything they did there, but we know that the main thing they did was pray (Acts 1:14). Then God pours out the Holy Spirit, and Peter stands up to preach. His sermon, as best we can tell, lasted for about ten minutes ... and three thousand people were saved.

Today, we shuffle the zeroes around: we pray for ten minutes, preach for ten days ... and only three people get saved. What a difference the placement of those zeroes can make!

When the early church was up against a wall, they retreated into prayer, all night if that's what it took.

The prayers of the church in Acts were not routine maintenance "organ recital" prayers ("God, be with Aunt Betsy's spleen, and Uncle Gordon's kidneys," etc.). We rarely (if ever) hear them praying for their safety. They simply prayed for boldness *in the Holy Spirit* to be faithful witnesses (Acts 4:29–31), and God answered so dramatically that the earth shook. And after that shaking by the Holy Spirit, the threats of their enemies no longer shook them—and they went out to shake the world with the gospel (Acts 17:6). Just like Jesus had promised, when they needed help, the good Father didn't give them a spirit of fear; he gave them the Spirit of boldness. Don't miss the order: they prayed; the Spirit shook them; then they shook the world.

When the Jerusalem authorities threw Peter into prison, the early church prayed "earnestly" for his release (Acts 12:5). Peter was released by God, and when he went to where they were gathered, in the middle of the night, he found them *still* praying (Acts 12:12). In other words, they didn't merely ask once, then flip on *Sports Center* and leave the situation to the "sovereign will of God." *They kept knocking, calling out to God, all night long.* And when it seemed like no one was home, they just knocked louder.

"On Earth as It Is in Heaven"

There's one more important thing for us to learn from Jesus' teaching on prayer in Luke 11. He gave his disciples a model prayer, and in that prayer he includes the phrase, "Your will be done on earth as it is in heaven." In that phrase he gives us a crucial insight into how prayer works.

As I pointed out earlier, when we pray, we should seek to perceive what "heaven" wants, either through the Word of God or the Spirit of God (or some of both), and then ask for those things in faith. The combination of his will and our faith produces a new reality on earth. The wave of our faith added to the wave of his revealed will results in the laser of his power.

The Saddest Verse in the Bible

Let's return again to Matthew 13:58. As I mentioned before, it just might be the saddest verse in the New Testament.

> And he did not do mighty works there because of their unbelief.

"There" was Nazareth, Jesus' hometown. Of all the places that Jesus must have *wanted* to pour out his saving power, Nazareth had to have been among the greatest. His childhood friends were there; cousins, aunts, and uncles. Yet he did *almost none* of his mighty works there— not because of his unwillingness, but because of *their* unbelief.

Oh, how I do not want that said about my family, my church, or my community! So I ask God to help me see my community through the lens of his promises. I don't want to get to heaven only to find out there was saving power he wanted to pour out that never was because no one asked.

Hudson Taylor, the pioneer missionary to China, wrote the following words in his journal more than a hundred years ago. They both inspire and haunt me:

> We have to do with One who is Lord of all power and might, whose arm is not shortened that it cannot save, nor his ear heavy that it cannot hear; with One whose unchanging Word directs us to ask and receive that our joy may be full, to open our mouths wide, that He may fill them. And we do well to remember that this gracious God, who has condescended to place His almighty power at the command of believing prayer, looks not lightly on the *bloodguilti-ness* of those who neglect to avail themselves of it for the benefit of the perishing....

In the study of that divine Word, I learned that to obtain success-ful workers, [what I needed was] not elaborate appeals for help, but first earnest prayer to God to thrust forth laborers....

I had no doubt but that if I prayed for fellow-workers, in the name of the Lord Jesus Christ, they would be given. I had no doubt but that, in answer to such prayer, the means for our going forth would be provided, and that doors would be opened before us in unreached parts of the Empire....

The sense of *bloodguiltiness* became more and more intense. Simply because I refused to ask for them, the laborers did not come forward, did not go out to China: and every day tens of thousands in that land were passing into Christless graves![2]

Bloodguiltiness. The stains of another's blood upon our hands. What a jarring image! And in case you think it is a little overdramatic, real-ize that God used it first, not Hudson Taylor: he told Ezekiel that if he failed to warn those God commanded him to warn, they would die in their sins, but God would hold Ezekiel guilty of their blood (Ezek. 33:8). Hudson Taylor thought of himself as "bloodguilty" if he failed to pray. If God is willing to pour out his powers of salvation, but we never ask him to do so, are we not guilty of the blood of those who would have been saved if we asked?

I confess I don't like meditating for long on the concept of "blood-guiltiness," but Paul seems to have thought about it sometimes too. When he left Athens and traveled to Corinth, he began preaching the gospel first to his fellow Jews, per his personal custom. But Luke writes,

When they opposed Paul and became abusive, he shook out his clothes in protest and said to them, "Your blood be on your own heads! I am innocent of it. From now on I will go to the Gentiles." (Acts 18:6)

He had done his Spirit-assigned job of preaching to them; now their blood was on their own heads.

Later Paul told the Ephesians, as he left them to go take the gospel to other places, "I am free from the blood of all." In taking the gospel to the places God had commanded, Paul had removed his bloodguiltiness. But the flip side is also true! For Paul not to have obeyed would have made him guilty of their blood. It is true that God does not need us.

But when he gives us an assignment or an opportunity, and we fail to take it, we become responsible for those whose "blood" we could have saved through our obedience.

God has placed his divine powers of salvation at our disposal, just as he had with Paul. You and I have been given the privilege of escorting certain people from darkness to light. What an unspeakable privilege! We have the power to *alter* the eternities of people — whole families (Acts 18:8), even whole nations.

That's a sobering thought. But his promises toward us if we obey and believe are staggering.

When Jesus called Peter to follow him, he told him to cast his net into the water; when Peter pulled up his nets, he had caught so many fish that his boat started to sink. "From now on," Jesus declared, "you're going to catch men like that" (Luke 5:10, my paraphrase). Do you realize that God has made this same promise of effectiveness to you, if you follow him? We have a chance to bring life to the nations!

Do we realize the great, eternal potential God has placed into our hands?

A Wave of Salvation in Southeast Asia

Earlier, I told you about standing on a shore in Southeast Asia in 2004, where a tsunami wave had killed more than 100,000 individuals, some of whom I had known personally and loved. On that shore I heard the Spirit of God whisper into my heart: "I want to send a wave of salvation. I will flood this land with my glory. Believe me. Ask me, and see."

I am trying to obey that Spirit-given directive. We constantly are holding this region out before our people, asking them to pray about being sent there. I believe God wants to send a wave of salvation, and he will, if we go. I have told our church that I want to be like the proverbial woodpecker who taps away faithfully on a telephone pole when a bolt of lightning flashes suddenly from the sky and splits the pole in two. The woodpecker, knocked off-balance and somewhat dazed, regains his composure and promptly flies off to gather a few of his friends. He brings them back to the pole and said, "There she is, boys. Look at what I did!"

I plan to be like that woodpecker in Southeast Asia and Raleigh-Durham, laboring faithfully when God sends the lightning bolt of his power, when he opens up heaven and floods this Negev region. When it happens, I'll back up and say, probably a little dazed: "Well, I always knew it would come. He told us it would."

Has God given you a place like that? A place where you know that God has stationed you to be a channel for his Spirit?

"Ask of me," he says, "and I *will* give you the nations as your inheritance."

Our most important assignment, I believe, is *to believe*. God overflows with all the compassion and power necessary to save, and he can do more in a few moments than we can accomplish in 10,000 lifetimes. So as we labor, we ask. We keep our hands to the plow, but always looking to heaven with the hope that he will send down the power of the Holy Spirit just as he promised.

The Secret Behind Spurgeon's Success

Charles Spurgeon, whom I have quoted frequently throughout this book, grew one of the largest churches in history, with over 10,000 weekly attenders in downtown London (and this was during a time when megachurches were unheard of!). An American pastor traveled all the way across the Atlantic to learn the "secret" of Spurgeon's success. Spurgeon told the pastor there really was no "secret," but if he had to identify something, it would be found in a room deep beneath the church sanctuary. He walked the pastor down to the church's basement, where he showed him three hundred people on their faces praying as the service went on upstairs.[3] Spurgeon rarely preached without hundreds of people on their faces asking God to send the Holy Spirit. Spurgeon told his own congregation:

> The prayer meeting is an institution which ought to be very precious to us, and to be cherished very much by us as a Church, for to it we owe everything. When our comparatively little chapel was all but empty, was it not a well-known fact that the prayer meeting was always full? And when the Church increased, and the place was scarce large enough, it was the prayer meeting that did it all. When we went to Exeter Hall, we were a praying people, indeed; and when we entered on the larger speculation ... of the Surrey Music-hall, what cries and tears went up to heaven for our success! And so

it has been ever since. It is in the spirit of prayer that our strength lies; and if we lose this, the locks will be shorn from Samson, and the Church of God will become weak as water...."[4]

"We owe everything" to the prayer meeting. There is no "secret" to the Holy Spirit's power, you see. It's a promise God holds out to all who will seek it through persistent prayer.

CHAPTER 16

The Way Up Is the Way Down

"What? Not help you? I bought you with My blood. What? Not help you? I died for you. Since I have done the greater, will I not do the less? Your requests are nothing compared with what I am willing to give."
— *Charles Spurgeon*

The Spirit is the first power we practically experience, but the last power we come to understand. — *Oswald Chambers*

I want to end this book by bringing us back to the one, core element behind all authentic Christian experience: the gospel. Jesus gave the Holy Spirit to serve the purposes of the gospel. The Holy Spirit first enables us to believe the gospel and then continually re-opens our eyes to its beauties. He takes up residence in us when we first believe it, and he fills us again and again as we re-believe it (1 Cor. 12:3; 2 Cor. 1:22; Gal. 3:1 – 3). He empowers us to carry that gospel throughout the whole world. The Holy Spirit is given *in* the gospel, for the purposes *of* the gospel. Thus, those who want more of the Holy Spirit's presence should press more deeply into the gospel; those who want to know the gospel more deeply should seek the help of the Holy Spirit; and we should expect those most filled with the Spirit to be the ones most passionate about the spread of the gospel.

The gospel begins with our brokenness and inability, not our power and potential. Billy Graham once said that rarely is it someone's sin that keeps them from heaven; usually, it is their good deeds. In the same way, it is our false sense of ability, not our inabilities, that keeps us from the power of the Spirit. Thinking that we can get along fine "apart from" him keeps us from the gift of power available in him (John 15:5).

When you finally come to that place where you realize you have no true power, then you are ready to receive his. The great irony in the Christian life, you see, is that the way up is the way down. The lower we sink in ourselves, the higher we rise in him.

"Therefore I Will Rejoice in My Weaknesses"

The first sign that the almighty God is working in your life is a rather ironic one. You feel like you are going "down"—that you are condemned, *losing* power, hopeless. In your weakness is the beginning of God's power.

I have always counted Elijah one of my favorite Bible characters. Here was a man who overflowed with spiritual power! He took on 850 prophets of Baal on top of Mount Carmel in a kind of "prophetic smackdown" all by himself. He challenged them to a contest to prove which god was the true God. Whichever god answers by fire, they agreed, was it. God not only sent down fire for Elijah, he sent down such an outpouring that it evaporated several barrelfuls of water that Elijah had poured on the altar. Jews regarded Elijah as one of the most powerful prophets ever to live. But when you read the account of his life, you'll see that he didn't start there.

Elijah's ministry began with Elijah telling King Ahab and his wicked-witch-from-the-west wife, Jezebel, that they are in sin (1 Kings 17). They threatened to kill him. Rather than being delivered through some act of power, Elijah had to run for his life. He *hid* out by a little creek on the backside of the wilderness called "the brook Cherith" (ESV). There, God provided rations of water and beef jerky through a raven courier service.

Elijah had made a bold statement to Ahab, but now he's hiding. Superheroes don't hide.

For the first time in his adult life, he is unable to provide for even his most basic needs! He literally had to depend on God to feed him for every meal, like a child. Does this sound like an "ascent to power"?

Then things got even worse. *God* dried up the brook (1 Kings 17:7), and instructed Elijah to go see a widow in Zarephath, from whom he would now have to receive his food and water. Widows were considered the poorest of the poor, and now Elijah has to go to one of them to seek provision! Oh, guess who else was from Zarephath? *Jezebel*. God sent Elijah deep into a place where he was more vulnerable than perhaps anywhere else in Israel, to be taken care of by the poorest of the poor.

I have a hard time thinking Elijah felt like he was "reaching his potential," "discovering his inner power," or "embracing his best life now."

But God had a bigger agenda for Elijah, you see, than simply helping him discover his inner warrior; he wanted to demonstrate *his* power *through* Elijah to all of Israel. On top of Mount Carmel, God wanted his people to wonder at his power to save, not Elijah's personal charisma. So God had to reveal to Elijah his weakness before filling him with his power.

The decisive contest on top of Mount Carmel, you see, was not about whose prophets were smarter, more prepared, or even more righteous. It was a contest about which god had *real* power. So to prepare Elijah for that moment, God *removed* Elijah's power so that Elijah would depend on something outside of himself.

Thus, it was at the brook Cherith and the widow's house in Zarephath (and not on Mount Carmel) that God prepared Elijah as his instrument. "Cherith," by the way, in Hebrew means "to cut down," and that's exactly what God did to Elijah early on. He cut him down to nothing in himself so he could be everything in God.

This is what God does with all those whom he wants to fill with the power of his Spirit. He leads them down a path of humiliation and failure. He breaks them. He makes them weak in themselves so they can fill up with the power of God.

The way up, you see, is the way down.

Is God doing something like that to you? Is he tearing you down? If so, I can assure you that it's not because he is angry with you or against you. Quite the opposite! He is preparing you.

Jesus said, "Blessed are the poor in spirit, for theirs is the kingdom of heaven" (Matt. 5:3). I have to admit that I've never wanted to be *poor* in anything, certainly not in something as important as "spirit." As an American, I want to be at least "middle-class" in spirit, believing that if I just try hard enough, I can pull myself up by my bootstraps and make things work. People who are rich or even "middle-class" in spirit, however, *will never know the power of God*. In fact, if you're rich in spirit, Jesus said it would be easier for a camel to pass through the eye of a needle than for you to know the fullness of God. God's power comes as a gift only to the empty-spirited. He blesses the poor in spirit because their empty spirits make good vessels for his own.

Here's the bottom line: You will never be full of the Spirit so long as you are full of yourself.

So where do you feel "full" right now? Do you feel as though you are a "pretty good" spouse, a capable parent, a competent administrator, a talented preacher, or an above average Christian? If so — bad news. You are unlikely to experience the Spirit's power in any of those areas.

Martyn Lloyd-Jones recounts hearing a group of older pastors, who had lived through the massive Welsh revivals of the early twentieth century, discuss a sensational new young preacher gaining great popularity in the countryside. One of the older pastors said, "Aye, but he's never been broken." Lloyd-Jones, a young man himself, was confused by what the old preacher meant, but said that all the pastors immediately began to nod, ruefully, in understanding. Only years later, he said, would he learn what that older man of God meant. Human talent can take us only so far; to have lasting, eternal impact, we have to be filled with God's Spirit. Really, to do *anything* of lasting significance, we have to be filled with God's Spirit. If we're going to be filled with the power of his Spirit, we have first to be divested of our own. To get us there, God has to break us.[1]

God chooses the foolish things of the world to shame the wise, Paul says. He picks the weak things to bring to nothing the strong. Why? So that the glory will go to God, not to people.

Dr. Adrian Rogers, former president of the Southern Baptist Convention, once looked out at his congregation of more than seven thousand and asked, "How many of you in here graduated valedictorian or salutatorian?" A smattering of hands went up. "Please stand up!" said Dr. Rogers. People clapped. "Now, if you were an all-American athlete, please stand." "If you went to college on scholarship ... if you were homecoming queen ... If you graduated with honors ..." Dr. Rogers went through a list of accolades, and by the time he finished, nearly one third of his audience was standing. Everyone clapped. Then, to those standing, Dr. Rogers said, "Well, I have good news and bad news for you. The good news is that God can use you ... *too*. The bad news is that you are not his first choice."

Just as the gospel is a gift of righteousness for those who know they are unrighteous, the Holy Spirit, the Spirit of the gospel, is power for those who know they are powerless. Thus, it is the strengths in our lives that are our greatest liabilities, because they keep us deluded into thinking that we are capable apart from God. And this is why Paul said,

> Therefore I will boast all the more gladly about my weaknesses, so that Christ's power may rest on me. (2 Cor. 12:9)

Paul saw his weakness as an advantage, because he knew in those places he *had* to depend on Christ's power. You see, *if dependence is the objective, then weakness becomes an advantage.*

Is this how you look at your life? Do you rejoice in weaknesses?

Are you "weak" financially, unsure how to meet your needs?
Weak relationally, lonely, bereaved, or single when you would really like to be married?
Weak in faith?
Weak against temptation?
Do you feel incapable as a parent, or a spouse?
Has God incapacitated you in some way?
Have you been denied some privilege you know that you have earned?

All of these weaknesses are invitations to lean into God's power.

A. W. Tozer once said, "It is doubtful whether God can bless a man greatly until he has hurt him deeply."[2] God wounds you now so he can use you later — just like Elijah.

Craig Groeschel tells the story of a little bird flying south for the winter. Being a poor planner, the little bird got a late start and got caught in a snowstorm. When ice formed on his wings, he crash-landed. He thought, "Great. Now I'm going to freeze to death." Then a cow came along and dropped manure on him. At first, the bird thought his situation had gone from bad to worse, but he realized that the manure had thawed his wings! He got so excited that he started to chirp and sing, but this attracted a cat, who pounced on him and ate him.

We can learn three lessons about life from this story:

- *Lesson 1: Not everyone who drops manure on you is your enemy.*
- *Lesson 2: Not everyone who digs you out is your friend.*
- *Lesson 3: When you're in manure, sometimes it's helpful to keep your little chirper shut and just wait it out.*[3]

When God makes you weak, it's not because he has forgotten you. Quite the opposite. He is inviting you to lean into the power of his Spirit. And that's the greatest invitation you'll ever receive.

Dependence, not strength, is God's objective for you. *And if dependence is the objective, then weakness is an advantage.*

Your strength is likely your greatest impediment. So rejoice when God makes you weak. He does so in order that you can become strong in his Spirit. Sometimes he puts you flat on your back so you will finally be looking in the right direction.

The Inevitable Crisis of Faith When the Spirit Speaks

Because it's not about *your* power, when the Holy Spirit beckons you to follow him into one of his assignments, you will almost always go through a crisis of faith. God will likely assign things to you that you feel entirely unable to accomplish. But if God wants to show off his power in you, why would he invite you to something you could already do without him? He often gives us things *much* larger than our abilities so that we have no choice but to depend on him and then give him the glory.

Isn't that what happened with Elijah? After watching 850 prophets of Baal dance and cut themselves for more than eight hours, Elijah simply got down on his knees and asked God to send fire. He didn't try to show that he could dance better, harder, or with holier moves than the false prophets. His hope was in the mercy of God—and a simple prayer of faith unlocked the power. After fire fell from the sky and consumed the offering, the altar, the twelve jugs of water Elijah had poured on the altar, and the dirt around the altar, no one left Mount Carmel saying, "Wow, what a prophet! Did you hear how eloquently he prayed?" Elijah might have been an eloquent speaker, but the outpouring from heaven was so strong that they could only say, "What a powerful *God*!" (1 Kings 18:22–39).

Over the years, I have compiled a list of things I believe the Spirit of God has called me to attempt. I rarely share the full list with anybody, mostly because I'm afraid they will mock it, or at least shake their heads in disbelief and say, "*You're dreaming.*" (In fact, I had a pastor say that to me just the other day!) I know that many of things I have written down are impossible unless God himself does them. But they are visions I believe the Spirit of God has put into me.

I believe everyone's "life goals" should include a few of those God-sized things. If everything you do is explainable by natural giftings, then at your funeral people will likely give you credit for your accomplishments. But if God does things through you that are "*impossible with men*," then at your funeral your friends are likely to give God the credit. The Spirit wants to glorify Jesus in your life, not you. Live today with your eulogy in mind, asking God to do through you what only he can get credit for. I want the summation of my life to be the words of Zechariah the prophet,

> "Not by might, nor by power, but by my Spirit," says the LORD. (Zech. 4:6)

I'm yearning for the Holy Spirit to write a story through me that only his power can explain. I hope friends will summarize my life not as "the Acts of J.D. Greear," but "the Acts of the Holy Spirit ... through and around J.D. Greear." He's writing the story of Jesus' salvation project through me and following it as he unfolds it has become the great adventure of my life.

What part of the story is he telling through *you*?

I hope this book has helped you see that the Spirit of God is beckoning you to follow him. Maybe he has been beckoning you for a while, but you have been unaware. I hope through these pages you have seen that throughout your life he has been pursuing, calling, preparing, and equipping you for his work.

The choice is now yours. He beckons you to follow him into a world of possibilities, impossibilities, dangers, and adventures. Remember, he didn't call you because he needed you. He called you because he loves you, he wants you to know his wonder and be amazed by his glory, and he wants to show off his power in you. He wants to give you the privilege of being used by him in the greatest rescue mission in the universe.

What lies ahead for you is so amazing that, if he let you see it all at once, it would probably blow your mind. Think about it: The angels, who see God's face every day, long to look into what you have — intimacy with God through the blood of Jesus and the fullness of the Holy Spirit. The Spirit, Paul says, is given to us as only a "down payment" of God's future plans for you (2 Cor. 1:22)! "Christ *in* us," Paul says, "our hope of glory!"

If you are a believer, the power that brought the worlds into existence and Christ back from the grave is inside of you, waiting to be released by a simple prayer:

"Yes, Lord, I will follow."

APPENDIX

A Word to Pastors

R. A. Torrey once lamented about seminary graduates in his day:

> We think that if a man is pious and has had a college and seminary education and comes out of it reasonably orthodox, he is now ready for our hands to be laid upon him and to be ordained to preach the gospel. But Jesus Christ said, "No." There is another preparation so essential that a man must not undertake this work until he has received it. *"Tarry* [literally 'sit down'] ... *until you are endued with power from on high"* (Luke 24:49).[1]

Have we, as evangelicals, overlooked this crucial component in our training the next generation for ministry? Are we producing leaders who are filled with the Holy Spirit—who know what it means to walk with him and move in his power? Or are we producing leaders who, though faithfully learning the lessons and busy doing the assignments, are attempting to do so apart from the power of the One who said, "Apart from me, you can do nothing"? Even worse, might we be completely unaware that we're even missing him?

Samson had gotten so self-confident that when Delilah cut his hair and he lost the power of the Spirit, "he did not [even] know that the LORD had left him" (Judg. 16:20). Might we not be in the same place today?

Furthermore, are we building our churches in ways that keep our people from seeking the empowerment of the Spirit in their own lives?

Jesus promised that his church would do even "greater" works than he did. He told us this would come when ordinary believers were filled with his Spirit and lived by his power. Our approach to building our churches often seems to turn that idea completely on its head. We act like the greatest ministry will happen when we position, platform, and megaphone one "anointed" mega-leader.

But if Jesus was telling the truth, the greatest power in the church is not to be found in the large ministries of a few anointed individuals, but when all members are equipped and sent out in the power of the Spirit. Jesus said that it was more advantageous for his Spirit to be in ordinary believers than for even he himself to remain with us. The Spirit *inside* of us is greater than even Jesus *beside* us.

Never forget that of the forty miracles recorded in the book of Acts, thirty-nine of them happen outside the church. If nothing else, that teaches us pastors that our greatest work is to build up our people to carry the power of God into the streets, not to preach sermons and create worship experiences that drip with the power of God. If you ask a church member to describe an encounter with the power of God, and they describe a moment that took place in one of your services, they are far from achieving their God-given potential for his kingdom. The greatest miracles are to happen through them in the streets, not us in the pulpit.

Ephesians 4:11–12 tells us that God gave pastors for the *equipping* of the saints in ministry. I often tell my church (tongue slightly in cheek), that according to this verse, when I became a pastor, I *left* the ministry. I became an equipper. My job is to help my people discover their Spirit-given giftings and then unleash them. Our great Savior did not send his Spirit into the hearts of every believer so that he could confine himself and his ministry to the physical presence of a few "anointed" pastors! He put his Spirit into our people so that they could accomplish the "greater" works. That's when the church will "turn the world upside down" again (Acts 17:6 ESV).

I once heard a pastor say, "The church is not a cruise ship; she's a battleship." I suggest that in light of Jesus' promise, we take the analogy one step further. Let's be aircraft carriers. Battleships fight their battles on or near the ship. But the *last* place an aircraft carrier wants to fight its battles is near itself! Aircraft carriers equip planes to carry the battle to the enemy.

The church's role is to equip believers to take the battle into the enemy's territory. Jesus said that when he began to build the church through us, even the gates of hell itself would not be able to keep us out.

The greatest promises of Jesus about the church relate to her sending capacity. So let's cease to be satisfied with building big churches and instead strive to see our churches become extraordinarily effective at equipping people to move out in the power of the Spirit. Let's cease judging a church's "success" by its seating capacity and put more emphasis on its sending capacity.

Pastors, have we taken Jesus' promises about the Spirit's potential in our people seriously?

Acknowledgments

Even a moment's reflection on how this book came to be fills me with a deep sense of the gratitude I owe to the following people:

To my wife, Veronica, my first and greatest partner in theological dialogue. She, in her own unassuming way, has taught me more about craving the presence of the Holy Spirit than anyone I know.

To the pastoral team and congregation of the Summit Church, who have eagerly walked with me as we sought to learn what it means to be a church filled with the Spirit.

To Tom Elliff, former president of the International Mission Board, who admonished me that it is high time for evangelicals to have another serious discussion about the Holy Spirit.

To my friends David Platt, Sealy Yates, Ed Newton, Josh Harris, Trevin Wax, Raudel Hernandez, and Chuck Reed, who not only helped me discover a lot of the truths in this book, but encouraged me to get them into a book.

To my Baptist and Reformed communities, who have instilled in me a deep love for the gospel and taught me to depend on the sufficiency of the Scriptures. *Sola fide; sola Scriptura; soli Deo gloria.*

To my charismatic friends, who have showed me that what God desires is relationship; that he seeks people who worship him in Spirit and in truth; and that he requires that in addition to doing justly and loving mercy, we walk humbly with him. To paraphrase Martyn Lloyd-Jones: I have spent half of my life learning the importance of doctrine and the other half learning that doctrine is not enough.

To Tim Keller and Mark Dever, whose frequent references to Martyn Lloyd-Jones in their preaching helped me bring it all together.

To the excellent editorial team at Zondervan, under the leadership of Sandra VanderZicht, whose skill in book crafting is exceeded only by their love for gospel and missional truth. To Steve Halliday, who encouraged me to write a book "for" something, not just "about" something; and who not only helped me translate many of these ideas into a readable form, but enlarged, deepened, and clarified them. To Jim Ruark, who patiently went over these pages line by line, putting up with a seemingly infinite number of small changes. No one was more excited to see this book go to print than Jim.

To David Thompson, Will Toburen, Rick Langston, and Jason Douglas, whose excellent leadership at The Summit Church allowed me the bandwidth to spend the necessary time studying and writing.

To Chris Pappalardo, my research assistant, whose brilliance and excellence in scholarship both better equips me to communicate these ideas and challenges me to be a better thinker.

Finally, to my kids, Kharis, Alethia, Ryah, and Adon. The desire to see you grow up and love God drove me to look to God for a power in parenting I did not have in myself. My prayer is that you come to walk with the Spirit our Lord Jesus sent to earth for our benefit, and that you love above all things that Savior the Spirit longs to exalt.

Bible Versions

Notes

Chapter 1: A False Dilemma

1. "The Holy Spirit's distinctive new covenant role, then, is to fulfill what we may call a floodlight ministry in relation to the Lord Jesus Christ.... When floodlighting is well done, the floodlights are so placed that you do not see them; you are not in fact supposed to see where the light is coming from; what you are meant to see is just the building on which the floodlights are trained.... This perfectly illustrates the Spirit's new covenant role. He is, so to speak, the hidden floodlight shining on the Savior." J. I. Packer, *Keeping in Step with the Spirit: Finding Fullness in Our Walk with God*, 2nd ed. (Grand Rapids: Baker, 2005), 57.

2. F. Dale Bruner and William Hordern, *The Holy Spirit: Shy Member of the Trinity* (Minneapolis: Augsburg, 1983).

3. John Newton, "Letter IV: Communion with God," in *The Letters of John Newton*, (Edinburgh: Banner of Truth Trust, 1960), 29.

4. Quoted in Iain H. Murray, *Lloyd-Jones: Messenger of Grace* (London: Banner of Truth, 2008), 136.

5. Martyn Lloyd-Jones, *Life in Christ: Studies in 1 John* (Wheaton, Ill.: Crossway, 2002), 386.

Chapter 2: Mystery and Clarity

1. Some translations, like the NIV, leave out "in the Spirit," preferring to see the Greek *pneuma* as referring to Paul's own spirit. The most literal Bible versions, however — namely, ESV, NASB, KJV, NKJV, and ASV — all translate *pneuma* as "in the Spirit." Perhaps even the ambiguity here is instructive. When our spirit is fused with God's Spirit, it's not always easy to tell where ours stops and his starts.

2. Acts 21:10: See Wayne Grudem, *Bible Doctrine* (Grand Rapids: Zondervan, 1999), 411.

3. Kevin DeYoung, *Just Do Something: A Liberating Approach to Finding God's Will* (Chicago, Ill.: Moody Publishers, 2009), 70–71.

4. Spoke audibly: Jer. 1:2; Ezek. 1:2–3; Hos. 1:1; Joel 1:1; Jonah 1:1; Mic. 1:1; Zeph. 1:1; Mal. 1:1.

5. Dreams: Gen. 28:10–22; Gen. 40, 41; Daniel 4:4–27. Visions: Amos 1:1; Obad. 1; Nah. 1:1; Hab. 1:1.

6. Angels: Gen. 22:11–18; Judg. 13:3–5, 9-20; All throughout the book of Zechariah, God speaks through an angel.

7. 1 Sam. 14:41. The apostles seem to repeat some version of this in the selection of an apostle to replace Judas at the end of Acts 1.

8. Judg. 6:36–40.

9. Num. 22:31–38.

10. Dan. 5:5–6.

11. Est. 4:15–16; 5:1.

12. 1 Sam. 14:6–15.

13. 1 Sam. 17.

14. John Piper, *Risk Is Right: Better to Lose Your Life Than to Waste It* (Wheaton, Ill.: Crossway, 2013), 24-26.

15. Bernard Ramm, *Rapping about the Spirit* (Waco, Tex.: Word, 1974), 7. Quoted in Graham Cole, *He Who Gives Life: The Doctrine of the Holy Spirit* (Wheaton, Ill.: Crossway, 2007), 42.

16. 1 Kings 19:11–13, emphasis mine. Note that Mount Horeb is another name for Mount Sinai, where God appeared to Moses and later the children of Israel in fire and earthquakes.

17. 2 Tim. 3:16–17; Deut. 32:47.

Chapter 3: The Mighty, Rushing Wind

1. I owe some of this insight to Andy Stanley from a discussion he gave on the church. See also http://www.etymonline.com/index.php?allowed_in_frame=0&search=kirche&searchmode=none.

2. John Piper, *Filling Up the Afflictions of Christ: The Cost of Bringing the Gospel to the Nations in the Lives of William Tyndale, Adoniram Judson, and John Paton* (Wheaton, Ill.: Crossway Books, 2009), 30, 47, 51.

3. Kenneth Scott Latourette, *A History of the Expansion of Christianity* (New York: Harper & Brothers, 1937), 1:116.

4. Mark Driscoll, *A Call to Resurgence* (Carol Stream, Ill.: Tyndale House, 2013), 153.

5. Charles Spurgeon, "A Sermon and a Reminiscence," *The Sword and the Trowel* (March 1873). Retrieved from http://www.spurgeon.org/s_and_t/srmn1873.htm (parentheses mine).

Chapter 4: Greater

1. Leon Morris, "Commentary on the Gospel of John," from the *New International Commentary on the New Testament* (Grand Rapids: Eerdmans, 1971), 646. Numbers mine.

2. Nik Ripken, *The Insanity of Obedience* (Nashville: Broadman, 2013), 19.

3. Timothy Keller makes this same point in "The Ascension" from the series *The Real Jesus Part 4: The Lord* (sermon, Redeemer Presbyterian Church, New York, NY, May 18, 1997), http://www.gospelinlife.com/the-ascension-6530.html.

4. Acts 5:12–16; Heb. 2:3–4.

5. Luke is the only Gospel writer to record the *bodily* descent of the Holy Spirit: His point is that everything from this point forward is going to be done in the power of the Spirit. "Luke places special emphasis on the Spirit during Christ's inauguration as a sign that *everything* in Jesus' ministry from that point forward would be charismatic." Roger Stronstad, *The Charismatic Theology of St. Luke* (Peabody, Mass.: Hendrickson, 1984), 45.

6. From Charles Spurgeon, *Morning and Evening*, July 9, http://www.spurgeon.org/morn_eve/m_e.html#07/09/AM. I edited a couple of archaic phrases out of the quote, but the essence is the same.

Chapter 5: God Doesn't Need You

1. Roland Bainton, *Here I Stand: A Life of Martin Luther* (Nashville: Abingdon, 1977), 203.
2. These words are Bainton's summarization of Luther's thought in *Here I Stand*, 181 (emphasis mine).

Chapter 6: God Steers Moving Ships

1. Ps. 32; 23:6; 16:11.
2. I first heard this analogy from David Platt in a sermon on Mark 8 that he preached in 2008 at a student conference at which we both preached at Champion Forest Baptist Church near Houston, Texas. To my knowledge, no recording exists.
3. This is according to the Joshua Project, a Christian missions research organization. See http://joshuaproject.net.

Chapter 7: In the Gospel

1. J. I. Packer, *Keeping in Step with the Spirit: Finding Fullness in Our Walk with God*, 2nd ed. (Grand Rapids: Baker, 2005), 57.
2. See, for example, 1 Cor. 2:2; 2 Cor. 3:18; Rom. 12:1–2; 1:16–17. I explain this concept at length in my book, *Gospel: Recovering the Power That Made Christianity Revolutionary* (Nashville: Broadman, 2011).
3. I heard this during one of Lloyd-Jones's sermons, but unfortunately, I can't remember which one.
4. Quoted in Martyn Lloyd-Jones, *Joy Unspeakable* (Wheaton, Ill.: Harold Shaw, 1984), 95–96.
5. For more on this, see Jim Cymbala, *Spirit Rising* (Grand Rapids: Zondervan, 2012), 57.
6. Jonathan Edwards, "Personal Narrative," quoted in C. Samuel Storms, *Signs of the Spirit: An Interpretation of Jonathan Edwards' Religious Affections* (Wheaton, Ill.: Crossway, 2007), 195.
7. The apostle John said that he wrote the book of 1 John so that believers could have "fellowship" with God, just as he had. Jesus was a God, he said, who he could see, and touch, and hear, and that's the *kind* of fellowship we should have too (1 John 1:1–3). But as John begins to unfold what that fellowship looks like, he talks about things such as knowing our sinfulness, sensing the light of his glory, experiencing his cleansing power, loving God's laws, knowing the majesty of his Lordship, and being filled with his love (1 John 1:7–9; 2:5, 9–10, 15, 27; 3:23–24; 4:2–3). Feeling these things unmistakably reveals that *we have fellowship with the Father.*
8. A. W. Tozer, *The Pursuit of God* (Ventura, Calif.: Regal Books, 2013), 28.

Chapter 8: In the Word of God

1. John Newton notes that pagans in Paul's days did such a thing with their "holy" books too. Using the writings of Virgil in such a way was so common it had a name: *Sortes Virgiliane*. See *The Letters of John Newton*, "Divine Guidance" (Edinburgh: Banner of Truth Trust, 1960), 79.

2. See also 1 Thess. 5:18.
3. Homily 7 on the First Epistle of John (Sermon on 1 John 4:4–12) http://www.new advent.org/fathers/170207.htm (my paraphrase).
4. 2 Tim. 3:16–17; 2 Peter 1:3 ESV.
5. I follow here the categories set out by Philip Jensen and Tony Payne in their *Guidance and the Voice of God* (Kingsford, Australia: Matthias Media, 1997), 90–98.
6. Peter Kreeft, "Discernment," http://www.peterkreeft.com/topics/discernment.htm.
7. The term "conscious cooperation" comes from Jensen and Payne in *Guidance and the Voice of God*. They believe, however, that the Spirit of God speaks to us in no other way, a conclusion with which I disagree. Still, I find ready agreement with them that the vast majority of things that require "conscious cooperation" are things written in his Word.
8. John Newton, "Divine Guidance," from *The Letters of John Newton*, 81–82, emphasis mine.

Chapter 9: In Our Giftings

1. See also 1 John 2:20, 27.
2. I first saw a diagram like the one above in Jim Collins's *Good to Great* (New York: HarperBusiness 2001). Collins uses it to show how companies can find their "sweet spot," the place they can really become a great company. Though his book was not written from a Christian perspective, I think the diagram illustrates nicely how we can find our spiritual gift. I've since seen this Venn diagram in places that predate Collins's book, so I'm not sure if it's original with him.
3. Rick Warren, *The Purpose Driven Life* (Grand Rapids: Zondervan, 2002), 236–39.
4. Gene Edward Veith Jr. summarizes Luther's thought this way in *God at Work: Your Christian Vocation in All of Life* (Wheaton, Ill.: Crossway, 2002), 10. Veith references Luther's "Exposition of Psalm 147."
5. By all accounts, this particular scene in the movie is fictitious, the creation of Colin Welland, the film's writer. But the internal struggle in Liddell that the scene depicts was real, and the words Welland puts in Liddell's mouth accurately communicate a belief long held by Scottish Reformed Christians, of whom Liddell was one.
6. A great resource for discovering more about God's purposes in our secular work is Timothy Keller, *Every Good Endeavor* (New York: Dutton, 2013).
7. Also, Mark Driscoll's *Who Do You Think You Are?* (Nashville: Thomas Nelson, 2013); see pages 121–37 especially. Others include *What's So Spiritual about Your Gifts?* by Henry Blackaby (Salem, Ore.: Multnomah, 2004); *The Sovereign Spirit: Discerning His Gifts* by Martyn-Lloyd Jones (Carol Stream, Ill.: Harold Shaw, 1986); and *Paul, the Spirit, and the People of God* by Gordon D. Fee (Grand Rapids: Baker Academic, 1996).

Chapter 10: In the Church

1. Eric Metaxas, *Seven Men: And the Secret of Their Greatness* (Nashville: Thomas Nelson, 2013), 62–63.
2. Gary Tyra, *The Holy Spirit in Mission: Prophetic Speech and Action in Christian Witness* (Downers Grove, Ill.: InterVarsity, 2011), 64.
3. Thabiti Anyabwile (summarizing Anthony Thistleton) from an unpublished (and untitled) sermon on 1 Corinthians 14:20–25 (9 Marks at Southeastern Conference, Southeastern Baptist Theological Seminary, Wake Forest, NC, Sept. 27, 2013), available at www.SEBTS.edu. I follow Thabiti's interpretation in my discussion of each of these five effects.
4. Ibid.

5. J. I. Packer, *Keeping in Step with the Spirit: Finding Fullness in Our Walk with God* (Grand Rapids: Baker, 2005), 174.
6. This is the proper balance of preaching! Some gravitate to rigid exegesis, and their preaching is devoid of Spirit-living application to the congregation. Others try to be in tune with the Spirit but do not do the work in exegesis. The best preaching combines *both*.
7. Tyra, *The Holy Spirit in Mission*, 77–78.
8. 2 Tim. 3:16–17; Acts 1:16; John 10:30; 2 Peter 1:20–21.
9. J. I. Packer says, "Paul's directive that when Christian prophets speak in the assembly, others must '… weigh what is said' (1 Cor. 14:29) shows that the potentially universal prophecy of the New Testament was less than infallible and irreformable and might need to be qualified." *Keeping in Step with the Spirit*, 173.
10. Wayne Grudem, *Bible Doctrine* (Grand Rapids: Zondervan, 1999), 408, 411.
11. 2 Peter 1:20–21; 2 Tim. 3:16–17; Matt. 5:18.
12. Vern Poythress, "Modern Spiritual Gifts as *Analogous* to Apostolic Gifts: Affirming Extraordinary Works of the Spirit within Cessationist Theology," *Journal of the Evangelical Theological Society* 39, no. 1 (1996): 71-101. Publisher and blogger Justin Taylor calls this "the best essay on spiritual gifts ever written."
13. From Lesslie Newbigin, *The Gospel in a Pluralist Society* (Grand Rapids: Eerdmans, 1989), 119-20, 133. Quoted in Tyra, *The Holy Spirit in Mission*, 146.
14. Tyra, *The Holy Spirit in Mission*, 77–78.
15. J. I. Packer notes, "Joel's prediction, quoted by Peter at Pentecost, was of universal prophecy as one mark of the age of the Spirit (Acts 2:17–21). Prophesying was thus an activity in which all believers were able and perhaps expected to share (see Acts 19:6; 1 Cor. 14:1, 23–25)." *Keeping in Step with the Spirit*, 172.
16. These three questions are adapted from a sermon by John Mark Comer on 1 Corinthians 14.

Chapter 11: In Our Spirit

1. John Piper, "Praying in the Closet and in the Spirit," (Jan. 3, 2010), http://www. desiringgod.org/resource-library/sermons/praying-in-the-closet-and-in-the-spirit (emphasis mine).
2. Charles Spurgeon, *Spurgeon on the Holy Spirit* (New Kensington, Pa.: Whitaker House, 2000), 102–3.
3. Ligonier Ministries, "Striking a Chord in the Heart of the Believer," *Table Talk* 14, no. 11 (1990): 13.
4. Cotton Mather, *Parentator: Memoirs of Remarkables in the Life and the Death of the Ever-Memorable Dr. Increase Mather* (Boston: B. Green, 1724), 189-91. Cited by Vern Poythress, "Modern Spiritual Gifts as *Analogous* to Apostolic Gifts: Affirming Extraordinary Works of the Spirit within Cessationist Theology," *Journal of the Evangelical Theological Society* 39, no. 1 (1996). I paraphrased Mather's words slightly because they are written in very old English, but I have accurately preserved his meaning. To note, Mather also issues several cautions and warns of counterfeits on pp. 191–96.
5. Poythress, "Modern Spiritual Gifts," n25.
6. The writer of Hebrews says that "[Our great salvation] was declared at first by the Lord, and it was attested to us by those who heard, while God also bore witness by signs and wonders and various miracles and by gifts of the Holy Spirit" (Heb. 2:3–4 ESV). God seems to have given the apostles an unusual endowment of supernatural powers for a time to authenticate the fact he was speaking to the world through them. But we see

the regularity of these spectacular occurrences dying down even through Acts. In Acts 3:1–11 Peter heals on demand. He didn't pray about it or even ask God to do it. He just said, "Be healed." But in 2 Timothy 4:20 (ESV), toward the end of his ministry, Paul said, "I left Trophimus, who was ill, at Miletus." That doesn't mean he doesn't ever do these things anymore, just that we should not expect them to be *as* regular or normative as they were in Acts, because that was, by any definition, a unique time.

7. Martyn Lloyd-Jones, *The Sovereign Spirit: Discerning His Gifts* (Carol Stream, Ill.: Harold Shaw, 1986), 89–90.
8. Ibid., 83.

Chapter 12: In Our Circumstances

1. I have omitted the details of this story because this information was obtained privately, and the leader in question has never expressed this publicly.
2. See also Colossians 4:3.

Chapter 13: When You Can't Feel God

1. C. S. Lewis, *A Grief Observed* (San Francisco: HarperCollins, 1961), 17.
2. Ibid.
3. The words here are those of Roland Bainton, summarizing Luther's teaching, from his biography of Luther, *Here I Stand: A Life of Martin Luther* (Nashville: Abingdon, 1977), 171.
4. Luther, quoted by David Steinmetz, professor of Old Testament at Duke Divinity School, "Calvin and Luther on Interpreting Genesis," (Reformation Heritage Lecture, Beeson Divinity School, Birmingham, AL, 1995), http://www.beesondivinity.com/podcast#!/swx/pp/media_archives/99668/episode/34564.
5. William L. Lane, *Commentary on Mark*, New International Commentary on the New Testament (Grand Rapids: Eerdmans, 1974), 516.

Chapter 14: Revival: When the Holy Spirit Moves in Power

1. http://www.bible-history.com/biblestudy/nineveh.html; http://biblematter.wordpress.com/2013/04/18/why-was-ancient-nineveh-called-the-city-of-bloodshed-2/; https://www.mpumc.org/uploads/file/Nineveh.pdf.
2. Derek Kidner, *Psalms 73–150: A Commentary* (Downers Grove, Ill.: InterVarsity, 1973), 440.
3. Martyn Lloyd-Jones, quoted in Collin Hansen, *A God-Sized Vision: Revival Stories That Stretch and Stir* (Grand Rapids: Zondervan, 2010), 14.
4. Ibid.
5. Ibid., 15.
6. Jonathan Edwards, quoted in Hansen, *A God-Sized Vision*, 179, revised to update some of Edwards's antiquated prose.
7. Timothy Keller, *Center Church* (Grand Rapids: Zondervan, 2012), 54.
8. Tim Keller, "Jesus Vindicated," plenary session at The Gospel Coalition 2013 National Conference, Orlando, FL, April 9, 2013, http://thegospelcoalition.org/resources/entry/jesus_vindicated.
9. Mark Shaw, *Global Awakening: How 20th-Century Revivals Triggered a Christian Revolution* (Downers Grove, Ill.: InterVarsity, 2010), 40–41. I have condensed Shaw's telling of the story.

10. This story came from Q&A I heard Dr. Keller give to pastors at the Gospel Coalition National Conference held in Orlando, FL, Apr. 8 – 10, 2013.
11. *The Letters of John Newton,* Letter IV, "Communion with God" (Edinburgh: Banner of Truth Trust, 1960), 31.
12. Heb. 12:14; Eph. 4:30.
13. 2 Cor. 3:18 – 4:4; Isa. 55:10 – 11; Rom. 1:17
14. Luther's Works, volume 51, *Sermons I,* "Eight Sermons at Wittenberg, 1522," 77.
15. For help on this, see my book *Gospel: Recovering the Power that Made Christianity Revolutionary* (Nashville: Broadman, 2011).
16. Peter says that failure to grow in grace results from "forgetting" that we have been cleansed of our sins.
17. James O. Fraser, missionary to China, quoted in A. Scott Moreau, *Introducing World Missions: A Biblical, Historical and Practical Survey* (Grand Rapids: Baker, 2009), 176.
18. This telling of the Pyongyang story borrows from Mark Shaw, *Global Awakening,* 39 – 42, but also from the following webpages: http://www.christianity today.com/ct/2007/januaryweb-only/105-32.0.html; http://www.cbn.com/cbnnews /world/2007/June/The-Pyongyang-Revival-100-Years-Later/; http://www.byfaith .co.uk/paulbyfaithtvmathewthoughts18.htm; http://www.omf.org/omf/uk/ asia/countries_and_omf_centres/korea/north_korea_prayer_blog/1_the_great_ revival_of_1907.

Chapter 15: You Have Not Because You Ask Not

1. Collin Hansen, *A God-Sized Vision: Revival Stories That Stretch and Stir* (Grand Rapids: Zondervan, 2010), 80 – 82.
2. From electronic version of book by Dr. and Mrs. Howard Taylor, *Hudson Taylor's Spiritual Secrets,* No. 5 of *Moody Giants* (1932: Moody, Chicago), http://www.woobiola.net/ books/taylor/jhtsecr.htm.
3. Elias Smith, ed., *Herald of Gospel Liberty* 102, issue 37 (1910): 1155.
4. Spurgeon, "Prayer Meetings" in *The C.H. Spurgeon Collection* (Rio, Wisc.: Ages Software, 1998 – 2001), 60:526.

Chapter 16: The Way Up Is the Way Down

1. Unfortunately, I do not remember which sermon Dr. Lloyd-Jones shared this story in!
2. A. W. Tozer, *The Root of the Righteous* (Camp Hill, Pa.: WingSpread Publishers, 2007), 144.
3. Craig Groeschel, "The Making of a Man of God: 1 Kings 17" (sermon given at Life Church in Edmund, Okla., May 10, 2009).

Appendix: A Word to Pastors

1. R. A. Torrey, *Power-Filled Living: How to Receive God's Best for Your Life* (New Kensington, Pa: Whitaker House, 1998), 226, quoted in Jim Cymbala, *Spirit Rising* (Grand Rapids: Zondervan, 2012), 38, emphasis original.